Israel: a Small America

AMERICA: A HUGE ISRAEL

The True History of America in the Middle East

Abdulhay Y. Zalloum

Order this book online at www.trafford.com
or email orders@trafford.com

Most Trafford titles are also available at major online book retailers.

© Copyright 2009 Abdulhay Zalloum.

Note for Librarians: A cataloguing record for this book is available from Library and Archives Canada at www.collectionscanada.ca/amicus/index-e.html

Printed in Victoria, BC, Canada.

ISBN: 978-1-4269-0617-6 (soft)
ISBN: 978-1-4269-0618-3 (ebook)

Our mission is to efficiently provide the world's finest, most comprehensive book publishing service, enabling every author to experience success. To find out how to publish your book, your way, and have it available worldwide, visit us online at www.trafford.com

Trafford rev. 10/7/2009

 www.trafford.com

North America & international
toll-free: 1 888 232 4444 (USA & Canada)
phone: 250 383 6864 ♦ fax: 812 355 4082

Table of Contents

ACKNOWLEDGMENTS   *xi*

INTRODUCTION: *xiii*

CHAPTER ONE
   THE ROOTS OF AIPAC INCREDIBLE POWER   *1*

Sign-on-Napkin Congress & One Dollar One Vote Democracy   *18*
The 2009 Israeli Assault on Gaza   20
AIPAC: a Part of an International Power Structure   22

CHAPTER TWO:
   THE VISIBLE AND INVISIBLES   *25*

The Templar Knights and the Masons   28
So: AIPAC Is Part of an International Power Structure   32
Think Tanks Created to Serve the Special Interests Group:
   CFR as Study Case   34
The CFR control of global media   36
How Dedicated Bureaucrats are Selected, Trained, and Deployed   40
The CFR creates Bilderberg Group and Trilateral Commission   46
How CFR and Think Tanks Operate   48

CHAPTER THREE
THE ROOTS OF ZIONIST AMERICA   *53*

Some History…   54
The Templars, Calvinism and Freemasonry   56
Christian Zionism & Restorationalism: 64
Islamophobia, a New Word for an Old Phenomenon   66
The First United States Interventions & Wars with Muslims   73
The First American Regime Change Plan in the Middle East   80
Two Hundred Years after Marine Bombardment of Derna   83

CHAPTER FOUR
THE AMERICAN CRUSADES   *89*

United States Role in the Ottoman Empire's Disintegration   89
Historical Overview   93
Napoleon's Invasion of Egypt & Syria: 97
Challenges to the Empire from Within   105
Mohammed Ali and Saddam Hussein   108
The Early missionaries   110
The First Years….   113
The Cultural Invasion Backed by the American Navy   114
A New Start   117
The New Target: Secularism through Nationalism   124

CHAPTER FIVE
SULTAN ABDUL HAMID II & THE FINAL DAYS *131*

Rejuvenating the Empire through an Islamic Agenda   131
Abdül-Hamid II   132

Late 19th Century American Christian Zionism Agenda 135

...a Different Agenda for Abdul-Hamid 138

Abdul-Hamid Reforms 140

America in Egypt & France in North Africa! 144

The Islamic & Arab policies were working well...but 146

Young Turks without a Turkey & a Masonic Jewish coup 152

Young Arabs and the 'Arab Revolt' 160

CHAPTER SIX
DISMEMBERING THE ARAB EAST INTO MINI STATES — 165

Deliberate Steps by CUP to alienate Arabs 165

Al Fatat & al Ahd secret societies 167

Initiation of Faisal in the Secret societies 169

Jemal Pasha Tightens his Reins 174

Hussein, From Sharif of Mecca to Arab King to Exile 176

The CUP Drags the Ottoman Empire to World War One 178

What a Coincidence! Or Was It? 180

Iraq's Occupation Was First Class War Aim 183

After Kitchener... 185

The Mesopotamian (Iraq) Campaign 187

The British Conquest of Palestine 188

Confronting the Jewish Immigrants 199

Faisal after World War One 204

A New Middle East at Cairo Conference 206

CHAPTER SEVEN
THE MANDATE: BUILDING JEWISH STATE INSTITUTIONS   211

The Intifada of Nebi Musa   212
A New British Civil Administration...Tension continues   214
The Jaffa Uprising...   216
A Zionist High Commissioner Rethinks Balfour...   218
More Jewish Immigration...The Wailing Wall Uprising   220
High Commissioner Chancellor in a Dilemma...   224
A White Paper and a New Policy...   225
A new Staunch Zionist for a High Commissioner   228
Al Qassam and the 1936 Palestinian Revolt   229
Jewish and British state Terrorism   232
Collective Punishment   238
The Origins of the Israeli Army Combat Doctrine   241
Montgomery Commanding the Anti-Palestinian Revolt   244
The 1939 White Paper...   245
Terrorism by two future Israeli Prime Ministers   248
British experts: Time to leave Palestine...   249
The End of British Mandate, UN Partition Resolution   250
Britain wanted to leave the Palestine Burden   252

CHAPTER EIGHT
A JEWISH STATE IN PALESTINE (1948-1967)   257

Unbalanced Political, Financial and Military Power   258
The Comparative Strength of the Arab and Jewish Armies   261
Between 1948 -1967: The Zionist Project Reached a Dead End   268

Jewish Demographic Revolution: More Mizrahi than
    Ashkenazi Jews   269

Discrimination against Oriental Jews and Resident Palestinians! 271

Economic Woes   275

Israel needed a War, Had Plans Ready and Created Pretexts
    for War   277

Seven Months before the War   281

....what to do with an Occupied West Banks...before its
    occupation   281

Israeli Provocations for War   284

War Plans against Syria   287

The War and an unimagined Easy Cheap Victory   290

Israel's New Borders, that's the Question Now!   293

The Ben Gurion Proposed Peace Plan   297

Transfer in Zionism Ideology   302

CHAPTER NINE
    ISRAEL: THE CRUSADES REVISITED   307

Peace Processes without Peace   307

Settlers Racism, Fascism and Terrorism Become Israel's State
    Policy   308

Settlers Lunatic Behavior and Government Collusion   312

1977 Begin's Likud Victory: A Turning point for Settlement
    Policy   315

Settlers Terrorism after Likud Election Victory   318

Meir Kahane: From New York to the Knesset   321

Temple Mount Zealots & Al Aqsa Mosque   324

Peace Processes without Peace   330

The Madrid Conference   331

The Oslo Accords   334

...Oslo II   337

...The Wye River Memorandum   338

...Barak, Arafat and Camp David   339

A Sharon Plan Backed by Bush Neoconservatists   341

...a second (Aqsa) intifada & reoccupying the West Bank   342

Mahmud Abbas after Yasser Arafat   347

Washington Promoting a Palestinian Civil War   350

OUR CONCLUSION: THE PARTY IS OVER   362

"The deep roots of Judeo-Christian values (historians) explore go back to the Protestant Reformation ... In the American context, historians use the term Judeo-Christian to refer to the influence of the Hebrew Bible and New Testament on Protestant thought and values, most especially the Puritan, Presbyterian and Evangelical heritage. These founding generations of Americans saw themselves as heirs to the Hebrew Bible ... These ideas from the Hebrew Bible, brought into American history by Protestants, are seen as underpinning the American Revolution, Declaration of Independence and the United States Constitution. Other authors are interested in tracing the religious beliefs of America's founding fathers, emphasizing both Jewish and Christian influence in their personal beliefs and how this was translated into the creation of American institutions and character. [1]

***

"HISTORY IS BUT A SERIES OF ACCEPTED LIES".[2]

1   Encyclopedia Wikipedia: Judeo-Christian culture
2   Lawrence of Arabia

ACKNOWLEDGMENTS

The research for this book took place over many years, as I collected many books on the subject. I was always attracted to buy books that were written by people who lived my experience on the other side of the fence. My private library ended up with dozens of books on the subject, but for the research of this book I am most grateful to the authors and publishers of fourteen books namely

1. *Born In Blood: The Lost Secrets of Free Masonry*, (John I. Robinson)
2. *The ascendance of Israel's Right* (Ehud Sprinzak}
3. *The Israel Lobby and U.S. Foreign Policy* (John J. Measheimer & Stephen Walt)
4. *The Lobby, Jewish Political Power and American Foreign Policy*, (Edward Tivnan)
5. *Palestine Peace Not Apartheid*, (Jimmy Carter)
6. *Power, Faith and Fantasy*, (Michael B. Oren)
7. *The Arab awakening*, (George Antonius)
8. *A Peace to End All Peace*, (David Fromkin)
9. *The Ottoman Centuries, The Rise and Fall of the Turkish Empire*,(Lord Kinross)
10. *One Palestine Complete*, (Tom Segev)
11. *1967* (Tom Segev)

12. *1948, The First Arab-Israeli War*, (Benny Morris)

13. *Zealots For Zion*, (Robert I. Friedman)

14. *The False Prophet*, (Rabbi Meir Kahana, Robert I. Friedman)

It happens that the majority of these authors are Jewish, and many of them were renowned Israeli academics, historians and writers. Since anybody who writes or insinuates any fact, and I repeat, fact, unfavorable to Israel will be readily accused of anti-Semitism, I heavily quoted these references which were well researched and professionally written; not that doing so will necessarily exempt me from anti-Semitism charges. In reality, I do not care. After all, I belong to the Semite race myself!

To all the authors I quoted I am grateful.

INTRODUCTION:

When I started writing this book, its theme and chapter synopsis were well defined, but I had no name for it, until I read an article by Israeli former Knesset member Yuri Avneri. The article was trying to explain why Obama, like most American politicians, crawl at the feet of AIPAC as a prerequisite for their election to public office, and once elected, for their political survival. In his article, Avneri, a superb author and a peace activist, concluded that America was a huge Israel and Israel was a small America. I immediately realized I had just found my book title.

This book's subtitle, *The True History of America in the Middle East* emulates the title of an American best selling book written by Boston University history Professor Howard Zinn titled *A People's History of the United States* which tells the other side of the historical story not normally told by corporate media, textbooks and encyclopedias. Zinn's book is a living proof that "History is but a series of accepted lies" as was stated by British intelligence agent Lawrence of Arabia. Certainly, most of history written by biased Western neo-orientalists is a "series of accepted lies" when it relates to the Arab and Muslim World. Many times, it is no more than sophistry ultimately geared to serve imperial ends.

I have lived through the life span of the State of Israel and more than a decade prior to its creation in 1948 in mandate

Palestine. I noted the chasm between reality as I lived it, and how it was reported by Western 'historians' or corporate media. I experienced the blowing up of the King David Hotel in 1946 by a Jewish terrorist organization led by Menechem Begin, who later became an Israeli prime minister, and who was awarded a Noble prize. The sound of explosion still resonates in my ears, and the sight of the ruins of the hotel that I saw the next morning remains fresh in my memory as if the explosion took place yesterday. The King David was very near to my Ummariyah School at Talbiyah, in West Jerusalem.

I left to the United States at age eighteen to pursue my higher education and remained in contact with it one way or the other for the past fifty five years, almost a quarter of the life of the American Republic. The subject of American involvement in the Middle East and roots of its attitudes towards Palestine, Arabs, Muslims and the world fascinated me not only academically but because it impacted my life drastically. Thus, my search and research continued for most of my adult life to resolve the puzzle of the Israeli American relationship and how such a small Jewish community can be so dominant and so powerful that it can 'shock and awe' American presidents, the congress and really the world.

In this book I argued that resulting from ideological and technological transformations after the Protestant revolution; a Judeo-Christian culture emerged in which it increasingly became more Judeo than Christian. Christian Zionism, I found, expressed itself from the very first days of European immigrants to America.

This culture was hostile to Islam and Muslims beginning with Christopher Columbus to George W. Bush.

I was hesitant at first to accept the Clash of Civilizations argument since, contrary to what is claimed, Islam accepts the 'other' (Judaism and Christianity), but the 'other' does not accept Islam. Muslim and Arab Elites hesitated to accept this clash theory as they themselves did not seek confrontations. They wanted not to believe that the secular West is driven by religious fundamentalism which was directed to satisfy the greed of the owners of the Judeo-Christian culture, the financial barons of the world. But the war of terror named in reverse as War on Terror revealed things for what they are. In his book The Clash of Civilizations Samuel Huntington wrote:

"The underlying problem for the West is not Islamic fundamentalism. It is Islam, a different civilization whose people are convinced of the superiority of their culture and are obsessed with the inferiority of their power. The problem for Islam is not the CIA or the U.S Department of Defense. It is the West, a different civilization whose people are convinced of the universality of their culture and believe their superior, if declining, power imposes on them the obligation to extend that culture throughout the world. "

The West, according to Huntington, wants to impose its Judeo-Christian culture on Muslims. And Muslims, except for a post-colonial Muslim power elite that was selected, trained, indoctrinated by the West are not buying that.

CHAPTER ONE

THE ROOTS OF AIPAC INCREDIBLE POWER

Many people from different creeds and nationalities around the world are puzzled by the influence and power of the Jewish community in the West in general, and the United States in particular. All agree it is by far disproportionate to their numbers in the societies in which they exercise enormous power.

As soon as Barack Obama won his Democratic Party presidential nomination he "ran to the conference of the Israel lobby, AIPAC, and made a speech that broke all records for obsequiousness and fawning" wrote the Israeli writer and former Knesset member Uri Avnery on June 10th, 2008 in his regular column at Ha'aretz, a leading Israeli newspaper. He added:

> "And lo and behold, the very first thing he does after securing the nomination of his party is to compromise his principles. ....And here comes Obama to crawl in the dust at the feet of AIPAC and go out of his way to justify a policy that completely negates his own ideas"

Avnery added that "what really matters is the similarity between the American enterprise and the Zionist one, both in the spiritual and the practical sphere. Israel is a small America; America is a huge Israel." I chose this sentence to be the title of this book. Avnery added that the Mayflower immigrants, who first arrived in North America, called themselves pilgrims. Early Zionist immigrants to Palestine called themselves olim- short of olim beregel, meaning pilgrims also. Both believed they were God's chosen people and both believed they had arrived in the 'promised land'. This is why the American early settlers named their new towns and cities by biblical and Palestinian names, including many Jerusalem(s) and Bethlehem(s) as well as two Mecca(s), three Medina(s), three Baghdad(s), an Aleppo, an Algiers, several Cairo(s) and Alexandria(s) throughout the new country. We may add that both committed atrocities and genocide against the indigenous people.

In May 2004, George W. Bush spoke at the annual policy conference of AIPAC. He commended AIPAC for its efforts "to strengthen the ties that bind our nations – our shared values, our strong commitment to freedom". He added that both countries "have much in common; we're both … born of struggle and sacrifice. We're both founded by immigrants escaping religious persecution in other lands. We have both built vibrant democracies, built on the rule of law and market economies. And we're both countries founded on certain basic beliefs: that God watches over the affairs of men, and values every life. These ties have made us natural allies, and these ties will never be broken". [1]

---

1   The Israel Lobby and US Foreign Policy John J. Measheimer & Stephen Walt, Farrar, Straus and Giroux, New York, st Edition 2007, Pg 78

Serious American scholars, politicians and writers ventured recently, against great odds, to research and explain the phenomenon of recent American policies being captive to Jewish power in the United States, even though they argued, such policies do not serve the American national interest. The Jewish Lobby AIPAC's incredible power was demonstrated in numerous cases to the extent that this lobby dominates congress and scares stiff presidents and high administration officials. The lobby and the power structure behind it try to steer issues related to Israel away from public discourse. They created a web of institutions to achieve this end. Any person who dares to stir up a serious debate whose outcome may not be agreeable with their agenda will be viciously attacked, if efforts to suppress bringing such debates or conclusions did not materialize.

As an example, two renowned American professors from the University of Chicago and Harvard University were asked by the Atlantic magazine to submit a study on the Israel Lobby. After working on the project for two years and revising the study per the request of the magazine, the editor finally advised them that the magazine decided not publish the article. "We worked on the article off and on over the next two years, in close collaboration with the Atlantic's editors, and we sent them a manuscript conforming to our prior agreements and incorporating virtually all of their suggestions in January 2005. A few weeks later, to our surprise, the editor informed us that the Atlantic had decided not to run the piece and that he was not interested in our attempting revise it."

The two professors decided to expand their article into a book. In their book they explained that the theme of the rejected article was simple and straightforward. They described the extraordinary level of material and diplomatic support that the United States is giving Israel, and they concluded that such support was not explained or justified for strategic or moral grounds. *"Instead, it was due largely to the political power of the Israel lobby."*[1] They suggested that these policies were not useful to the national interest; to the contrary they are harmful to American national interests and ultimately Israel's long-term interest. To illustrate the volume of such support the two professors wrote:

> "The most obvious indicator of Israel's favored position is the total amount of foreign aid it had received from America's taxpayers. As of 2005, direct U.S. economic and military assistance to Israel amounted to nearly $ 154 billion dollars (in 2005 dollars), the bulk of it comprising direct grants rather that loans.[2] As discussed below, the actual total is significantly higher, because direct U.S. aid is given under unusually favorable terms and the United States provides Israel

---

1   The Israel Lobby and US Foreign Policy John J. Measheimer & Stephen Walt, Farrar, Straus and Giroux, New York, 1st Edition 2007, Pg viii

2   According to the "Greenbook" of the U.S. Agency for international Development (USAID), which reports "overseas loans and grants", Israel received $153,894,700.000 (in constant 2005 dollars) from the United States through 2005, See http://qesdb.usaid.gov/gbk

with other forms of material assistance that are not included in the foreign assistance budget."[1]

Ironically, that is about a 100 000 U.S. dollars for every Israeli family of four, at a time when 45 Million Americans are classified as poor by the official United States Bureau of Statistics in Washington. This is contrary to the American saying "charity begins at home".

After exploring other media avenues, including the prospect of publishing the expanded study in a book, they did not find interested parties. It had to be published in London by the London Review of Books and it was posted at Harvard Kennedy School of Government website. The arguments in the book were so powerful and convincing it attracted the wrath of the Jewish lobby which immediately branded the two professors as anti-Semite. It has become a habit to blackmail researchers or anybody who happens to disagree with the lobby and Israel. After the stir that was caused after publishing the article in London, their book was published in the United States.

Israeli former Knesset member, author, writer and peace activist commented on the professors' book. I myself could add to the book a whole chapter from personal experience.

---

1   The Israel Lobby and US Foreign Policy John J. Measheimer & Stephen Walt, Farrar, Straus and Giroux, New York, Ist Edition 2007, Pg 24

"In the late 50s, I visited the US for the first time. A major New York radio station invited me for an interview. Later they cautioned me: 'You can criticize the President (Dwight D. Eisenhower) and the Secretary of State (John Foster Dulles) to your heart's content, but please don't criticize Israeli leaders!' At the last moment the interview was cancelled altogether... In 1970, the respected American Fellowship of Reconciliation; invited me for a lecture tour of 30 universities, under the auspices of the Hillel rabbis. When I arrived in New York, I was informed that 29 of the lectures had been cancelled.... In the end, all the lectures took place under the auspices of Christian chaplains".

I especially remember a depressing experience in Baltimore. A good Jew, who had volunteered to host me, was angered by the cancellation of my lecture in this city and obstinately insisted on putting it on. We combed the streets of the Jewish quarters - mile upon mile of signs with Jewish names - and did not find a single hall whose manager would agree to let the lecture by a member of the Israeli Knesset take place...

That year, during Black September, I held a press conference in Washington DC .... The journalists came straight from a press conference with Prime Minister Golda Meir, and showered me with questions. Almost all the important media were represented - TV networks, radio, the major newspapers. After the planned hour was up, they would not let me go and kept me talking for another hour and a half. But the next day, not a single word appeared in any of the media. Thirty-one years later, in October 2001 I held a press conference on Capitol Hill in Washington, and exactly the same thing happened: many of the media were there, they held me for another hour - and not a word, not a single word, was published."

Edward Tivnan also wondered how the Jewish community of only 6 million Americans became so politically influential, and wondered if the U.S. and Israel's interests were the same. When he decided to write a book on the subject, those whom he talked to thought the subject would make a good story:

"But there was one problem: 'Nobody will talk to you'; I was informed over and over again. The subject was too hot, too touchy, too politically dangerous for all concerned. Jewish leaders, the lobbyists, their friends – and enemies – in Congress preferred to keep this subject under wraps. I was told that if I was to be as fair as I claimed, I would have to be critical of Israel and the American Jewish community (even my well-informed Jewish friends conceded that was a given) and the slightest criticism of either was bound to invite the charge that I was 'pro-Arab' or 'anti-Israel' or worse still, 'anti-Semitic'". [1] Tivnan added:

"Others had a darker view. Former career foreign – service officers and ex-ambassadors to Arab countries warned that "no New York publisher will publish such a book". When I explained I already had a commitment from a major New York publisher, they waved a hand and explained that distributors would reject it or that local Jewish groups would pressure bookstores to remove it from the shelves." [2]

I bought this book during my stay in Boston, during the graduation of my son in the mid eighties. At a meeting with an oil industry colleague who was the Director General of The State Company for Oil Projects, and became First deputy to Iraq Defense Minister Hassan Kamel, I quoted some stories from the book and then I gave the book to him saying, I'll buy another one. Months later, I was back in the States and tried one book store after another, and I learned that the book was out of stock and out of print!

In his book former President Jimmy Carter wrote that he was visited by Yitzhak Rabin who was then Israel ambassador to the

1   The Lobby, Jewish Political Power and American Foreign Policy, Edward Tivnan, Touchstone, Ist Edition 198, Pg 8-9
2   The Lobby, Jewish Political Power and American Foreign Policy, Edward Tivnan, Touchstone, 1st Edition 198 , Pg 9

United States while Carter was governor of Georgia, and he invited him to visit Israel which he did in 1973. Carter's name apparently was in the mills as a Democratic Party presidential candidate, and if we may call that invitation actually an interview that took on a different name. Carter visited Israel and when he learned about the "ejection of Palestinians from their previous homes" Carter admitted that he compared that to the "forcing of Lower Creek Indians from Georgia land where our family farm was now located... They were moved to make room to our white ancestors". He left Israel "convinced that the Israelis were dominant but just... I was excited and optimistic about the apparent commitment of the Israelis to establish a nation... dedicated to the Judeo-Christian principles of peace and justice, and to live in harmony with all their neighbors". So Carter passed the interview and shortly afterwards he became a president of the United States of America. As president he realized that Israel was not indeed intent on making peace with its neighbors as he could not force Begin to implement even the agreement Begin signed at Camp David. Carter wrote:

"It is not likely that any combination of Arab powers or even the powerful influence of the United States could force decisions on Israel concerning East Jerusalem, the west Bank, Palestinian rights, or the occupied territories of Syria. These judgments will be made in Jerusalem..." [1]Carter's sin according to AIPAC, was he believed peace is achievable if only Israel can adopt reasonable policies. "Many Arab regimes have become increasingly

---

1   Palestine Peace Not Apartheid, Jimmy Carter, Simon & Schuster, New York, 2006, p 69

preoccupied with domestic problems which include resurgent religious identity, rising expectations among more tendency for these regimes to free themselves from their Palestinian burden."[1] The problem, said the former president of the United States was that the "United States is almost alone in its undeviating backing of Israel". To give Israel political cover against the will of the international community, the United States has used its veto power 42 times since 1973, and in most of these instances it was only the USA and Israel against the world.

Moderate Arab States stalled and delayed the convening of an Arab foreign ministers meeting for days and objected to convening an Arab Summit. Hamas and Gaza were left to their destiny facing the fourth most powerful military army in the world with more than 5000 civilians killed

The New York Times ignored Jimmy Carter's book as if it did not exist. Facts do not seem to be 'news fit to print'. It did not review the book and then only published a negative comment from a former Carter employee and only after Carter's book forced itself on the New York Times own Best Seller list for five consecutive weeks. Responding to smears and vicious attacks, Carter wrote in the Los Angeles Times:

> "For the last 30 years, I have witnessed and experienced
> the severe restraints on any free and balanced discussion
> of the facts ... It would be almost politically suicidal

---

1   Palestine Peace Not Apartheid, Jimmy Carter, Simon & Schuster, New York, 2006 ,P 14

for members of Congress to espouse a balanced position between Israel and Palestine, to suggest that Israel comply with international law or to speak in defense of justice or human rights for Palestinians."

Carter was accused of being an anti-Semite, worst yet, a pro-Nazi. He was attacked for saying even less than Yossi Sarid, a former Israeli minister, and peace activist, in an article at the leading Israeli newspaper Ha'aretz on 26 April 2008.[1] The article, commenting on Carter's book was titled: Yes, It Is apartheid. Sarid concluded in his article:

"It is entirely clear why the word apartheid terrifies us so. What should frighten us, however, is not the description of reality, but reality itself. Even Ehud Olmert has understood at last that continuing the present situation is the end of the Jewish democratic state, as he recently said."

The journalist Michael Massing reports that a congressional staffer sympathetic to Israel told him, "We can count on well over half the House – 250 to 300 members – to do reflexively whatever AIPAC wants." Similarly, Steven Rosen, the former AIPAC official who has been indicted for allegedly passing classified government documents to Israel, illustrated AIPAC's power for the New Yorker's Jeffrey Goldberg by putting a napkin

---

1   http://www.informationclearinghouse.info/article19811.htm

in front of him and saying, "In Twenty – four hours, we could have the signature of seventy senators on this napkin".[1]

The charges of anti-Semitism, pro-Nazism or accusing serious studies of being conspiracy theories is becoming a joke, yet a joke that many people distaste. It is a form of blackmail and pre-emption to police thought, all aiming at keeping such issues away from public discourse, so that the sign-on- napkin senators and those who elected them remain uninformed.

Though these books addressed the Jewish power in the United States, they did not address Jewish power in other parts of the world. Lloyd George, the British prime minister in world war one, for instance, wrote in his memoirs when in the 1930's the general feeling in England was that supporting Zionism in Palestine was a mistake, that he had to "make contract with Jewry" because the Jewish race was so powerful and he needed them to win the war.

"The British promise of a Jewish National Home, when given on November 2, 1917, …created a mere ripple of public interest that contrasts strongly with the flow of ill-consequences that it generated for Britain. To the Jews who went to Palestine, and to many who did not, it signified fulfillment and salvation, but it brought the British much ill-will, and complications that sapped

---

1   Michael Massing, "The Storm over the Israel Lobby", New York Review of Books, June 8, 2006; and Jeffrey Goldberg, "Real Insiders", New Yorker, July 4, 2005

their power. Measured by British interests alone, it was one of the greatest mistakes in our imperial history."[1]

Quoting L. Stein's book *The Balfour Declaration* , he claimed that the British Government when issuing the Balfour Declaration:" was thinking of the rapidly deteriorating situation in Russia, of the apathy towards the war of a considerable sector of American Jewry, of the propaganda value of a pro-Zionist declaration…"[2]

"The British hope was that the influence of Russian Jewry would both keep (Russia) in the fighting line and prevent the Russian grain trade, which was largely in Jewish hands, from being diverted to the Hungry Germans." [3]

If the American presidents or congressmen are awed by Zionist pressure what was the reason the icons of the British Empire themselves were not less afraid than their American peers? Ben Gurion wrote in his memoirs and as recorded by the Israeli historian Tom Segev:

"In turn, top British officials continued to treat Weizmann (leader of the Zionist Organization) with honor, despite the erosion of his position in the Zionist movement. Sir Archibald Sinclair, leader of the Liberal Party, hosted him at his home for dinner;

1   Britain's Moment in the Middle East 1914-71, Elizabeth Monroe, The Johns Hopkins University Press,2nd edition 1981, P 43

2   Britain's Moment in the Middle East 1914-71, Elizabeth Monroe, The Johns Hopkins University Press,2nd edition 1981, P 44.

3   Britain's Moment in the Middle East 1914-71, Elizabeth Monroe, The Johns Hopkins University Press,2nd edition 1981, P 43

Winston Churchill was among the guests. Churchill got drunk, called Prime Minister Stanley Baldwin an "idiot", and promised Weizmann that he would support the Zionists even if they did horribly stupid things. Churchill turned to Clement Attlee, who would himself become prime minister, and pointing at Weizmann, declared, He is your teacher, he is my teacher, he was Lloyd George's teacher – we will do whatever he tells us."[1]

The Jews had significant roles in the downfall of the Tsarist and Ottoman empires.

"Alexander Israel Helphand, who had adopted the underground pseudonym of "Parvus", was a Russian Jew whose professed political objective was the destruction of the Czarist Empire. Where Lenin was merely indifferent to the prospect of German victory, Helphand was positively enthusiastic about it. As it happened, Helphand possessed the money and political contacts that enabled him to pursue his pro-German inclinations." [2]

1   One Palestine Complete, Tom Segev, Henry Holt & Company, New York 1st American Edition 2000 , Pg. 397
2   A Peace to End All Peace, David Fromkin, Henry Holt &Co, New York,1989, Pg 242

Under the sub-title : A Taboo Subject, Mark Weber wrote in The
Journal for Historical Review (http://www.ihr.org) , January/
February 1994,volume 14 number 1

> "Although officially Jews have never made up more
> than five percent of the country's total population,
> they played a highly disproportionate and probably
> decisive role in the infant Bolshevik regime, effectively
> dominating the Soviet government during its early
> years ...

With the notable exception of Lenin (Vladimir
Ulyanov), most of the leading Communists who
took control of Russia in 1917-20 were Jews. Leon
Trotsky (Lev Bronstein) headed the Red Army
and, for a time, was chief of Soviet foreign affairs.
Yakov Sverdlov (Solomon) was both the Bolshevik
party's executive secretary and -- as chairman of
the Central Executive Committee -- head of the
Soviet government. Grigori Zinoviev (Radomyslsky)
headed the Communist International (Comintern),
the central agency for spreading revolution in foreign
countries. Other prominent Jews included press
commissar Karl Radek (Sobelsohn), foreign affairs
commissar Maxim Litvinov (Wallach), Lev Kamenev
(Rosenfeld) and Moisei Uritsky.

Lenin himself was of mostly Russian and Kalmuck ancestry, but he was also one-quarter Jewish. His maternal grandfather, Israel (Alexander) Blank, was a Ukrainian Jew who was later baptized into the Russian Orthodox Church."

It is of interest for us to see how the Jews influenced Russia after the collapse of communism and the USSR. [1]

"A few days ago MSNBC posted on the Internet a list of what it called 'Russia's Robber Barons: the Twelve Men Who Own Russia's Economy,' along with brief biographical sketches of each of these newly made billionaires. It is interesting to note that none of these billionaires had as much as $10,000 to his name ten years ago. ... Of these 12 robber barons listed by MSNBC eight are Jews.... That is indeed remarkable in a country with only about one-half of one per cent Jews in its population...

Boris Berezovsky, Vladimir Gusinsky, Mikhail Khodorkovsky, Vitali Malkin, Mikhail Fridman, Alexander Smolensky, Vladimir Vinogradov, and Anatoly Chubais are Jews, self-acknowledged Jews... all of them new billionaires who have backed Boris Yeltsin with money and media support ...

---

1   Dr. William Pierce article titled 'The Russian Economy wrote: (Free Speech - September 1998 - Volume IV, Number 9)

Jewish billionaire Boris Berezovsky has been described by Forbes magazine as the godfather of Jewish organized crime in Russia...Berezovsky certainly seems to be the Jew who has the strongest grip on Boris Yeltsin. He likes to boast that he's the man who got Yeltsin elected to the presidency... After Yeltsin's second election in 1996 he appointed Berezovsky to the National Security Council.... When it became public knowledge that Berezovsky is an Israeli citizen, however, Yeltsin was obliged to dismiss him.

Dr. Pierce wondered about how such robber barons can maintain their grip on the Russian people:

"And the answer is that they get away with it in Russia the same way they get away with it in America: they control the news and entertainment media... Berezovsky, for example, controls Russia's biggest television network, ORT, as well as a number of newspapers and magazines. Vladimir Gusinsky, who also is the president of the Russian Jewish Congress -- and like Berezovsky an Israeli citizen -- owns Russia's second-largest television network and a number of newspapers and magazines, as well as one of Russia's largest banks".

The Jewish Masonic alliance created what the British ambassador to Istanbul called "The Jew Committee for Union and Progress- the C.U.P (Union Committee for Union and Progress) which deposed Sultan Abdul-Hamid and exiled him to Salonika where he was confined in a villa owned by a Jew. The ambassador wrote the Foreign Office, that a web of Jewish- Masonic network throughout the Ottoman Empire was conspiring for the downfall of the Ottoman Empire."

Jewish lobbies draw their organizational and political power from secret or semi-secret organizations and societies that operate like intelligence agencies in compartments, and utilize acquired centuries and generations of procedures and ways of perfecting their 'deniability'. Bill Casey, CIA former director general, once explained that in the covert and non-transparent world, you form pictures as if you are making a mosaic picture. Only after putting the pieces together, can they become a picture? Circumstantial evidence therefore can be used to decipher the actions of such secret societies. This book will try to put together the mosaic pieces for the reader, so that he can see the picture.

Sign-on-Napkin Congress & One Dollar One Vote Democracy

On February 12, 2008 Secretary of Homeland Security Michael Chertoff, gave a lecture at Harvard University's Kennedy School of Government while serving in the second George W. Bush administration. His talk was titled, "Why Washington Doesn't Work" in which he said:

> "The obstacles to change in Washington are
> more structural (I translate: systemic) than partisan,

according to Secretary of Homeland Security Michael
Chertoff.... . The impediments to change — largely
powerful individual and group self-interest —make it
hard to drive dramatic change in Washington, he said,
and "frustrate the pursuit of the common good."

In my lecture, also at Harvard University's Kennedy School of
Government about six weeks later on March 18 2008, I wondered
how the public good can be achieved by sign-on-napkin senators.
The system is working as indeed it was designed to work, serving
those special interests. How can the pursuit of the common good
be ever achieved if 70 senators will sign on a blank check or an
empty napkin within 24 hours?   George Soros, an icon himself
of those special interests knows best when he argued in his book
The Crisis of Global Capitalism that:

"Capitalism and democracy obey different rules....The
interests that are supposed to be served are different.
In capitalism it is private interests, in democracy it is
the public interest. In the United States, this tension
is symbolized by the proverbial conflicts between
Wall Street and Main Street."

It indeed frustrates the common interest and it can only do so
using sign-on-napkin senators in a one-dollar-one-vote democracy.
Wall Street and multinational corporations are part of the wheel
structure of power of which AIPAC is only one visible component
which 'shock and awe' the congress and presidents anytime of the

day or night! The lobby and all what it represents will use all its power to try to keep facts that will expose it or Israel out of public discourse. How else can they have senators to vote reflexively to their demands or sign on an empty napkin? After being fed up with robber barons and corporations, a former U.S president, Rutherford B. Hays said: "This is a government of the people, by the people, and for the people no longer. It is a government of corporations, by corporations, and for corporations".

A former Jordanian prime minister told us at a dinner table that included also a former Jordan justice minister and the governor of Aljazira State in Sudan that during the peace negotiations between Jordan and Israel, President Clinton tried to influence Jordan to conclude its peace treaty with Israel by granting Jordan few hundred million dollars. Then Clinton looked at Yitzhak Rabin who was in the meeting and told him: "Itzhak, you will help me to get this through with congress wouldn't you?" Here was a United States president asking the help of a foreign leader, an Israeli prime minister to help him secure his promise with the sign-on-napkin Congress of the lone superpower of the world.

The 2009 Israeli Assault on Gaza

Israel and the United States saw that Hamas and Islamic Jihad were obstacles to 'a peace' drafted by Israel to resolve its demographic problems in a so-called two-state solution in which the new

Palestinian entity will assume the security and municipality burdens on behalf of Israel no more. Even a three-state solution was recently advanced by neoconservatives.

The United States and Israel were surprised when Hamas won the majority of seats of the Legislative Council in the 2006 elections that were monitored and certified as free by international observers. 'The only democracy in the Middle East' and the United States started their campaign to change the results of the elections as soon as the election results were revealed, first by arresting the Hamas members of the Legislative Council and simultaneously backing CIA sponsored PLA security apparatus to undermine the Hamas-led government. When Hamas foiled the coup of these security forces in Gaza, a siege on Gaza was enforced. All crossing points in and out of Gaza were blocked including the Egyptian Rafah crossing point. Seven Hamas ministers and two dozen Hamas elected members of the legislative council were arrested and jailed by Israel, and a crackdown on Hamas was imposed in the West Bank.

Since eighteen months of siege failed to undermine Hamas and as the term of Mahmud Abbas was to end the first week of January 2009, and since the second Bush administration will end January 20, with Israeli election due in February 10 2009, the anti-Hamas allies launched an offensive spearheaded militarily by Israel, backed financially and diplomatically by the United States and its allies hoping the removal of Hamas will pave the way for the two-state solution which became an Israeli strategic objective and which was on the front burner of the Obama Administration which is dominated by the 'Clinton Jews' as one British writer wrote to Israeli writer Avnery.

Barak Ravid, Avi Issachar and Zvi Bar'el wrote in the Israeli daily Haaretz on January 6, 2009 an article titled:

> Egypt's Mubarak to EU: Hamas must not be allowed to win in Gaza. "Hamas must not be allowed to win its conflict with the IDF, Egyptian President Hosni Mubarak on Monday told a delegation of European foreign ministers in a closed conversation."

Moderate Arab States stalled and delayed the convening of an Arab foreign ministers meeting for days and objected to convening an Arab Summit. Hamas and Gaza were left to their destiny facing the fourth most powerful military army in the world with more than 5000 civilians killed and wounded, half of them women and children, and the infrastructure of Gaza was totally destroyed.

AIPAC: a Part of an International Power Structure

Though the books mentioned above restrict their research to the extraordinary phenomenon of Jewish power in the United States nowadays, they all stopped short of explaining the real power structure grid of which that lobby belongs and derives its power from. This is what we call the invisible grid of international power representing mainly global financiers, hedge funds, stock exchanges, multinational corporations, think tanks, and corporate media. This book will argue that this invisible power structure had long established non-transparent roots for centuries, and AIPAC is the only visible piece of this structure. The book also connects the relationship of that power structure with Muslims, Arabs and Palestinians in particular.

Professor Carroll Quigley of Georgetown University also a Pentagon consultant, "was especially impressed by the old foreign affairs establishment, part of a larger Anglo-American financial and corporate elite and what he called a 'power structure between London and New York which penetrated deeply into university life, the press, and the practice of foreign policy.' He saw the prestigious Council on Foreign Relations as a concerted, if not conspiratorial, international network." Quigley taught that the platform of both parties is almost identical. A student of Quigley commented that according to Carroll Quigley "it won't matter whom you vote for on November 3 (for the presidency "[1]

1   Roger Morris, as quoted in Partners In Power

CHAPTER TWO:

THE VISIBLE AND INVISIBLES

Is AIPAC on its own, or is it part of an invisible power structure that can 'shock and awe' U.S. presidents, Congress or a whole administration? Did this invisible power emerge spontaneously, or was it the result of a historical process that is now deeply entrenched in a Judeo-Christian Anglo-Saxon culture that evolved as the West was transformed from a feudal to industrial and capitalist society?

Ever since the Protestant revolution and Reformation, a Judeo-Christian culture emerged that became increasingly more (Judeo) than Christian. As capitalism took hold, and Reformists including Calvinism gradually and progressively sanctioned usury, which was banned by all religions, prominence to capital role in society took hold and thus capitalism was fueled which was a system developed around capital being the major factor overshadowing other factors in the production equation. Jews were historically very involved in the money business, not the least because they were banned in many European (but not Muslim) lands from land ownership. Having the capital and centuries old experience in the money business, they dominated the financial world and wielded extraordinary power where they could tip a war in favor of a king or emperor to whom their lending may be extended or by denying it to his adversaries.

The first international banking was probably started by an obscure religious order that not much about its background was known. Few years after the first crusaders successfully conquered Jerusalem, Hugh de Payens, a vassal of the count Champagne, petitioned King Baldwin II on behalf of 8 others and himself to establish them as a religious order. They claimed they wanted to devote themselves to the military protection of pilgrims:

"They sought permission for, and were granted, quarters for their new order in a wing of the royal palace in the temple area. This was the former Mosque al Aqsa, said to have been built on the site of the original Temple of Solomon. From this location the group took its name....Over the centuries to come they would be referred to as the Order of the Temple, the knights of the Temple of Solomon in Jerusalem, and a number of other variations. Two things remained standard however. Whatever the form of their name, it was always based on the Temple of Solomon and it always took second place to the popular name they bear still, the Knights Templar." [1]

Between 1118 and 1127 the new order took in no members and not much about its activities were recorded. When they

1   Born In Blood: The Lost Secrets of Free Masonry, John I. Robinson,. M. Evans & Company/New York,1989, p 66

decided to break out, King Baldwin II wrote a letter to Bernard, abbot of Clairvaux, who was known as a second pope, requesting him to assist the order to get a Rule from the Pope of Rome, which he did. Bernard championed their cause, and through the Kings of Europe the Templar Knights were granted treasure and land. When Hugh de Payens left Jerusalem, he was an obscure leader of an order of 9 people and when he returned to Jerusalem he became the grandmaster of an order sanctioned by the Pope with lots of gold and silver and 300 knights sworn to die in his defense. Within a few years the Templar Knights became the bankers of the crusaders and the Pope, with whom they maintained very close ties. They accepted safe deposits. Even England stored part of the crown jewels with them. Their 'banking' outlets were called commanderies. They acted as agents for collection. They took government contracts to collect taxes. They acted as mortgage bankers lending money on property income. They initiated the service of paper for money. These papers were honored at any of the Templar commanderies, thus being forerunners to checks or sight drafts.

The Jews of Europe were not permitted to own agricultural lands or other means of production and the Jewish communities, especially in Venice perfected some banking techniques, including making loans to rulers. But such activities were not made in public or in institutions. The Templar financial activities broadened the scope of these activities and institutionalized them.

The Templar Knights and the Masons

Two main characteristics were common to the Templers and the Jews: they both made the restoration of the Temple and building a Third Temple a core of their beliefs, and they both were pioneers in banking and financial services. An interesting question may be whether these were they only things they had in common? Was there more to their relationship? The Templars operated an intelligence network and agents in the principal cities of the Middle East and Europe and operated in secrecy:

"Taken all together, the intelligent network of codes, signals, identification techniques, and surreptitious dealings associated with continuous military and financial operations, coupled with a fierce dedication to secrecy in initiations and meetings provided an ideal base to construct a secret society." [1]After fallout between the Templars and the King of France who appointed a Pope of his own, the Templars were rounded up in France and their grandmaster was burned to death. French Templars escaped to England, but when the Pope requested that the King of England persecute the Templars, they went underground with their treasure and records intact.

In his book, *Brothers in Blood- The Lost secrets of Freemasonry*, author John J. Robinson who conducted his research for his book in cooperation with the Masons wrote:

---

1   Born In Blood: The Lost Secrets of Free Masonry, John I. Robinson,. M. Evans & Company/New York,1989

"Now I would test the possibility that there was indeed a connection between Freemasonry and the French speaking Templar order, by looking into the lost meanings of those terms, not in English, but in medieval French. The answers began to flow, and soon a sensible meaning for the name Hiram Abiff, the murdered architect of the Temple of Solomon, who is the central figure of Masonic ritual." [1]

Whereas Robinson had to visit many lands and do extensive research to reach a logical conclusion that was constructed piece by piece due to the secret nature of the Masonry secretive nature, nowadays one only needs to visit the Mason's Meridian Lodge No. 691 website to read under the Subtitle Masonic *Connection:*

"All Knights Templar are members of the world's oldest fraternal organization known as "The Ancient Free and Accepted Masons" or more commonly known as "masons". However, not all masons are Templars. Templary is but a part of the Masonic structure known as the "York Rite of Freemasonry".[2]

Freemasonry developed to a point that makes us state without exaggeration that it has become central to the Judeo-Christian

---

1　Born In Blood: The Lost Secrets of Free Masonry, John I. Robinson,. M. Evans & Company/New York,1989 , p xvii

2　http://www.islipmasons.org/knights_templers.htm

Western civilization of capitalism in the past few centuries.
Robinson wrote:

> "George Washington, a Mason, took his first
> Presidential oath of office on a Bible borrowed from
> a Masonic Lodge in New York City, and the oath was
> administered by Chancellor Robert R. Livingston,
> another Mason and, at the time, Grand Master....
> In addition to Washington and Monroe, the Masonic
> roll of presidents of the United States includes Andrew
> Jackson, James K. Polk, James Buchanan, Andrew
> Johnson, James A. Garfield, Theodore Roosevelt,
> William Howard Taft, Warren G. Harding, Franklin
> D. Roosevelt, Harry S. Truman, Lyndon Johnson,
> Gerald Ford, and Honorary brother Ronald Reagan.

> World War II was fought by British Masonic
> Leaders Sir Winston S. Churchill, Field Marshal
> Earl Alexander of Tunis, Field Marshal Sir Claude
> Auchinlech, Marshal Lord Newhall (Royal Air Force),
> and general Sir Francis Wingate. American Masonry
> was well represented by Generals Mark Clark, Omar
> Bradley, George Marshall, Joseph Stillwell, and
> Douglas MacArthur.

> One hardly knows where to stop in recounting
> Masonic influence on all aspects of western life in the

past 270 years, whether that influence be political, military, or cultural…. ". [1]

We can conclude that the Western civilization that followed Reformation and Protestantism was *a Judo-Christian and not a Christian* civilization, and progressively more Judeo than Christian. It started with a revolt against the Catholic Church and slowly ended with outright hostility to mainstream Christianity through Calvinism and the numerous sects of Restorationalists who openly stated their enmity to mainstream Christianity and even advocated and did change the New Testament as Calvin and others did openly. It is noted that all these Judeo-Christian white Anglo-Saxon Protestantism (WASP) sects were united in their enmity to Islam and their zeal to restore the Jews to Palestine and rebuild the Temple of Solomon. Christian Zionists and Jewish Zionists shared that goal. The stated ultimate goal of Masons is also to rebuild the Temple. The New Testament slowly but surely and the Old Testament became one and the same.

Thus, the Israeli Lobby power comes from the combination of these revisionist Christian sects, the power of Jewish money being the pillar of capitalism and the secret organizations operating undercover that orchestrate the global politics and economics through its network of overt and covert societies, institutions, foundations and dedicated members of carefully screened and selected elites who are aided to positions through which their master plan is implemented. Regardless of the obvious different

---

1   Born In Blood: The Lost Secrets of Free Masonry, John I. Robinson,. M. Evans & Company/New York,1989, Pg. 176 – 177

motives for the Christian and Jewish Zionists, Christian Zionists are taken for a ride as expressed by Lenny Davis who said when told:

> "That the Christian Zionists diverge from Jewish
> beliefs after the arrival of the Messiah in Israel, said:
> "Sure, these guys give me the heebie-jeebies. But until
> I see Jesus coming over the hill, I am in favor of all
> the friends Israel can get." [1]

So: AIPAC Is Part of an International Power Structure

Supra-national worldwide political, economical, financial and military substructures exist today that all together form a wheel of power that steers globalization today. AIPAC is one component of these sub-structures. Modern communications in the information age enabled the integration of these immensely powerful substructures into one wheel of power. In my Harvard Kennedy School of Government lecture of March 18, 2008 I defined globalization or the so-called new world order as actually a hypocritical understatement which in reality *is a* process that transforms nation-stations into banana republics to serve the special interests that own the wheel of power that steers the world via an American Empire now, and a British Empire yesterday. In

---

1   Painting Islam as the New Enemy, Abdulhay Zalloum, Pg 211

reality, not much has changed between yesterday's imperialism and today except for form but not substance. Robert Cooper, an advisor to the British prime minister, wrote in the October 2001 issue of Prospect Magazine comparing the conditionalities of the IMF to-day and imperialism of the Anglo-French of nineteen century when they decided in 1875 to directly control the finances of Egypt to ensure the repayment of debt: "How different is this from what Lord Cromer and others did in Egypt...Sounds remarkably like a rather strict IMF program." It was an East India Company yesterday and a Chevron today, and a Rothschild yesterday and many Rothschilds today.

If one reads Ignatius Donnelly's speech at St. Louis Populist Convention in the last quarter of the nineteenth century, one would think someone is describing the ills of today. Connelly said:

"We speak in the midst of a nation that was brought to the verge of moral, political, and material ruin. Corporation dominates the ballot box, the legislatures, the Congress, and touches even the ermine of the bench...The newspapers subdued or muzzled..."

This Western capitalist imperialism is dominated by an Anglo-Saxon Judeo-Christian imperialism of the world through a web of multinational corporations, corporate media and financial, military, and political institutions, planned, created, dominated and steered by this power structure yesterday and today. These groups succeeded for some time to privatize and hijack the power of governments, lately under the label of privatization.

These "power groups promoting and driving the New World Order are doing so in full public view: i.e., multinational corporations (e.g., the Fortune Global 500s accounting for over 80% of U.S. economic activity); the global financial infrastructure (which includes banks, investment funds, stock exchanges and commodity market operators); multimedia monopolies; major Ivy League universities; international multilateral organizations (such as the World Bank, the IMF/International Monetary Fund, the IADB/Inter-American Development Bank, the BIS/ Bank of International Settlements, the UN/United Nations and the WTO/World Trade Organization) and, most important, key government posts in the United States, Israel, the United Kingdom and other industrialized nations."[1]

Think Tanks Created to Serve the Special Interests Group: CFR as Study Case

A group of influential bankers, lawyers, politicians, and academics who were attending the Paris Peace Conference in 1919 met at the Majestic Hotel in Paris. As it became obvious that the imperial power is moving from Britain to the United states, the power structure prepared for a smooth transition and more insidious ways of exercising their power. They decided to create a web of think tanks, as exclusive lodges through which they can design the post war orders accommodating the imperial

---

1   Salbuchi Global Research Articles by Adrian Salbuchi] Global Research, December 2, 2006

global interests and objectives of the Anglo-American alliance. Twin think tanks were created, one in London named Royal Institute of International affairs (RIIA) and one in New York under the name of Council on Foreign Affairs (CFR). Both think tanks were promoting a social and political order, promoted at the time by "such Masonic fronts as the Fabian Society financed by the Round Table Group which was in turn created, controlled and financed by South African magnate Cecil Rhodes, the international financial dynasty of the Rothschilds, various UK-based Ancient Rite Masonic Lodges, and the British Crown. The CFR got its initial support from the most wealthy, powerful and influential families in the United States, such as Rockefeller, Mellon, Harriman, Morgan, Schiff, Kahn, Warburg, Loeb and Carnegie, Adrian Salbuchi/Global Research Articles.

The treasurer of Rockefeller's Standard Oil Co., Charles Pratt, donated the 68th Street mansion for the New York headquarters of the CFR. The CFR established sister institutions in Canada, South Africa, New Zealand, Australia, Sweden, Netherlands, India and Japan. Since the Rockefeller group and the J.P. Morgan group drafted the legislation which created a private Federal Reserve System to control America's money and banking in 1913, the Rockefeller faction and the New York Council on Foreign Relations have been decisive in its policy control. In the postwar period, William McChesney Martin, Arthur Burns, G. William Miller, Paul Volcker, Alan Greenspan and the present Fed chairman Benjamin Shalom Bernanke all have served as heads of the world's most powerful central bank, the Federal Reserve and all belonged to the same Jewish faith. All were first, members of the CFR.

Among the first CFR directors was Allan Dulles who was a key figure in the United States intelligence community and who founded the Central intelligence Agency (CIA), Walter Lippmann a confidant and advisor of President Wilson and a media icon, many corporate lawyers from J. P. Morgan and other financial institutions, and of course Isaiah Bowman who in 1919 led the team to re-draw the map of Central Europe. Isaiah Bowman also led the secret War and Peace Studies Group that designed the new world order after World War Two, who based on its recommendations the United Nations, the IMF, the World Bank and GATT were created in 1944 in a meeting at Bretton Woods.

From its very early days until today, control of media was planned and achieved. CFR members owned and managed the new emerging radio networks such as NBC, ABC, and CBS radio networks. With newspapers already under their control, including the New York Times, the Washington Post, The Wall Street Journal, and Chicago Tribune, controlling U.S. media was complete. These same networks owned the TV stations and this control was by sight, sound and letter.

The CFR control of global media

Since World War II and the creation of the Psychological Strategy Board in the CIA and State Department, the CFR and the inner circles of the U.S. Elite has devoted enormous resources to control of media. Today, American media is more tightly controlled by members of the CRF elite than the media in Communist China or the tightest dictatorship. The control is subtle so that most Americans are blind to the fact their every political thought is being spoon-fed and manipulated from above.

During the Cold War, a Soviet media group visited the United States to see the "free" media in a democracy. At the conclusion of their tour they were asked if they have any questions.

The Soviet delegation expressed admiration for the degree to which the media was controlled in the United States. They said they heard the same message in every state they visited whether by radio, TV or newspaper. They would love to learn how that was perfected, and went on to say that whoever is controlling the U.S. media was doing a better job than they were in the Soviet Union.

To reflect their changing priorities in the era of the recent globalization of their control since the early 1990's, the major media giants have been reorganized and centralized, globalized in a few hands. The largest media group today is AOL-Time Warner, which in turn controls CBS television, CNN, HBO the largest U.S. pay-TV network, Time magazine group, the largest magazine publisher which includes Sports Illustrated and numerous others; Warner Bros. and other Hollywood film studios. AOL is the largest private Internet provider in the U.S. Gerald Levin is the Chairman of AOL-Time Warner.

The second largest U.S. media giant is the Walt Disney Co. headed by CEO Michael Eisner, an outsider with no ties to the Disney family. Disney today controls several TV production companies including Touchstone TV, Buena Vista TV, and Hollywood film companies including Walt Disney Motion Pictures, Touchstone, Caravan and Hollywood Pictures. It also owns Capital Cities/ABC the second largest TV network with many subsidiaries in Europe.

The third member of the U.S. media cartel is Viacom Inc. It also owns the cable sports network ESPN, Women's Wear Daily, Viacom Inc., Paramount Pictures and recently bought CBS from Time Warner. Viacom controls the worldwide youth market through its cable network MTV, which promotes violence and sex via song videos, and Nickelodeon, Showtime. MTV shows its rock-rap videos to 210 million homes in 71 countries. It is one of the world's most influential communications companies.

Australian-born media mogul Rupert Murdoch is the owner of the fourth largest U.S. media group, News Corporation. He owns Fox TV, whose programs are dominated by neo-conservative propaganda in favor of Israel. Murdoch also owns the New York Post and numerous other newspapers including the neo-conservative Weekly Standard of William Kristol. Murdoch's former business associate, Haim Saban, a Hollywood billionaire who is close to Ariel Sharon and a pro-Israel hawk, recently bought Germany's largest TV group, Pro-7 Media.

The fifth largest media conglomerate is the Newhouse Group, of billionaire Si Newhouse. Newhouse owns 12 TV stations, 87 cable TV systems, the largest circulation Sunday magazine, Parade, New Yorker, Vogue, Mademoiselle, Vanity Fair magazines, the Cleveland Plain-Dealer, Newark Star-Ledger, and New Orleans Times-Picayune.

The striking fact about this concentration of media power today in America is that all the top companies are controlled by CFR members, from Disney to Time Warner to Fox News to Viacom. Perhaps as significant is the fact those CFR members controlling the giant American media conglomerates today are all Jewish. This reality is open for anyone to see, but it is considered so explosive that it is taboo to mention this most clear and obvious fact. If anyone attempts to ask the most basic question about how such a monopoly of power in the media could be controlled by one small ethnic group whose views on U.S. foreign policy might be tainted by a pro-Israel bias, charges of anti-semitism immediately surface. The fact remains that U.S. media today is more concentrated than ever in history, and the control is held by members of the CFR, almost all of whom happen to be Jewish.

The CFR was and is today an elite, private group whose members are chosen by committee for their loyalty to the secret globalist agenda of the Elite. Its members, today just over 3,000 prominent people, control government, both political parties, banking and private industry. Of the 3,000 CFR members, there is inner elite, called by former U.S. Air Force intelligence liaison to the CIA, Colonel Fletcher Prouty, the Secret Team. This Secret Team is approximately 100 select CFR members who in turn control the U.S. State Department, CIA, Defense Department, FBI, U.S. Treasury and all key arms of the U.S. Government.

The new American imperialism, rather than use formal colonies to build its empire, used the ideology of free markets, of open trade, to insure its industry and banks dominated and continued to grow, at the expense of its rivals. With agencies such as the United Nations, with its control of new organizations of economic and financial rule, the International Monetary Fund, World Bank and later, GATT for control of trade, the United States emerged from the Second World War at the peak of its power. It controlled the vast bulk of world monetary gold. It controlled the seven seas, controlled 40% of the world's wealth and industrial capacity, and had escaped the destruction and economic hardship of war.

How Dedicated Bureaucrats are Selected, Trained, and Deployed

To start with let us define the relationship between the invisibles, holders of the real power, and the visible who are selected by them to execute their agendas. The relationship between a devoted elite's class chosen from academics, politicians and bureaucrats and the global financiers and robber barons was defined clearly by Walter Lippmann. A founding member of CFR and a media icon of the permanent establishment in the twentieth century, he divided America's class system into a "special class" – "the responsible men" whose business was to define the national interest – and a largely ignorant "public," who must be steered by that special class. The economist and writer F. William Engdahl quotes Lippmann's view in his book, *Century of Wars*: "This elite would become the dedicated bureaucracy to serve the interests of private power and private wealth, but the truth of their relationship to the power and private wealth should never be revealed to the broader ignorant public. They wouldn't understand." He continues: "The general population must have the illusion that it is actually exerting 'democratic' power. This illusion must be shaped by the elite body of 'responsible men' in what was termed as 'the manufacture of consent'." This "dedicated bureaucracy" is what we call the visible. Real power is with the invisible.

As a case study we will discuss Henry Kissinger and Condoleezza Rice as outstanding members of the dedicated class. An ambitious young Harvard Professor, Henry Kissinger, was sponsored by the CFR in 1957 to head a new CFR study group for the 1960's. Kissinger's 1958 book, *Nuclear Weapons and Foreign Policy,* came out of the CFR project, and Kissinger was hired as a White House adviser by President Kennedy three years later as a result. He became an icon of the invisible power structure coming on and off the government to implement CFR hidden agendas.

Isaiah Bowman, who led the Peace and War Studies group that constructed the post-World War II order, sponsored a publication by Robert Strausz-Hupe, who founded in 1955 the Foreign Policy Research Institute (FPRI). The institute was initially part of the University of Pennsylvania. Strausz-Hupe began, in 1957, publishing the quarterly Orbis, a journal of world affairs. On its editorial board was William Yandell Elliot, from Harvard School of Government, and his student, Henry A. Kissinger, both members of the founding editorial board of advisors. The institute's long-term mission was to promote an American empire, without nation-states, in a post-Soviet world. The lead article of the first issue of Orbis, by Strausz Hupe, titled *"The Balance of Tomorrow"* (reprinted in the winter 1992 issue, after the fall of the Soviet Union, in order to re-commit FPRI to its founding imperial mission) said: "The issue before the United States is the Unification of the globe under its leadership within this generation. How effectively and rapidly the United States will accomplish this task will determine the survival of Western culture, and conceivably the survival of mankind. ...will the coming world order be the American Universal empire? It must be that - to the extent that it will bear the stamp of the American spirit." The new threat to this vision and the new American empire will be coming from Asia, according to the Orbis article. "The American empire and mankind will not be opposites, but merely two names for the universal order ..." Wasn't the gist of the letter of 60 Americans promoting American values as universal, written after September 11 2001, similar to FPRI's mission that was started in 1955? The mentor and professor of the clash of civilizations heroes Huntington, Kissinger, Brzezinski, was on the founding editorial board and Huntington himself, as well as Princeton University-based British geopolitical professor Bernard

Lewis (who was the first to coin the term clash of civilizations), were on FPRI's advisory board. After the collapse of the USSR the U.S. started its drive to implement a New World Order: an American Empire.

On August 23, 1990, three weeks after the Iraqi invasion of Kuwait, Brent Scowcroft, and President George Herbert-Walker Bush's national security advisor used the term "New World Order" for the first time. He told reporters: "We believe we are creating the beginning of a New World Order out of the collapse of the U.S.-Soviet antagonisms." The president addressed the U.S. Congress few weeks later, on September 11, 1990: "A new partnership of nations has begun …. The crisis in the Persian Gulf, as grave as it is, also offers a rare opportunity … out of these troubled times … a New World Order can emerge."

Let us discuss George W. Bush and Condoleezza Rice. When the invisibles decided for George W. Bush to become a candidate for the presidency, he knew very little about foreign policy. During an interview with an American magazine he was asked who Taliban was. Bush thought (very seriously) that it was a Rock n' Roll band. To cover such deficiency two professors from the dedicated bureaucrats, Condoleezza Rice and Paul Wolfowitz were assigned the job of nurturing Bush. Since the fall of 1998, Bush, Rice and Wolfowitz have held, every Sunday night, a three-way conference call to set the plan for the following week's work plan. The next Monday morning, a bigger team would conduct another conference call to set the details of the week's agenda decided upon by Bush, Rice and Wolfowitz. The bigger team included mostly Bush Sr. administration figures, staunch believers in the New World Order and members of the Zionist lobby, such as Richard Armitage, Richard Perle and Dov Zakheim. After the election was won by Bush's son, the participants in the election campaign were given key positions in the new administration to implement the next phase of remaking the world order according to the Shadow Power Structure master plan.

We have explained how presidents-to-be are trained. To explain how the dedicated bureaucrats are recruited, nurtured, and promoted, we will take the case of Condoleezza Rice. She was born in Birmingham, Alabama, in November 1954. Due to discrimination and segregation against blacks in the South, and increased tensions between whites and blacks, her father moved to Denver, Colorado. He became a professor at the University of Denver. She obtained her PhD in international relations in 1981 from the University of Denver under the tutelage of Josef Korbel, Professor of International relations.

In a September 26, 1999 article in the Guardian, Rice said she became a close friend of Josef Korbel's and a frequent visitor to his home. There she met and befriended his daughter, Madeleine Korbel Albright, who would become secretary of state during Clinton's presidency. Albright would claim to be Christian until, one day, after assuming her secretary of state position; a reporter revealed that Albright had a Jewish cousin who lived in a kibbutz in Israel. Albright then admitted her Jewish background and claimed to be excited by her new discovery, at age 60! Josef Korbel had been a diplomat in the pre-war Czech Foreign

Service. He moved to London where he became a key member of Benise's Czech government in exile. He was sentenced to death in absentia by the communists, so he moved with his family to the United States.

Rice moved to teach at Stanford University where, very quickly, she became a full professor. She joined the Hoover Institution on War, Peace, and Revolution and continued to be a Senior Fellow. Under a fellowship from the Council on Foreign Relations she moved to Washington DC, where she worked on nuclear strategic planning in the office of the Joint Chiefs of Staff. In 1989, she joined the National Security Council (NSC) under Brent Scowcroft as chief Soviet specialist. In May 1990, she was promoted to become NSC's senior director for Soviet and Eastern European Affairs. On August 9, 1990, one week after Iraq's invasion of Kuwait and the launching of the New World Order, she was promoted to become Special Assistant to Bush. She supervised the critical years of the transformation of the Soviet Union from a superpower to a third rate power with nuclear teeth. After she left the Bush administration, and until she joined the campaign of his son, she was allied with the multinationals of finance and oil industries and was a board member of many corporations, including Chevron Oil Company, Hewlett Packard Foundation, Charles Schwab, and on the international advisory board of J.P. Morgan.

The CFR creates Bilderberg Group and Trilateral Commission

In 1954, the Elite members of the CFR realized that they required an Atlantic organization which would implement and control policies in the emerging postwar Western Europe, aside from the military policies of NATO. At a private hotel, Hotel Bilderberg, in Holland, the CFR strategists organized an ultra-elite annual series of policy discussions. They were hosted by an American paid asset, paid by secret bribes from the Lockheed Corporation, Prince Bernhardt of Netherlands. Bernhardt had served during the war as an officer in the Nazi elite SS, and was close to SS chief Himmler. After the War, "the Dutch playboy prince" as the press dubbed him, was a useful façade for the US to organize its European affairs via the Bilderberg Group.

Some 100 leading corporate and government leaders from North America and Europe would meet once a year at a secret location, where they banned all press, and discussed pre-planned policy initiatives. The process became known as the Bilderberg Group for the hotel in Holland where the group first met.

In May 1973,   in a secret meeting at the private island retreat of the Swedish Wallenberg family at Saltsjoebaden outside Stockholm, the Bilderberg Group met and planned the economic process of the 400% price shock in oil, a process which Henry Kissinger was to organize as Secretary of State. Of course, it was all blamed on greedy Arab OPEC oil Sheikhs, but the scheme and its implementation down to the last detail was the work of Kissinger and Bilderberg elites organized by the U.S. CFR.

The shadow power structure financed the creation of another international private entity to organize this, the Trilateral Commission. Tri means three in Latin. The three great centers of U.S. power globally, were North America, Western Europe and now Japan.

The Trilateral Commission had as first Executive Director a Henry Kissinger protégé, Zbigniew Brzezinski. Brzezinski had been director of the Russian Studies Institute of Columbia University at the time, an institute funded by the Rockefeller Foundation. Jimmy Carter, then an unknown governor of Georgia, was selected to become a Trilateral founding member, and his Presidency from 1977-1980, was dominated by Brzezinski, CFR member, Cyrus Vance, and other members of the Trilateral Commission.

For the past three decades, the policies outlined at the 1975 Trilateral meeting have been implemented, step-by-step to the point of September 11, 2001, when fear of new terror attacks led the American population to accept police state controls as never in its history. Those who re-read the 1975 Huntington *Crisis of Democracy*, could see the direct parallels between 1975 and 2001. Not by coincidence. Huntington was the author of the provocative article, Clash of Civilizations, which "predicted" wars between Western Christianity and the Islamic world. Huntington first published his thesis in the magazine of the CFR, *Foreign Affairs*.

These organizations, the Council on Foreign Relations, the Bilderberg Group and the Trilateral Commission are the arms and legs of what some insiders refer to as the Secret Team, the U.S. power Elite, through which they organize the world to their gain, as they define it. However, these are only the more visible groups. Behind these are invisible networks of private, secret societies, known as freemason lodges, which organize millions worldwide behind a power agenda, which has been described as an "Interlocking Directorate." The world headquarters for the powerful Ancient & Accepted Scottish Rite of freemasonry was moved from Charleston South Carolina to Washington D.C. This is no coincidence. It is one of the most powerful and secret organizations in the world. It is deeply involved in occult activities such as the support for the rebuilding of the Temple of Solomon in Jerusalem at the holy Al Aqsa Mosque site. Its members are secret, but are known to include the leading members of the Council on Foreign Relations, Bilderberg and Trilateral Commission.

How CFR and Think Tanks Operate

The blueprint for current United States foreign policy was written back in 1992 by the office of then-Defense Secretary, Dick Cheney, in the first George H.W. Bush Administration, shortly after the first Gulf War, Operation Desert Storm. Cheney set out a new doctrine that called for U.S. power in the twentieth century, to be aggressive and unilateral, in order to secure American dominance of world affairs by force if necessary. This "peace through strength" policy has been unfolding from the day George W. Bush took office in January 2001.

The strategic planning was done during the Clinton administration with funding from the military-industrial complex, energy companies, and right-wing foundations. Over time, those working on these new plans evolved into the think-tank they called Project for the New American Century (PNAC). PNAC, established in 1997, had Dick Cheney of Halliburton Corporation, the world's largest oilfield services and military construction company, Donald Rumsfeld, and Paul Wolfowitz.

The elite PNAC circle also included most of the neo-conservative hawks in the Bush Administration whose lies and fabrications led to the war in Iraq. John Bolton, later in charge of arms control and proliferation policy in the State Department; Lewis Libby, Cheney's Chief of Staff; Avram Shulsky, Stephen Cambone and Dov Zakheim of the Pentagon, all were involved. Richard Perle and Karl Rove played key roles in the report as founders of PNAC, along with Jeb Bush the Florida Governor whose state gave George W. the White House in 2000 with unusual help from the Supreme Court.

Was it a coincidence that shortly before September 11 2001, CFR held a conference to determine the effect of a terrorist attack on the financial markets? On July 12-13, 2000, CFR ran a scenario titled "*The Next Financial Crisis: Warning Signs, Damage Control, and Impact*". Earlier scenarios that were not made public, included how a major terrorist attack would cause a meltdown of the U.S and world economy and steps to prevent such a meltdown in a very volatile system. The scenario was part of a public report on the "Financial Vulnerabilities Project". The public scenario assumed that somehow, the United States president will be incapacitated and the "establishment" will have to step in. Interestingly, when September 11 attacks occurred, Vice-President Dick Cheney took charge and went to the situation room with the "establishment", as the president of the United States was out of Washington, in Florida. Of course Cheney, the more seasoned establishment figure, kept the president informed about the events. The financial markets were kept under reasonable control, considering the circumstances. On September 14, 2001, the CFR updated the 2000 scenario at a meeting it held at the St. Regis Hotel in Washington DC. The event was named "The U.S. Commission on National Security for the 21st Century: After the Attack A New Urgency". Former CIA director R. James Woolsey was one of the CFR members who played a key role in the "Financial Vulnerabilities Project". CFR promoted the reorganization of domestic intelligence and emergency management organizations. Bush Jr. complied, and three days later the Homeland Defense Security Agency (HDSA) was announced. Pennsylvania Governor Thomas Ridge was named to head NDSA and was given Cabinet-member status.

On flight RJ 194 from New Delhi to Amman, I was seated next to a retired Israeli general who was a military governor of the West Bank and later on became   administrator of the occupied territories. He was in transit to Tel Aviv via Amman. During our six hour plane journey, we spoke about a range of subjects.

What's pertinent to our subject in this introduction is the power of the Jewish lobby. The general said that he was in the States at the time of the Bush Cheney versus Gore Lieberman presidential elections. Most of Israelis holding American passports went to the States to cast their votes for the Al Gore/ Lieberman ticket since Lieberman was a Jew. An AIPAC member told the general not to worry. Bush and Cheney are in this pocket, Gore and Lieberman are in this other one.

Real power was and remains in the hands of the few, the invisibles who define agendas for both political parties. Presidents and their administrations are actors to market and execute their agendas.

"Come let us declare in Zion the word of God", said William Bradford, quoting Jeremiah as he stepped into the American land off the Mayflower, the now famous ship that carried 101 Puritans of the early Immigrants in 1620. America was the incarnation of the Biblical Promised Land.

CHAPTER THREE

THE ROOTS OF ZIONIST AMERICA

The majority of the earliest settlers were Puritans. They were the early European immigrants who voyaged on the Mayflower. They were a secret sect, who believed the Church of England needed to purify itself from false ceremonies and non-Scriptural teachings. They formed secret congregations, but once exposed they fled to Leiden, Holland en masse in early 1609. While in Holland the Puritans petitioned the Dutch government to "transport Israel's sons and daughters ...to the land promised their forefathers...for an everlasting inheritance."

The Puritans, who stamped their identity with that of the Jews, gave the towns in the new country scriptural names such as Zion, Shiloh, Salem, Jerusalem, and Bethlehem. To Bradford and his companions had finally arrived in the New Promised Land. He later on became the governor of the Plymouth colony. As most of the immigrants to the East Coast were Puritans, the study of Hebrew was encouraged and it was made mandatory at major East Coast universities. The Old Testament was revived and several new varieties of Protestantism sprang up such as the Baptists, Presbyterians and Methodists, and their Bibles were written mostly based on the Old Testament. These new sects constitute the core of Christian Zionism today.

Some History...

Since the Reformation England rediscovered the Jewish Bible, the Old Testament. Books previously discouraged or banned by the Catholic Church were promoted. The media machine of that time, a chorus of writers, poets and philosophers were employed to promote the wedding "the genius and history of us English to the genius and history of Hebrew people." This resulted in a Judeo-Christian culture in England that continued to move closer to the Old Testament. The Hebrew language was revived and Old Testament names became popular among the English people. But the most prominent secret sect that identified itself totally with Jews and the Old Testament were the Puritans

They opposed mass, and opposed church marriage. They abandoned conventional churches. Their worship place they called 'meeting house' with no crosses. They faithfully observed the Sabbath and did not celebrate Christmas and Easter. And they came to America with their prejudices against Islam and Muslims or the Orient or the East as it was also called. After the Mayflower, over the next twenty years, 16,000 Puritans migrated to the Massachusetts Bay Colony, and many more settled in Connecticut and Rhode Island. The American Puritans, just like their co-religious sect in England, strongly identified with both the historical traditions and customs of the ancient Hebrews of the Old Testament. They assumed that their immigration from England was a replay of the Jewish exodus from Egypt. England to them was Egypt and the English king was the pharaoh. They considered the Atlantic as the Red Sea and they considered the New Land as their new promised land, the Land of Israel, and the Indians were the ancient Canaanites. They thought of themselves as the new Israelites. Thanksgiving -- first celebrated in 1621, a year after the Mayflower landed, was conceived as day parallel to the Jewish Day of Atonement, Yom Kippur. It was a day of fasting, introspection and prayer.

Most of the immigrants from Europe until the middle of the 1700s were splinter sects such as the Puritans and the Quakers, an extremist Puritan sect who did not believe in ministers and for whom a Society of Friends meeting together was good enough to bring down the Holy Spirit. Among the immigrant sects were the Calvinists, who early on had challenged the Catholic belief on several issues, as well as the French Calvinists (the Huguenots), the Mennonites, a Swiss sect of Anabaptists who rejected infant baptism, and the Amish.

These immigrants came to America to escape persecution and the one thing that seems to unify them was their Protestantism and closeness to Jewish traditions. To them the Crusades against Muslims was not a distant past. The early wave of these immigrants inscribed on a rock next to their new North American colony:"The Eastern nations sink, their glory ends, and empire rises where the sun descends".

It is believed that freemasonry entered America with the early immigrants from England at least from the mid 1600s. John Robinson wrote:

> "We have seen John Locke incorporate Masonic charges in the constitution he wrote for the proposed colony of South Carolina over half a century before Freemasonry became public (in 1717), including a prohibition against lawsuits for money damages... South Carolina became a bastion of Freemasonry in the United States ...The city of Charleston was the port of entry for what became Scottish Rite Masonry...." [11]

The Templars, Calvinism and Freemasonry

The Puritans and most early American settlers were Calvinists, including the French Huguenot and Dutch settlers on New York which was called New Amsterdam. In 1536 Calvin published the first edition of his work the 'Institutes of the Christian Religion' and Commentary on the Bible thus becoming an international influence on the Protestant Reformation. He belonged to the second phase of Reformation.

Calvinism set the stage for the development of capitalism as his views revolted against the condemnation of usury. In a letter,

---

1   Born In Blood: The Lost Secrets of Free Masonry, John I. Robinson,. M. Evans & Company/New York,1989, *P 285 Robinson*

he criticized the use of certain passages of scripture that was used to oppose usury and charging of interest. He reinterpreted some of those passages and advised that other passages were no longer valid because of the changing times. Thus, in his opinion it is permissible for money lenders to charge interest for lending their money. The Jews of Europe benefited most from Calvinism. Since they were prohibited from owning agricultural land or other means of production they were mostly involved in trade and lending money mostly to rulers. With capitalism fueled by money lending and the emergence of the industrial revolution, Jewish power grew proportionately with that revolution and its prerequisites for capital and banking.

This secret organization's first public appearance was in Jerusalem shortly after the crusaders conquered the city in 1099. The Crusaders committed genocide as they entered Jerusalem as one of the reports to the Pope read,

> "If you would hear how we treated our enemies at
> Jerusalem know that in the portico of Solomon and
> in the Temple our men rode through the unclean
> blood of Saracens, which came up to the knees of
> their horses".

The Jews crowded into their principal synagogue hoping the Crusaders would spare them for being non-Muslims, nevertheless, their synagogue was burnt and they were all killed. Raymond of Aguilers, writing about the mutilated corpses that covered the temple area, quoted Psalm 118:

"This is the day the Lord has made. Let us rejoice and be glad in it". [1]

This mysterious group was generally referred to as the Knights Templar. They sought permission for, and were granted permission to place their headquarters in the Aqsa Mosque which they claimed to be the sight of the Temple of Solomon.

> "One theory proposed, for example, was that the Templars had deliberately chosen that al Aqsa Mosque as their headquarters because it was on the site of the Temple of Solomon, and that in their secret meetings the Templars were keeping alive the order of Freemasonry, which had been founded in the building of that temple". [2]

They became the bankers for the crusaders, issued the first letters of credit, and printed their own money that was honored through any of their numerous branches in Europe and the Holy Land. They acted as agents for collection, maintained trusts, managed properties and dispersed payment to heirs. All these services was performed for a fee. They acted as property managers and mortgage bankers and they issued paper for money which was like sight drafts or checks which were honored in any of their commanderies. They actually became the first multinational

---

1   Born In Blood: The Lost Secrets of Free Masonry, John I. Robinson, . M. Evans & Company/New York,1989, Pg 65

2   Born In Blood: The Lost Secrets of Free Masonry, John I. Robinson,. M. Evans & Company/New York,1989,Pg. 287

financial institution! With the lapse of time, they developed into several variations. But:

> "Whatever the form of their name, it was always
> based on the Temple of Solomon and it always took
> the second place to the popular name they bear still,
> the Knights Templar."[1]

After two centuries of crusades, European kings and princes got tired of the Crusades, especially after their defeat. They lost steam and started fighting amongst themselves, though they continued to give only lip service to Crusades which in reality were not part of their agenda. Only the Pope and the French Grandmaster of the Knights Templar, Jacques de Molay did not give up and continued trying to assemble a new Crusade. For this purpose, the Papal office prepared a merger plan between the Knights Templar and the Hospitallers, another crusading order that emerged during the Crusades which busied itself mostly in nursing and social work.

De Molay and the Templars had every reason to believe that they were on good terms with King Philip, while he was secretly planning for their destruction. They allowed him into the Paris temple for the treasury of France, loaned him money for his wars to acquire British kings continental possessions, and even gave him a loan for the dowry of his daughter Isabella who was to marry England's King Edward's son who became Edward II. The

---

1   Born In Blood: The Lost Secrets of Free Masonry ,John I. Robinson,. M. Evans & Company/New York,1989, Pg 66

Knights Templar largest treasure and properties were in France, and King Philip intended to expropriate it all to himself.

The covert operation against the Templars was assigned to De Nogaret, a first class underworld operator. De Nogaret was known for his capacity to carry out big secret missions. On one day only, in July 22, 1306, De Nogaret arrested all the Jews in France and exiled them all, without their properties a few weeks later. Using a planted spy in a prison cell with a former Templar, De Nogaret was able to extract confessions from the former Templar on some of their secrets. The former Templar confessed to blasphemous practices he claimed were practiced by the Templar order. He said that new members, as part of their initiation rituals, were requested to trample or spit on the cross. They must pledge to put the Templar order and its wealth above any principle, and they must understand that revealing any of the order's secrets will bring them immediate death. This information was sent to the Pope

Even though it appeared as if the Templars knew something was going on, as they tightened security throughout their commandaries, de Molay remained unsuspecting since the Templar order was not subject to the laws of France or any secular king or emperor for any offense, and they were exempted from all forms of torture. Even on the very night that King Philip started his secret operations against the Knights Templar, de Molay was entertained at King Philip's palace with the highest honors in the company of nobility. The next morning, Friday October 13th 1307, sealed orders were sent to all French provinces for the simultaneous arrests of all Templars. Philip's troops descended on every Templar commandery to arrest 15 000 of them, in an area of one hundred and fifty thousand square miles! Their wealth was seized. On November 22, the Pope issued a bull in which:

> "he praised King Philip, stating the official papal position that the charges against the Templars appeared to be true and calling upon all the monarchs of Christendom to arrest and torture all the Templars in their domains. From that date onward the Pope pursued the Templars with enthusiasm."[1]

When the Grand Master de Molay was later arrested he confirmed the charges confessed by the former Templar, though he denied them later, claiming his confessions were to save him from torture. Later on de Molay was sent to his death by burning under a slow charcoal fire.

> The monarchs of Portugal and Spain were more concerned about fighting the Muslims in Spain than on incriminating the Templars, who after all, were helping them in their fight against the Muslims. The Templars changed their name to become the Knights of Christ and as such they reported to the king rather than the Pope. In Germany: "the Templar preceptor Hugo of Gumbach clanked into the council of the

---

1   Born In Blood: The Lost Secrets of Free Masonry, John I. Robinson,. M. Evans & Company/New York,1989, Pg. 133

archbishop of Metz, arrayed in full battle armor and accompanied by twenty of his brother knights. Hugo proclaimed to all present that the Templar order was innocent of all charges and that Grand Master de Molay was a man of religion and honor. Pope Clement V, on the other hand, was a totally evil man, illegally elected to the Throne of Peter, from which Hugo now declared him deposed."[1]

This was a revolt against the Pope and the Catholic Church. Was Martin Luther a disguised monk and a Templar who repeated Hugo of Gumback's charges against the Catholic Church and its Pope two centuries later?

In England Edward II was skeptical about arresting the Templars, as they had a strong influence in the country and in the royal court. He did not act until January 1308 allowing the Templars' grand master de la More to complete the move of his order's documents, jewels and treasures underground. When de la More was arrested, he was given comfortable accommodation and a royal allowance. The few Templars arrested were put under house arrest. Thus, the English Templar order practically remained intact. When the Pope enquired why the Templars were not tortured, Edwards claimed England had no torture experts, so the Pope decided to send him twelve of them. Yet, many of the Templars under arrest were allowed easy escape. This explains

---

1   Born In Blood: The Lost Secrets of Free Masonry, John I. Robinson,. M. Evans & Company/New York,1989, pg 137

why England and then Scotland became the haven of the Knights Templar who went underground and became a secret society.

The Scottish kings and revolutionaries ignored the Papal order as they valued the Templars assistance, and gaining independence from England was their first priority. Eventually, England and Scotland united and the Templars ended on top of things exerting great powers discretely. Their secret organization became known as the Free Masons. The United Kingdom became the bastion of Freemasonry as evidenced from the list of British kings who were confirmed Masons and this has remained the case until today.

Robinson wrote:

> "We have seen that there are only two organizations that have found their principal identifications in the Temple of Solomon: Freemasonry and the Crusading Order of the Temple, the Templars. The great mass of circumstantial evidence has clearly indicated that the common identification was no mere coincidence, but rather that the secret organization was born in the ashes of the public organization that had been condemned by both the church and state in an era of the most brutal bodily punishments ."

In both countries of England and the United States the Hebrew language was revived. The new varieties of Protestants started to use Hebrew names. By the 1720s, it was possible to study Hebrew at Harvard College under the tutelage of Professor Judah Monis. In 1777, Hebrew became a required course in the freshman curriculum at Yale University. Colonial Protestants had an interest that stemmed from a belief that the Old Testament, the Hebrew Bible, laid the ground for the Christian "New Testament." New England clergymen in particular, assumed that an accurate reading of the Old Testament was best done in its original language. To this day, two Hebrew words (*Urim v'Thummim*) appear at the center of the official Yale University seal. These two words appear eight times in the Hebrew Bible. Not only Yale, but also Dartmouth and Colombia placed Hebrew logos on their emblems.

Christian Zionism & Restorationalism:

According to Wikipedia encyclopedia

"Christian Zionism or Restorationalism, is a belief among some Christians that the return of the Jews to the Holy Land, and the establishment of the State of Israel in 1948, is in accordance with Biblical prophecy. Some Christian Zionists also believe that the "ingathering" of Jews in Israel is a prerequisite for the Second Coming of Jesus. This belief is primarily, though not exclusively, associated with Christian Dispensationalism, mainly in English-speaking countries outside Europe. The idea that Christians should actively support a Jewish return to the Land of Israel, as a means fulfilling a Biblical prophecy has been common in Protestant circles since the Reformation. The term Christian

Zionism was popularized in the mid-twentieth century. Prior to that time the common term was Restorationalism."

Restorationalist organizations according to Wikipedia:

"include Christian Conventions, Churches of Christ, Disciples of Christ, Independent Christian Churches/Churches of Christ, Jehovah's Witnesses, the Latter Day Saint movement, Seventh-day Adventists and others. These groups teach widely divergent theologies, but they all arose from the belief that the true pattern of the Christian religion died out through apostasy many years before and was finally restored by their churches. Some believe that they alone fully embody this restoration exclusively; others understand themselves as conforming to a rediscovered pattern of original Christianity that is now found in many churches, including their own."

These new varieties of Christianity (if it is Christianity at all) wrote their own version of the Bible, which was continuously, edited getting closer to the Old Testament by the day! The early Protestant missionaries to the Middle East considered Arab Christians as misguided and needed to be converted just as much as the Muslim Arabs. That was one reason they were strongly opposed by the Maronite Church in Lebanon, even more than by the Muslims!

We may want to conclude that the secret and un-transparent forces existed for some centuries. They revolted against the Catholic Church in Europe, and these same forces dominated the immigration and organization of theology and politics with the aim of constructing of the Temple of Solomon. To do this, Jerusalem and Palestine must be reclaimed from Muslim hands and the forces that must do it must succeed at what 200 years of Crusades could not achieve. Thus, when General Allenby occupied Jerusalem in 1917 it was proclaimed that "Now the Crusades had ended." The bells of Westminster Church started ringing for the first time after the start of the First World War. Lloyd George, the British prime minister, and Lord Balfour, the foreign secretary both were jubilant. Both of them were restorationalists and both described themselves publically as Zionists!

We already noted that the French Revolution was led by Masons, and so was the American Revolution. George Washington, most of his generals, most of those who wrote the American constitution and many American presidents took the Masonic oath. All American presidents were Protestants except for John F. Kennedy who was a Catholic, and he was assassinated before he could complete his first presidential term. Christian Zionism was entrenched in the West many generations before Herzl's Zionism.

Islamophobia, a New Word for an Old Phenomenon

As early as the seventeenth century, Alexander Ross published in 1649 –*Alcoran*- with his stated purpose to expose the falsehood of Islam. In 1734 lawyer George Sales wrote another version and his goal was to assist Protestants "to attack the Koran with success." A copy of this book was found in the Library of Thomas

Jefferson, a main figure among those who drafted the American constitution and who later became a U.S. president. The scanty knowledge on Arabs, Muslims and the Muslim lands continues until this day. This scanty knowledge is mixed with racism and certainly with hatred resulting from a failed two hundred years of crusades.

The moors, the Turks, the Arabs, the East, the Orient, the Middle East or any name you may call the Muslims, is still to the West in general, and the United States in particular, the 'ultimate other', a region and people of a different but distinct culture, and a different social structure and civilization. Early immigrants coming from Europe carried their prejudices against Islam with them to the New Lands. :

> "Although early America prided itself on religious tolerance, that forbearance rarely extended to Islam which was scarcely considered a religion at all. "Oren P 42. Oren wrote that most Western scholars admit that most of those immigrants, even contemporary Americans "knew very little about Islam" and Muslims and their scant knowledge about Muslims and their countries was basically drawn "from the Bible and 'A Thousand And One Arabian Nights' that was translated in America in 1708." [1]

---

1   Power, Faith and Fantasy, Michael B. Oren, W.W. Norton & Co.,
     New York, 2007, pg. 42].

Samuel Langdon, a Harvard President many generations ago, said, "Mohammad was a false prophet.....and an emissary of Satan." Samuel Huntington, a professor at Harvard in the 21st century and a former National Security Establishment figure stated bluntly in his book:

> "The underlying problem for the West is not Islamic fundamentalism. It is Islam... "[1]

Wall Street Journal reported on March 8, 2007 under the title: Bernard Lewis Applauds the Crusades:

> "Famed Princeton Islamic scholar Bernard Lewis drew a standing ovation from a packed house of conservative luminaries Wednesday night in a lecture that described Muslim migration to Europe as an Islamic attack on the West and defended the Crusades as a late, limited and unsuccessful imitation of the jihad that spread Islam across much of the globe."

This speech was given by Lewis at the American Enterprise Institute which gave the George W. Bush administration many of its neoconservatives and was attended by Vice President Dick Cheney, Supreme Court Justice Clarence Thomas, Richard Pearle and many of Washington's political heavy weights. The Wall Street Journal article added:

---

1   The Clash of Civilizations, Samuel Huntington, Simon & Schuster, 1997.

"The 90-year-old Lewis, seen by some as the intellectual godfather behind the administration's decision to invade Iraq, warned in his lecture that the West — particularly Europe — was losing its fervor and conviction in the face of an epochal challenge from the Islamic world. The Islamic world, he said, was now attacking the West using two tactics: terrorism and migration. He listed ideological fervor and demography as two of the chief strengths that the Muslim world had in its favor in its face off against the West, but fell short of offering any prescriptions for what Europe should do to stem the flow of immigrants from North Africa, South Asia and the Middle East." The Wall Street Journal continued: "In the AEI speech, he made the point that the Crusades, as atrocious as they were, were nonetheless an understandable response to the Islamic onslaught of the preceding centuries, and that it was ridiculous to apologize for them."

Applauding Lewis intellectualism and advice, U. S. Vice President Dick Cheney remarked: "…in this new century, his wisdom (Lewis's) is sought daily by policymakers, diplomats, fellow academics, and the news media."

'Islamophobia', a term that was first coined in 1976, gradually crept into public discourse reaching its climax after September 11, 2001. The shortest definition for Islamophobia is the prejudice against or the demonization of Muslims, though the British Runnymede Trust, an independent anti-racist think tank chaired by Professor Gordon Conway of the University of Sussex issued a report defining Islamophobia as having eight distinct features: [1].

1. Islam is seen as a monolithic bloc, static and unresponsive to change.

2. It is seen as separate and "other". It does not have values in common with other cultures, is not affected by them and does not influence them.

3. It is seen as inferior to the West. It is seen as barbaric, irrational, primitive, and sexist.

4. It is seen as violent, aggressive, threatening, supportive of terrorism, and engaged in a clash of civilization.

5. It is seen as a political ideology, used for political or military advantage.

6. Criticisms made of "the West" by Islam are rejected out of hand.

7. Hostility towards Islam is used to justify discriminatory practices towards Muslims and exclusion of Muslims from mainstream society.

8. Anti-Muslim hostility is seen as natural and normal.

The decision to ignore complex realities that magnified recent discourse and tension between Muslims and the West in general

---

1   Islamophobia: A Challenge for Us All, Runnymede Trust, 1997, p. 1, cited in Quraishi, Muzammil. Muslims and Crime: A Comparative Study, Ashgate Publishing Ltd., 2005, p. 60. ISBN 075464233X

and the neoconservatives of the United States in particular exacerbated an already dire situation. Unfortunately, efforts were not directed to create dialogue and better understanding because the neoconservatives, who many believe hijacked the American republic, are working hard to hijack the world through globalization, topping the list Muslim oil and other resources. As 70 percent of the oil reserves remaining in the world that fuels the capitalist industry and war machine is under Muslim lands, the neoconservatives waged their generational war on the one ideology they believed is standing in their way for a globalized empire.

Jeremy Seabrook wrote in the Guardian: [1]

> "Officially, all right-thinking people have forsworn racism ... Islamophobia is the half-open door through which it makes its triumphal re-entry into respectable society."

But the hate campaign of neo-conservatism and its chorus allowed racism to enter America through fully opened doors. After six Muslim Imams were requested to leave a U.S. Airways flight before take off in November 2006, a radio station that covers Washington D.C., Maryland and Virginia conducted a hoax that was very revealing. Here is how the Council on American-Islamic Relations described the event in a press release: [2]

---

1   "Religion as a fig leaf for racism", The Guardian, July 23, 2004
2   http://cair.com/default.asp?Page=articleView&id=2415&theTyp e=NR

(WASHINGTON, D.C., 11/27/06) - A parody of anti-Muslim bigotry on a Washington, D.C., radio station drew support for treating American Muslims in a manner similar to how the Jewish community was targeted in Nazi Germany....In his 630 WMAL program on Sunday, November 26, (2006) talk show host Jerry Klein seemed to advocate a government program to force all Muslims to wear "identifying markers." He stated: "I'm thinking either it should be an arm band, a crescent moon arm band, or it should be a crescent moon tattoo." Klein said: "If it means that we have to round them up and do a tattoo in a place where everybody knows where to find it, then that's what we'll have to do. ..."Richard" in Gaithersburg, Md., said: "Not only do you tattoo them in the middle of their foreheads; you round them up and then ship them out of this country, period." "Heath" in Upper Marlboro, Md., said: "I don't think you go far enough...you have to set up encampments like they did during World War II like with the Japanese and Germans." Later in the program, Klein revealed that his call for discriminatory actions against Muslims was "baloney." Klein said: "I can't believe any of you, any of you, are sick enough to have agreed for one second with anything that I have said in the last half hour."

Jacob Weisberg wrote political articles to Newsweek, New Republic and the New York Times Magazine before joining Slate in 1996. He is a columnist for the Financial Times also. Weisberg commented on Bernard Lewis speech at the American Enterprise Institute: He wrote in Slate's online magazine: [1]

> "What did surprise me was Lewis' denunciation of Pope John Paul II's 2000 apology for the Crusades as political correctness run amok. ...Were you to start counting the ironies here, where would you stop? Here was a Jewish scholar Lewis criticizing the pope for apologizing to Muslims for a holy war against Muslims, which was also a massacre of the Jews."

The First United States Interventions & Wars with Muslims

When the American colonies declared their independence the core Muslim State was the Ottoman Muslim State headed by a Khalifa known also as Sultan, who according to Islam is the political and religious leader of Muslim lands. In Islam, what is to God is to God and what is to Caesar is also to God. The French Revolution and its twin, the American Revolution, both led by Masons advocated secularism: the separation between State and Church. Though this may be possible in Christianity since

---

1   http:/www.slate.com March 14,2007- Party of Defeat: AEI Weird Celebration

indeed there were two entities, a state and a church, this does not apply to Islam which has no church or clergy as both functions are one and the same. Thus, for the West the divorce between State and Church was made final and official. Not so for the Muslims. To adherent Muslims, secularism or the separation of Islam from everyday life is asking Islam not to be itself. Muslim scholars believed, and still do, that the Western powers have as an objective to impose secularism, a Judea-Christian Masonic invention on the Muslim world. To bring about this objective, Western missionaries worked side by side and hand in hand with the Western colonialists, and many times ahead of them to pave the way for Western colonialism and imperialism. Secularism in the Muslim lands became an imperial western objective that was meticulously pursued until it was realized officially in 1924.

The Ottoman Muslim State in 1776 was made up of a highly autonomous confederacy that comprised most of today's Eastern Europe including Serbia, Greece, Bulgaria ,parts of Romania and Ukraine, present Turkey, present Middle East States of Syria, Lebanon, Palestine (and Israel) ,Iraq, the Gulf States, Egypt, Libya, Tunisia, and Algeria. Thus, about eighty percent of the Mediterranean coasts were under Muslim control. The regional states (Wilayat) of the Ottoman Muslim State, especially those of North Africa, considered the Mediterranean, their lake, a Muslim lake, and any other party entering their lake must pay a fee which was called a tribute, something like a Panama Canal or a Suez Canal fee. This was an accepted fact of life in 1776 that Britain, as well as most of North Europe were paying a tribute to the North African states of present Libya, Tunisia, Algeria and Morocco. These states were known to Muslims as Bilad Al-Maghreb, but to the West as the Barbary States. American ships entering the Mediterranean before 1776 when the American colonies were part of Britain were covered by the tribute paid by Britain. It was not so when they separated from Britain and declared their independence.

The North American colonies traded with the Middle East since as far back as the 17th century. In 1625, the Moroccan navy captured a ship that departed from the North American colonies. In 1678 the Algiers navy seized a Massachusetts ship and 13 vessels from Virginia. But by 1770, one fifth of the American exports went to Mediterranean ports and the trade was growing. The new independent United States tried at first not to pay tribute. Since it had no official navy, which was yet to be approved by Congress, American citizens, especially the merchants, assembled a navy between 1776 and 1783, an unofficial naval force to confront Algerian navy to protect their trade in the Mediterranean. The private American naval force was totally destroyed or sunk by the Moroccan navy and in 1784 Morocco captured the American ship Betsy. Two months later, two more American ships, the Dauplin and the Maria were captured by Algiers and 21 American sailors were arrested. As a result, the Congress enacted the law to create the American navy in 1784 and its mission was to protect trade in the Middle East! But also, Congress instructed that there be negotiations with [the Barbary States] to discuss the issue of paying them tribute.

America's ambassador to London and later United States President John Adams was instructed to start diplomatic negotiation with the North African States. He met in 1785 with Abd al-Rahman Al-Ajar, the political representative of the Pasha of Tripoli. Al-Ajar explained the logic behind the North African states policy towards ships entering the Mediterranean, which Al-Ajar described as an Islamic sea and "no nation could navigate that sea without a treaty of peace with them." He concluded that the United States must pay a tribute of one million dollars, a substantial amount if one knows that the United States budget was about ten million dollars only! William Jefferson, who also became a president later on, joined Adams and had talks with Tunis envoy al-Ajar and had no better luck than Adams. Adams recommended to Washington to pay the tribute, which he preferred to call the bribe, as the alternative was war which the United States could not afford and could not win at that time. Grudgingly he in his memoirs that: "Christendom has made cowards of all their sailors before the Standard of Mohamet." Congress also instructed Adams, Jefferson and Franklin in June 1786 to make peace with Morocco. The peace treaty was signed and the ship Betsy was released and a 20 000 dollar tribute was paid. An American council was assigned to Tangiers. The Betsy had been recaptured however, this time by Tunis.

The U.S. Government sent John Lamb as its envoy to Algiers in 1786 to release the American prisoners captured two years earlier. His mission ended in failure as he failed to meet the demand of the Algerians. The issue of the North African threat to American national security was exploited to maximum limits. Until then, the United States had no constitution even though each individual state had theirs. The Middle East threat was overblown for internal political designs. Using this exaggerated threat allowed those advocating for a strong federal government and army to win. Historian Thomas Bailey commented that in some way, the Bay of Algiers "was a founding father of the Constitution." Maybe North African Muslims can be called the fathers of American Navy, because North Africa was used by American politicians to advocate for the creation of a U.S. Navy. The congressional resolution in 1794 authorizing the creation of a Navy specifically stated that such Navy must be adequate for the protection of commerce of the United States against Algerian corsairs.

In 1790 Thomas Jefferson became Secretary of State. With a U.S. navy, he was spoiling for a fight with the Barbary States. He recommended to Congress that the U.S. go to war with Algiers. Congress refused and instead approved a $140 000 tribute payment. In March 27, 1794 George Washington signed a bill authorizing the building of six frigates.

The 'George Washington' was the first U.S. Navy ship to enter the Mediterranean and that was in 1800. It was carrying a $500 000 tribute to Algiers. Algiers, though autonomous, was part of the Ottoman Muslim State and thus contributed to the finances of Istanbul. At Algiers, the Crescent, a 36 gun boat was waiting. That ship was part of previous tributes paid by the U.S.A. to Algiers. After paying the $ 500 000 to the Dey, the commander of the George Washington was informed that his journey was not over. He had to carry material to the Sultan Khalifa in Istanbul. Afraid of having his ship confiscated if he refused, he complied. So the George Washington was loaded with 150 sheep, many ostriches and parrots, sweets and more than a million dollars of gold, jewels and goods. The commander agonized throughout the trip to Istanbul and it bothered him so much when he noted that the Algerians so punctually kept their five daily prayers, rain or shine, struggling in rough waters to stay put while praying in the direction of Mecca.

Jefferson, now a U.S. president, was determined to confront the North Africans as he now had a Navy. With Congress still against the declaration of war, he side-stepped Congress and he ordered the new American Navy to start policing the Mediterranean waters. He ordered the Navy to repulse any aggression by "sinking, burning or destroying their ships." Thus, going to War without Congress became a practice of many later U.S. presidents. Again, Jefferson wanted to intimidate the Pasha of Tripoli, Yusuf Qaramanli with the issue of the tribute. Qaramanli was so enraged, that on May 14, 1801 the Pasha's soldiers went to the American Consulate in Tunis and cut the pole of the standard of the American flag, an act of war. Jefferson wanted war and now he got it. The U.S.A. sent a squadron made of the Essex, the President, the Philadelphia and the Enterprise with the instruction of blockading the port of Tripoli and shelling the city to scare Qaramanli until he surrendered. The instruction for the commander of the squadron was to use its "best exertions to keep the enemy's vessels in port....and subdue, seize and make prize" of any attempting to escape.

The mission started its operations by having the Warship 'the Enterprise' raising a British flag. As such, it advanced to a point blank range from the ship Tripoli. The Enterprise then suddenly raised the American flag and stormed the Ship 'Tripoli' killing 30 of its crew of 80 sailors, arresting its captain Rais Mohammad Soussa, and belting and flogging him in public. A landing party from the squadron went to shore, set 11 feluccas loaded with wheat afire on May 25, 8001. Recovering from the surprise attack, Qaramanli boats managed to escape the blockage and set their own blockade for the American squadron. The marine force that landed on the shore, had 15 members killed, the first marines causalities in the Middle East! The American squadron commander had to surrender to Qaramanli with a white flag in hand.

In August 1803, USS Philadelphia heading a U.S. Navy squadron entered the Mediterranean. They encountered the Moroccan ship 'Almarkoba', attacked it and arrested its passengers. On its way to Tripoli, they attacked Tripoli boats opposite the Tripoli coast. The Tripoli boats withdrew, probably in a tactical move, closer to their shores, but were followed by the USS Philadelphia. Its captain claimed he hit a coral, at which time in the afternoon of October 31, 1803, nine Tripoli boats closed in on the Philadelphia, arrested its captain along with his 307 marines. They were all stripped of their clothes and taken as prisoners to shore. The Tripoli boats tugged the Philadelphia to shore as well and Yusef Qaramanli, the pasha of Tripoli decided to rename it 'the Gift of Allah'. But the Americans came back on the 'USS Intrepid' and on the night of February 16, 1804, a party of American marines dressed as Maltese sailors, got to the Philadelphia and set it on fire. Pope Pius VII considered this an act that did "more for Christianity than the most powerful nations of Christendom have done for ages."

Qaramanli was offered $ 100 000 for the release of the captain and crew of the Philadelphia but he refused. He demanded 1.5 million U.S. dollars! So the US Navy was again called to act against Tripoli. A party of marines, led by Joseph Israel ,under the cover of night were carried close to Tripoli shores by the Intrepid which was also carrying 15 000 pounds of gun power. The mission was to destroy the Qaramanli fleet at port under the cover of night. Obviously they were spotted by Tripoli boats, and the force that landed was killed and the Intrepid itself exploded with its tons of gun powder producing lighting light flares and thunderous loud explosions. Again, when the U.S. squadron commander asked Qaramanli for permission to bury the crew, Qaramanli insisted that their bodies be left to the dogs.

The First American Regime Change Plan in the Middle East

John Eaton, an adventurer by nature, who fought Native Americans enthusiastically, was chosen as America's first council to Tunis in 1799. Then he carried with him the tribute to Tunis, which included two American made warships. He was duly respected according to diplomatic norms with a salute from firing cannons. The Bay of Tunis however, presented a bill for $800 being the cost of gun powder used for the occasion. Eaton became convinced that the answer to America's problems in North Africa was an American force of marines to occupy one of those states to strike fear into the hearts of its rulers. He left his Tunis post and went back to Washington where he and his hard-line supporters promoted his vision. His plan finally was based on a regime change for Yusef Qaramanli. The plan was to use Yusef brother Hamid, who was exiled to Egypt after Yusef took over power. So with Hamid siding with the American plot, Eaton could form an army based on few Americans and other mercenaries. President Madison encouraged Eaton to feel free to apply his "zeal and ….calculations" to help Hamid in overthrowing his brother. Eaton must not expect his covert operation to have overt American intervention. To give him diplomatic protection he was named Agent of the United States to the Barbary States. Eaton sailed for Egypt soon after.

The first two things he did were to locate Hamid Qaramanli, whom he finally located at Burj El-Arab. Then he promoted himself to general! And he started to assemble his army which finally numbered about 400. It was made of unspecified numbers of American marines, 90 Tripolitans, 63 European mercenaries [or contractors per today's terminology!) as well as 250 Bedouins. Hamid pledged to set the American prisoners free when he assumed the post of his brother. The trip across the desert was characterized by severe weather, tough terrain, dwindling provisions and frequent fighting between the Muslim and Christian soldiers of his army. On more than one occasion Eaton army Bedouins were about to revolt and even Hamid himself had second thoughts about the merits of his mission against his brother. Eaton had arrangements with the U.S. Navy that an American war ship would meet him at the Bay of Bomba, thirty miles west of Tobrok, loaded with supplies and ammunition. Sure enough, USS Argus arrived loaded with supplies and food. With new supplies and refreshed, Eaton's army continued to Derna, the second largest port of the region. The plan was for it to be the launching pad to Tripoli. Eaton's army arrived at the gates of the port city on April 15. Self-made general Eaton demanded that the governor surrender his city. The governor's response was: "my head or yours." Now American battleships the 'Argus, the Hornet and Nautilus' that were hovering within range from Derna started to bombard the city's defenses. Eaton started his attack. He was shot through the wrist and two of his marines along with many of his army were killed or wounded. Three thousand troops of Qaramanli suddenly arrived, encircling Eaton and his army and they started a counterattack. Sixty of Eaton's army was killed at the first charge. Eaton and his army were now under siege. The U.S. had to conclude an agreement with Qaramanli. President William Jefferson appointed Tobias Lear as representative of the United States. Lear thought that only through peace with Yusuf Qaramanli could America have its prisoners released and normalize relations with Tripoli. He negotiated with Yusuf and agreed to exchange one hundred Tripolitan prisoners with 296 captive American marines and their commander, plus a cash payment of $60 000. By the end of May, the USS 'Constellation' advised the besieged Eaton of the agreement. Hamid was handed to his brother, and he lived peacefully in Tripoli thereafter. On June 4, 1805, USS Constitution arrived at the harbor of Tripoli and carried away the American prisoners and their commander. And America's first armed attempt for a regime change in the Middle East ended in failure! Yet until this day, US marines hymn includes the lyric 'to the shores of Tripoli" even though there was not much for them to brag about at the battle of Derna!

The United States grew stronger and bigger. By 1815 President James Madison sent an American fleet against Algiers, Tunis and Tripoli forcing them to stop attacking American ships. That put an end to a thirty years war between American and the Muslim North African States.

Two Hundred Years after Marine Bombardment of Derna

The international issue of Newsweek of May 12, 2008 (p 30) carried an investigative report titled Destination: Martyrdom. The report was to determine why the city of Derna was the base for so many volunteer suicide bombers during the war in Iraq.

When in 2007, American marines raided the headquarters of an Iraqi resistance group, the Mujahedin Shura Council at the Northern Iraqi town of Sinjar, they started to analyze the files and nationalities of 606 fighters background and were stunned to find out that 112 came from Libya including 52 from the small city of Derna with a population of 50 000. Saudis numbered 244 but on per capita basis, the Libyans represented the highest percentage, and the city of Derna was by far the highest producer of Jihadi suicide bombers. Take the case of 20 year old Abd al-Salam Bin-Ali who was born and raised in Derna. He was blind in one eye, graduated as a veterinarian; he was jobless in an oil rich country that left his city and most of Eastern Libya very underdeveloped. He repeatedly watched the 'The Lion of the Desert' a 1981 epic of Libyan resistance starring Antony Quinn who acted as Omer Al Mukhtar, the charismatic, white-robed Muslim holy warrior who led the revolution against the brutal Italian occupation. Al Mukhtar became known as the Lion of the Desert. For 20 years, Mukhtar's guerrillas harassed the Italian forces until he was finally captured in 1931.

"Italy's practices were brutal. According to one Libyan census, the native population dropped from 1.2 million in 1912 to 825.000 in 1933: 'the direct result of Italian policy', says Ronald Bruce St. John, a widely respected scholar of Libya who adds that Italy's tactics included concentration camps, deliberate starvation and 'mass execution that bordered on genocide'".[1]

Qarna was the sight of the American Marines first battle in the Middle East, supported by mercenary 'contractors'. The city was bombarded by the American fleet in the early 1800s.

---

1   Newsweek, May 12, 2008 (p 30)

If the marines still remember 'the shores of Tripoli' until this day in their Hymn, so do the people of Derna remember the American bombardment of their city. Abd Al Salam also tuned in to Aljazeera and other Arab satellite channels and was horrified by the causalities and destruction he saw happening to the Iraqis and their infrastructure. He told his mother that he wanted to go and fight the Americans in Iraq, but retracted to comfort his mother when she got upset. Then one day he disappeared. After few weeks, the family received a call from him. He said he was now in Ramadi. "I am in Iraq," he said!

Concerned about the number of Libyans joining the Iraqi resistance, the U.S. State Department in November 2007 sent a delegation led by Gen. Dell Daily to Tripoli to meet with senior Libyan officials. The Libyans at first could not believe the numbers provided by the Americans until they were shown the documents from Sinjar. According to later American reports, the U.S. was pleased with the level of cooperation provided by the Libyan authorities in combating 'terrorism'. The Newsweek report concluded:

> "Despite the Sinjar revelations, few U.S. officials believe that Kaddafi is sending fighters to Iraq. A wave of Jihadists returning to Libya from Iraq with new skills would be at least as big a nightmare for him as it is for Americans."

Anti-American resistance is deep rooted as can be concluded by the Newsweek interviews with some relatives of the Mujahidin.

When the reporter advised the Mayor of Derna about the number of his citizens who volunteered as Mujahidins he did not believe it until again he was confronted with the documents. Then the Mayor said:

> "If this number is true, it's very bad. It's bad for politics. But it's not bad for Muslims to do their duty. America said that this war is for freedom. And it's not."

The Sarna city mosque's 60-year-od muezzin, Anuri Al Hasadi, was just arriving from afternoon prayers when a Newsweek reporter stopped by to ask him about his 18 year old relative Ashraf who volunteered as a Mujahid and was now in Iraq. At first Anuri did not want to answer but then he suddenly erupted. "Oil! Oil!" he cried. "America needs oil. It's America's fault."

28-year-old Abdelhakim Okaly slipped out of Derna in the late spring of 2007. Even though his relatives request the city immigration office to deny him a travel permit, as they worried he may go to Iraq, they noted that Abdelhakim was increasingly irritated by what he considered the brutality of American occupiers of Iraq. He came from a well to do family, and had a chance to join the family business, but insisted he chose to take up the call of Jihad against the American invaders.

The brother of Abd al Salam al-Ali, Abdelhamid, said he has now come to terms with his brother's death. "When he was killed, I was really very happy", he says, frowning and wringing his hands. "In my opinion he was right to go. He was right to go. We see people getting killed for nothing. I used to think about going myself". Now Abd al Hamid is the family's sole support. "I can't go now", he says quietly. "It's only me now".

Asa McFarland, a Massachusetts
Presbyterian, declared in 1808:
"When that (Ottoman) empire falls...the Jews
will begin to be restored to Palestine ...and Christ
will take to himself his power and reign."

The way the State Department described Gersson (American consul in Jerusalem appointed in 1844) as someone who had lost half his mind while the other half was erratic, may be applied to many Judeo-Christian fanatics that have flooded the Holy Land since Ibrahim Pasha's permissive law. Harriet Livermore was one of those. The daughter of a New Hampshire congressman, she established her own sect of Baptism and left to the Middle East. She met a Lady Hester, another 'weak mind'. They both decided to combine forces but finally disagreed on which of them was elected to hold the hands of Jesus as he re-enter Jerusalem! Palestinians today have to deal with such lunatics!

CHAPTER FOUR

THE AMERICAN CRUSADES

United States Role in the Ottoman Empire's Disintegration

Soon after President Madison sent the American Navy to subdue the North African states, a cultural invasion of the Middle East was planned. A group of American clergymen, industrialists and businessmen formed in 1810 the American Board of Commissioners for Foreign Missions with the purpose of fostering missionary centers in the non-Protestant world. America, they claimed, had a divinely assigned role to act as a "light unto nations." To American Protestants, the Eastern Christians, Greek Orthodox and Armenians were spiritually misguided, but could be easily converted. They called them "Christians in name" only. The Muslims, they thought were spiritually nil and were desperately waiting for salvation.

Many clergymen started to advocate evangelizing the Jews and uniting the Old Israel with the New. A Massachusetts Presbyterian, Asa McFarland declared:

"When that (Ottoman) empire falls…the Jews will begin to be restored to Palestine …and Christ will take to himself his power and reign."[1]

In 1816, an issue of Niles Weekly Register wrote that when the "weak and imbecile" Ottomans are ousted from Palestine, the Jews will return and swiftly make that desert "blossom like roses." It was a predetermined agenda of the Protestant missionaries to assist in the disintegration of the Muslim Ottoman State so that their restorationalism could be realized.

Before departing from Boston to the Holy Land and becoming the first missionaries to the Middle East, two 25 years old preachers addressed the crowd at Boston's Old South Church and what became the missionaries program for the Muslim world. Levi Parsons was the first to speak:

> "'They who taught us the way to salvation were Jews', Parsons began. They had faithfully preserved the Bible, had worked, suffered, and died defending 'our' religion, he attested. 'Our God was their God. Our heaven is their heaven'. Most crucially, Parsons recalled, they had provided humanity with its Savior. 'Yes, brethren, he who now intercedes for you before the throne of God … is a Jew!' To show their gratitude for the Jews' munificence, he concluded, Christians must strive to restore that people to sovereignty in its ancestral and biblical home.

---

1   Power, Faith and Fantasy, Michael B. Oren, W.W. Norton & Co., New York, 2007,P 89

Parsons explained how the Jews had been living for eighteen centuries in political limbo, homeless, and shorn of independence. The time had now arrived, however, to redress that inequity. 'Admit', he said, 'there still exists in the breast of every Jew an unconquerable desire to inhabit the land which was given to the Fathers; a desire, which even a conversion to Christianity does not eradicate'. That land was Palestine, once splendorous but now not an independent state nor even a distinct province, but a sparsely inhabited Turkish backwater waiting for its rightful owners to regain it. And reclaim it they would, Parsons ventured. Were the Ottoman occupation of Palestine to vanish, 'nothing but miracle would prevent their (the Jews) immediate return"'. [1]

Parsons said that the return of the Jews to Palestine was a necessary condition for the emergence of a Messianic Jewish polity, thus fulfilling the prerequisite for the "Second Coming". The second preacher, Pliny Fisk spoke about redemption and Palestine. Ending the speech he said:" Every Eye is fixed on Jerusalem." The Church crowd burst into tears. Thus, from this Church which was the stage for instigating Americans to dump the East India Tea into the sea and spark the American Masonic-led revolution, the spark of the new Crusade was ignited, this time again from Boston, U.S.A. The two preachers toured the

1   Power, Faith and Fantasy, Michael B. Oren, W.W. Norton & Co., New York, 2007, Pg 80-81

whole country and were well received and they received donations from the various churches for their Crusade, not unlike the tours of the Pope before the first European Crusade. John Adams, a future president, wrote according to Mordicai Noah in 1819: "I really wish the Jews again in Judea an independent nation." Zion, which was America to the early pilgrims, now became Palestine to those American crusaders.

The agenda of the missionaries therefore became clear: the return of the Jews to Palestine, and the destruction of the Muslim Ottoman State that, according to the missionaries, were occupants of Palestine. The new Crusade began and the missionaries were the Crusaders spearhead. Ninety Eight years later, Palestine was occupied by the British to create that Jewish polity in Palestine. General Allenby said as he entered Jerusalem in 1917:"Now the Crusades had ended."

To that end, the missionaries worked patiently and planned and executed a cultural invasion that assisted, along with other factors, in the disintegration of the Ottoman Muslim Empire. The American ambassadors assigned to the Ottoman capital Istanbul (or Constantinople) were either Christian Zionists or Jewish Zionists such as Straus, the brother of the Macy's department stores owners who, according to the British ambassador in Istanbul who served in Istanbul about the same time as Straus, participated actively with the Jewish Masonic C.U.P to depose Sultan Abdulhamid, who refused Herzl's offer a few years earlier, to trade Ottomans permission of Jewish immigration to Palestine against payment of all the Empire's debt! Some historical background is needed so we can understand the geopolitics surrounding the Middle East which was part of the Ottoman Empire.

Historical Overview

For us to understand the environment which was prevailing in the first half of the nineteenth century we must review the geopolitics of the Middle East which was part of the Ottoman Empire, which also was the Muslim core state.

The Ottomans derived their name from Osman, the founder of what became the Ottoman Muslim State or Empire as it is called in the West. His tribe came from Central Asia fleeing the Tang Chinese Empire. They settled in Turkish Anatolia which was made up of Ghazi provinces occupied from a weakened Byzantine Empire. The provinces belonged to the Seljuk Muslim State. Osman's father Ertugrul settled in Western Anatolia, he and his tribe converted to Islam and fought with the Seljuks, and finally led one of the ten Ghazi provinces under the Seljuks. He was succeeded by his son Osman who in 1299 declared sovereignty of his province and started to expand it by unifying the Ghazi provinces. This state continued to expand until it spread over three continents, became the prime world power for some time until its dissolution in 1923. It became the Muslim core state whose head according to Islamic tradition became the Khalifa of all Muslims, entrusted in seeing God's Koran and Sharia'a laws implemented. Since there is no Church in Islam, there is no separation between state and church. Orhan, Osman son, expanded the growing empire and crossed the Dardanelles strait, in 1362. But the Ottoman Empire reached its zenith when Mehmed II captured the Byzantine Empire's capital, Constantinople that was renamed Istanbul in 1453.

As per Encyclopedia Wikipedia:

"At the height of its power (16th–17th century), it spanned three continents, controlling much of Southeastern Europe, the Middle East and North Africa, stretching from the Strait of Gibraltar (and, in 1553, the Atlantic coast of Morocco beyond Gibraltar) in the west to the Caspian Sea and Persian Gulf in the east, from the edge of Austria, Slovakia and parts of Ukraine in the north to Sudan, Eritrea, Somalia and Yemen in the south. The Ottoman Empire contained 29 provinces, in addition to the tributary principalities of Moldavia, Transylvania, and Wallachia."

For six centuries the Ottoman State became the center of the world situated between the East and the West, controlling the Mediterranean as an Ottoman Muslim lake for a considerable portion of its life. It inherited not only Constantinople but actually the Byzantine Empire as well. A distinctly Ottoman Islamic culture resulted from adopting, adapting and elaborating on Byzantine and other cultures of its ethnic and religious groups within the state. The empire passed through essentially five stages:

Rise (1299–1453)

Growth (1453–1683)

Stagnation and reform (1699–1827)

Decline and modernization (1828–1908)

Dissolution (1908–1922)

Applying Muslim law, the Sharia'a, the Ottoman Muslims never forced their non-Muslim subjects to convert to Islam unwillingly. Thus, in the Ottoman Christian possessions in Europe, although there were some converts to Islam, a great number of the population remained Christian. During the Spanish Inquisition, the Jews were evacuated to the safety of the Ottoman Muslim State particularly to Salonika, Cyprus and Constantinople. As we will see later, it was Salonika that became the center for the dissolution of the Ottoman Empire.

By the beginning of the nineteenth century, the survival of the Ottoman State was mainly because of a delicate balance of power amongst the European and Russian Empires whose rivalry for influence and territories in the Ottoman State resulted in a policy of keeping the empire sick, ensuring that all efforts for reform or rejuvenations are aborted, until the day the powers may agree on how to divide the spoils of the Ottoman State. Napoleon invaded Egypt, which was under Ottoman sovereignty in 1798. He assembled at Toulon a large fleet and army, not disclosing its destination or purpose.

Ottomans realized that ethnic conflicts were promoted by the powers and were not related to the issue of Ottoman governance. They noted that every effort to reorganize or reform was aborted.

Greece declared its independence from the Empire in 1829 after the end of the Independence. When the Ottoman and Egyptian armies and fleets were about to eradicate the Greek Revolution, European powers destroyed the Ottoman and Egyptian navies.

Nationalism was first encouraged in the Danubian Principalities and Serbia; in 1875 Serbia, Montenegro, Bosnia, Wallachia and Moldova declared their independence from the Ottoman Empire.

After the Russo-Turkish War of 1877-78, independence was formally granted to Serbia, Romania and Montenegro, and autonomy to Bulgaria, with the other Balkan territories remaining under Ottoman control. Yehuda Solomon Alkalai, a Serbian Jew encouraged a return to Zion and independence for Israel during these times.

Following defeat in the Russo-Turkish War of 1877-78, Egypt, which had previously been occupied by the forces of Napoleon of France in 1798 but recovered in 1801 by a joint Ottoman-British force, was occupied in 1882 by British forces on the pretext of managing the finances of Egypt to enable it to pay its debt. It was made a protectorate in 1914 along with Sudan

Ottoman North African provinces were lost, one after the other, starting from Algeria (occupied by France in 1830), Tunisia (occupied by France in 1881) and Libya (occupied by Italy in 1912.)

Napoleon's Invasion of Egypt & Syria:

To understand the state of balance of power politics in the Nineteenth century when the American missionaries started to arrive, we present the Napoleon invasion to Egypt and Syria as an example of the geopolitics of those days, and illustrate that foreign powers did not allow the fall of the Ottoman Empire when Mohammad Ali's son Ibrahim was on his way to Istanbul with nothing to prevent him from taking over the Ottoman capital. Not only did the European powers destroy his fleet, they forced him to adopt free trade IMF style, and reduce tariff on European goods which resulted in the destruction of his industry and aborted all his reforms. But first, let us discuss Napoleon invasion, its motives, and how it went astray.

Napoleon orders as the aim for his Egyptian invasion were

> "to clear the English from all their oriental possessions…
> and notably to destroy all their stations at the Red Sea
> ;to cut through the Isthumus of Suez and to take the
> necessary measures to assume the free and exclusive
> possession of that sea to the French Republic." [1]

Napoleon sailed with 300 ships and 40 000 troops to invade Egypt, an Ottoman province at the time. He ultimately arrived at the city of Cairo on July 25, 1798 after uneventful battles with the Mamelukes who were supposed to be defenders of Egypt on

---

1   The Ottoman Centuries, The Rise and Fall of the Turkish Empire, Lord Kinross, Perennial, 2002, Pg 424

behalf of the Ottoman Empire. The Egyptians were stunned when they saw the French entering Cairo, echoing the easy American entry to Baghdad on April 9, 2003. It was the "shock and awe " 1798 style. Initially, the French soldiers bought everything more expensively to lure the population to their side. French soldiers walked the streets unarmed. So did American marines in 2003. Napoleon brought with him to Egypt 36 scholars to understand Egypt, its culture and change its laws from religious to secular, a strategic goal not only for Napoleon but for the West including the American missionaries. If the Americans were claiming they were bringing democracy loaded on Cruise Missiles, so did Napoleon who claimed that his invasion brought enlightenment. He ruled by proclamations, like Bremer, the first American proconsul to Iraq did. And again as George W. Bush claimed, Napoleon claimed that he came to liberate the population from their rulers' oppression! A standard cliché! Change the dates, few names and it's the same story.

When Napoleon entered Cairo he called the dignitaries (the sheikhs). He told them that he wanted to rule the country by a group of ten and set up the laws. That is how America ruled Iraq after the 2003 invasion as they created the Central Provisional Authority, the CPA. So Napoleon had his CPA. He made the newly built palace of Mohammad Bey al Elfi, the former governor as his headquarters. So Napoleon had his Green Zone just like Bremer made Saddam Hussein's presidential palace complex in downtown Baghdad his green zone. After the population of Cairo (and Baghdad!) woke up from their "shock and awe" they didn't like what they saw: a foreign occupier and they started their insurrection! The French responded by setting up cannons (of course they did not have F-16s) and firing them at what they determined to be the command center of resistance, the Al Azhar University Mosque. Napoleon wanted to stay the course, so he sent one general after another. He sent General Dupuy and his troops to conduct 'Operation something' to stop the demonstrations and insurrections. Riots that turned into rebellion started in October 1798. General Dupuy was killed along with many of his soldiers! Napoleon thought he got the insurgency leadership, including the chief of the Corporation of the Blind, who was executed along with four others. The French even poisoned the dogs because the dogs would sound a warning as French soldiers approached. Also they demolished parts of the city including some mosques, homes, and palaces. That must have been Napoleon's Fallujah. Napoleon noted that the Ottomans, the Mamelukes and the British were forming an axis of evil to evict him out of Egypt so he decided to declare a preemptive war so he invaded Palestine but was defeated at Acre. So he returned to Egypt and left for France secretly on August 22, 1799, his mission unaccomplished. It seems that he was rewarded for his defeat and he was proclaimed as the First Consul of France in 1799, just like George W. Bush was rewarded for his Iraq fiasco with a second term!

General Kleber was left in charge in Cairo. He was killed by a Muslim foreign insurgent named Suleiman Alepin. A foreign Muslim insurgent?! A Jihadist? Or was he from Al Qaeda - never mind that it did not exist at that time. Alepin was executed along with two others and Kleber was succeeded by General Jacques Menou who later converted to Islam. He became General Abdulla Jacques Menou. He married an Egyptian and had a son he named Said Soliman Murad. But finally, a coalition between the British, the Mamelukes and the Ottomans drove the French out. The second in command, who later became the head of the Ottoman forces, Mohammad Ali became commander in 1803 and Viceroy of Egypt reporting to the Ottoman Sultan by 1805. The interaction of Mohammad Ali with the British army and operatives during the war against the French gives credibility to the assumption that Mohammad Ali was tacitly approved by the British Empire, otherwise he would not have had their support. British imperial influence remained considerable in the Ottoman Empire during the progressive stages of indirect influence in the early 19th century to outright occupation in 1882 to declaring Egypt as a protectorate of His Majesty the King of England. British troops remained in Egypt until 1954.

After consolidating his power in Egypt, Mohammad Ali ruled for over 43 years (1805-1848), and embarked on ambitious industrialization and modernization projects. In agriculture he expanded the area under cultivation, and planted several crops that were geared for exports such as long-staple cotton, sugarcane, indigo and rice. He operated a centralized agricultural system where farmers were allocated the area and the crop they should grow The government sold the crop for a mark-up and used the surplus income for the construction of public works projects including irrigation, canals, roads, dams, and barrages as well as financing industrial projects and the military. Modern factories were set up for weaving cotton, jute, silk, and wool as well as manufacturing sugar, glass indigo, and tanning. Machinery was imported and foreign advisors were employed. About 4 percent of the population became employed in the industry. As was practiced in Europe he imposed embargoes and tariffs to protect the industry against cheap imports especially during its formative years. He was steadily moving to achieve a favorable trade balance. He built a strong army and naval force that the Ottoman Sultan, to whom he officially reported, used once in a while when needed. Mohammad Ali's son was dispatched to fight the Wahhabi movement in Arabia, and assisted the Sultan to fight the rebellion of Greece in the 1820s. The European powers were alarmed at the rising strength of Mohammad Ali. An European Allied fleet sunk the entire Egyptian navy on October 24, 1827 at Navarino on the southern coast of Greece.

When Mohammad Ali's son Ibrahim Pasha proved to be a brilliant general and he waged successful wars and conquered Sudan (1820), Western Arabia, and Syria (1831/1832), Mohammed Ali entertained the idea to take over Constantinople (Istanbul) and replace the Ottoman Sultan, and thus, rejuvenate the Muslim empire. His son Ibrahim defeated the new Ottoman army in the battle of Konya on December 21, 1832 in Anatolia and nothing would have stopped from reaching Istanbul and realizing his goal. This time Russia intervened and a compromise resulted whereby Ibrahim was confirmed as an official governor

(Wali) of Syria, and Mohammad Ali received Crete and Hejaz as compensations. Most of the European powers preferred a weaker Ottoman empire that would disintegrate when they could agree to whom and where its pieces should fall. They decided to check Mohammed Ali's rising power as they saw it as threatening to them in this strategic part of the world.

The best way to limit Mohammad Ali's power would be to strain his financial resources. Since the United Kingdom induced the Ottoman to sign the Treaty of Balta Liman in 1838 in which free trade terms favored the UK, Mohammad Ali was asked to do likewise. Since doing so would result in reduced tariffs and would bankrupt his treasury, he refused to oblige. Consequently, British and Ottoman forces drove Ibrahim Pasha out of Syria after its occupation and rule for about a decade. The British fleet bombarded his troops in Beirut in September 1840. The Egyptian army was forced to retreat. Ibrahim Pasha lost Acre in November and a British naval force anchored at Alexandria. Mohammad Ali was forced to accede to British demands according to the treaty of 1841. The most significant points of this treaty were that Mohammed Ali had to give up all the acquired territory except Sudan, but worst yet he was compelled to agree to the Anglo-Ottoman Balta Liman Free Trade treaty which established "free trade" terms. This meant that Mohammad Ali was forced to abandon his economic policies and establish new tariffs that were more favorable to imports. This resulted in the decimation of the local industries that took decades to establish. Also, limitations on the size of his army were imposed. The year after the treaty was enforced the tax arrears came down by 80 percent, Egypt debt went up to 2.4 million pounds and Mohammad Ali had a nervous breakdown that lasted severely for one week. His health continued to decline, he was deposed in July 1848, his son 'Ibrahim died in November 1848 and Mohammad Ali himself died in August 1849. By 1879 Egypt's debt, under the watch of British advisors went up to 100 million pounds and Britain decided to occupy Egypt and manage its finances.

Here is how the above was explained in the Library of Congress country study on Egypt:[1] "The historian Marsot has argued that Britain became determined to check Muhammad Ali because strong Egypt represented a threat to Britain's economic and strategic interests. Economically, British interests would be served as long as Egypt continued to produce raw cotton for the textile mills of Lancashire and to import finished goods from Britain. Thus, the British and also the French were particularly angered by the Egyptian monopolies even though Britain and France engaged in such trade practices as high tariffs and embargoes to protect their own economies. Strategically, Britain wanted to maintain access to the overland route through Egypt to India, a vital link in the line of imperial communications." This policy became an established British policy as formulated by Lord Palmerstone, the British minister of foreign affairs and continued until WW1. Britain preferred a weakened but intact Ottoman Empire that would serve its strategic and commercial interests and allow it to maintain its influence in the region, rather

---

1   http"//countrystudies.us/Egypt/21/htm

than from a unified, militarily strong state that may threaten its interests.

Thus, the imperial policies to keep a weak Muslim state and the compulsory policies of "free trade" and other economic or even social policies resulted in the continued political and economical supremacy of Western empires. These policies were mostly responsible for the status of the Muslim world today, and it is not Islam or Islamic culture that prevented the Muslim world from rejuvenating itself.

Yet, though the idea of a canal connecting the Mediterranean with the Red Sea was conceived as early as the first decades of the 19th century, work started on the Suez Canal in 1859, and the canal was finally opened in 1869. Debt traps had been an old and are still the practice of Western empires and their financiers. The European powers introduced credit to Egypt at such high rates, and it eventually accumulated to an extent that gave Britain and France the excuse to foreclose on the Egyptian economy. Khedive Ismael, Mohammad Ali's grandson, was in such a financial mess that in 1875 he had to sell Egypt's shares of the Suez Canal to the British for 4 million pounds. It was Disraeli, who closed the deal and it was the Jewish financial house of the Rothschilds that gave the British government a loan to conclude the deal. With British advisors all over the place, Britain occupied Egypt on the pretext that it must control its finances for loan repayments in 1882, and then proclaimed Egypt a protectorate at the advent of World War One.

Challenges to the Empire from Within

In the 18th and 19th century, two movements challenged the Ottoman Caliphate. The first was the Wahhabi movement. A native of Najd who was well travelled, preached passionately to purify Islam from the many practices that had crept into it over the centuries and to return to the pure sources of Koran and Sunnah, as practiced during the Prophet's days. The House of Saud adopted his teachings. The Wahhabis started to spread their doctrine outside the peninsula and they made a thrust into Iraq and reached the gates of Baghdad in 1799, the year Napoleon invaded Egypt. The Wali in Baghdad had to make a treaty with them. Two years later they sacked Karbala. They turned westward and occupied Mecca and Medina, and northward and reached Damascus and Aleppo. The Ottoman Sultan instructed Mohammad Ali to restore the holy places and he sent his army headed by one of his sons to the Peninsula in 1811 in a campaign that lasted until 1818 in which the Holy Cities were re-captured and Mohammad Ali's forces occupied the Wahhabi's stronghold of Dir'iya.

The second challenge came from Mohammad Ali and sons. In 1820 he sent his armies south and occupied Sudan. Per the Sultan's request, after he occupied Crete in 1822, his navy was sent to Greece in 1824 to assist in putting down the Greek Revolt. He landed in Morea, conquered the peninsula, captured Athens and put down the revolt. Alarmed by this success and Mohammad Ali's potency, the Powers of Europe decided to wage a joint attack to sink Mohammad Ali's and the Sultan's fleets, which they did at

Navarino in 1827. Mohammad Ali rebuilt his forces very quickly, and he wanted Syria as a reward for helping the Sultan in Greece. By July 1832, his invasion of Syria, led by his son Ibrahim Pasha was complete.

Mohammad Ali was ambitious and wanted to establish an Arab Empire and become Caliph himself. Ironically, he was not an Arab, but an Albanian Muslim, but ethnicity was not strong amongst Muslims and Islam placed no limitations on the origins of a Caliph as long as he was capable and met the pre-requisites of Islamic knowledge and adherence. Mohammad Ali did not speak Arabic well, nor was he religious. And yet, he wanted to promote Arabism and become the caliph of Muslims. It is on record that Western powers or at least some of them encouraged him to do so. France was in favor. It was in favor of anything that would block the way of Britain to India. Also, he received concrete suggestions from Austria, through Count Prokesch-Osten who outlined the Austrian position in a note dated May 17, 1833. But strong opposition came from Palmerstone of Britain. Ibrahim Pasha continued his invasion and defeated the Sultan's forces near Istanbul. Nothing would have stopped him from taking over the capital except for the Powers intervening by pressing his father to stop him and withdraw to Syria. Even there, Britain drove him out of Syria. The countdown for Mohammad Ali started. He was forced to sign a free trade treaty that destroyed Egyptian economy, and he was forced to limit the number of his armed forces. Finally he was deposed.

Mohammad Ali's rule in Egypt was the closest to what one may call a secular regime. In the short period that Ibrahim Pasha ruled Syria, he changed the system and laws to a secular-like regime, and his new educational system was organized with the assistance of a Frenchman, Dr. A. Clot who was an advisor to Mohammad Ali in Egypt and who according to George Antonius,

> "was genuinely devoted to ...the cause of national regeneration in Egypt; and one of his concerns in the higher schools which he directed was to inculcate a true sense of Arab national sentiment". [1]

Antonius continues:

> "The rule of tolerance established by Mohammad Ali had one unpremeditated result: it opened the door to Western missionary enterprise; and, by so doing, it gave free play to two forces, one French and the other American, which were destined between them to become the foster-parents of Arab resurrection."[2]

According to Encyclopedia Wikipedia : "Ibrahim Pasha, born in the town of Kavala, in the Ottoman province of Rumelia, currently located in the Macedonian region of Greece was the

---

1   The Arab awakening, George Antonius, Simon Publications, 2001, Pg. 40
2   The Arab awakening, George Antonius, Simon Publications, 2001, Pg. 35

son of a repudiated Greek Christian woman and a man named Tourmatzis." He was adopted by Mohammad Ali.

Mohammed Ali and Saddam Hussein

A quick review to old practices of Western empires and the lone empire of the day may be interesting. We will compare Egypt in the 19th century and Iraq in the 20th and 21st centuries and see how striking the similarities between the ways of the Anglo-Saxon empires the British of yesterday and the Americans of today:

- Both Saddam Hussein and Mohammad Ali were strong men who consolidated power, sometimes ruthlessly.
- Both came to power at least by tacit agreement of the prevailing imperial power of their day, Britain in the case of Mohammad Ali, to preserve a weak Ottoman empire, and the United States in the case of Saddam Hussein to fight local communists in Iraq that joined the government of Abdulkarim Kassem at first, and to fight the Islamic Revolution of Iran.
- Both adopted secularism, an outstanding demand of the West from Muslims
- Both built a strong army and an industrial base to support it. In both cases the build-up was blessed by empires.
- Mohammad Ali's army was used to wage wars on behalf of empires and Saddam waged proxy wars, knowingly or

unknowingly on behalf of empires, such as the Iranian Iraqi eight years war.

- Both formed strong armies beyond the acceptable limits of the empires, and in both cases the empires demanded a reduction quantitatively and qualitatively of the armed forces capabilities. Once they did not comply they were doomed.

- Saddam nationalized Iraq's main crop, the oil industry and Muhammad Ali managed state-controlled system of Egypt's main crops of agriculture and imposed embargos and tariffs to protect his nascent industrialization projects. Both actions were not to the likening of the empires.

- Mohammad Ali's armed strength was checked. His fleet was totally destroyed by a coalition of allied European powers of the day. He was left with a calculated accepted strength for about a dozen years afterwards. Also, Saddam's armed forces were destroyed to a predetermined level in the 1991 Gulf War, and were left for a dozen years as well, before he was removed.

- Mohammad Ali, with British fleet guns pointed towards Alexandria, was forced to adopt a free trade agreement in 1841 where he had to remove his tariffs and allow British goods to flood the Egyptian market thus killing the Egyptian nascent industry. After occupation and with American troops all over the place, Iraq had to adopt free trade and free enterprise which bankrupted all the state companies that were operating under Saddam including both civil and military industries resulting in hundreds of thousands of unemployed.

The Early missionaries

Parsons and Fisk, the restorationalist preachers mentioned earlier, began their six weeks journey in 1820 from New England and their destination was Smyrna, today's Izmir in Turkey. Their choice of destination was due to its large Eastern and Greek Orthodox Christians, whom Fisk and Parsons, like all missionaries, considered their faith to be long-corrupted Christianity. But they found comfort in their being Christians though, they thought, in name only. They were shocked at how different that world was from theirs whether in architecture or culture, and they started learning the language and traditions. They bought the local attire and turbans. They received instructions from Samuel Worcester, secretary of the American Board that their mission could be anywhere in the Middle East, Palestine, Syria, Egypt and Persia included. In December 1820 Parsons left Fisk in Smyrna and he voyaged towards Jerusalem. He wrote *"The permission to anticipate the special welfare of Zion is an unspeakable privilege."* English missionaries already in the area advised him to arrive in Jerusalem during Easter and Passover pilgrimages so he could remain inconspicuous. They recommended he wear a turban, and appear as a literary gentleman.

Parsons arrived in Jerusalem after three months. He was dazzled by Jerusalem, which he considered the center of the world.

He visited the Wailing Wall and claimed to be the first American to do so. He was distressed that he could not evangelize any of the Jews or Eastern Christians living in the city. He found that they enjoyed religious freedom, yet he was distressed that he could be allowed neither to reside in Jerusalem nor to build a Protestant church there. Jerusalem, he found, was something special to the Ottoman Muslims being the venue of the Al Aqsa mosque and the center of the three Abrahamic religions. Foreigners were allowed to visit but not reside in the city to ensure continued Muslim majority. Muslims fought the Crusades some two hundred years to re-take Jerusalem and the Holy Land. The Ottoman Muslims wanted to keep it that way. Parsons spent 80 days in Jerusalem and then he headed back to Smyrna.

Greece was a part of the Ottoman Muslim State possessions since the 15th century. As the Ottoman state weakened and instigated by European powers, the Greek revolted against the Ottoman rule. Smyrna, having a large Greek population was subjected to sectarian fights. Fisk and Parsons were evacuated by the American warship USS America. It became a practice of the American Navy in the Mediterranean to project its power throughout the 19th century to protect the missionaries against any danger or obstacle that might stay in their way. Both preachers were transported to Alexandria. Parsons was sick with dysentery and he died shortly afterwards. Fisk was now alone but not for long.

The American Board sent a replacement to Parsons, Jonas King, a professor at Amherst College, along with a printing press to be based in Malta. In Malta, Fisk and King met a Joseph Wolff, the son of a Rabi, who claimed he converted to Catholicism and now Protestantism. The trio decided to go to Jerusalem via Egypt. In Egypt they met Bashir II, a Muslim who converted to Maronite Christianity and a Druze prince. Somehow, resulting from these shady meetings in Egypt, the missionaries changed plans and headed for Beirut. Fisk now decided to make Beirut as his base for several reasons. First, it was situated on the sea and he and his colleagues could be evacuated easily by the standing American fleet in the Mediterranean. Second, it had a well established English diplomatic representation which was very willing to assist its co-religious missionaries when and if needed. Third, the Mount Lebanon District had a large population of Druze and Eastern Christians, and Fisk thought it may be good ground for his missionary work to save their souls. To beef up the Beirut station after Jonas King returned to the States in 1823, the American Board sent two missionaries instead: Isaac Bird, a graduate from Yale, and William Goodell, a graduate from Dartmouth. They both came with their wives. They were to assist Fisk in his first American school project. Fisk convinced the American Board that since it was very hard to convert the elders, they should work on their children and help them adapt to the American ways and possibly save their souls through Christ. The American Board was elated and proclaimed that the:

"Standard of truth and righteousness has been erected. The Chaplin of the US senate proclaimed that he now sees the day when missionaries loaded with books will feel their way into the farthest retreats of Mohammedan darkness." The cultural Crusade had begun.

The First Years....

The first few years did not go exactly as Fisk wished. His school was boycotted by Muslims and Maronites alike, and only a few Jewish children, who sold their New Testament Bibles for paper, enrolled. The missionaries could only convert one Muslim who was thrown into jail until his death. So Fisk went on preaching missions every now and then. In 1825, he left to Jerusalem. He was caught distributing religious tracts, an unlawful act, so he was arrested, put in chains, and sent to jail. It was only after the personal appeal of the British council that he was set free. Fisk planned to return to the States on leave in October 1825. He decided to visit Nazareth before he leaves. En route, he distributed tracts and tried to preach what people did not want to hear, he was beaten very badly by the crowd. He was borne back to Beirut, and never recovered. He ended up with an agonizing death.

The schooling project did not progress, until an event changed things. It was the Egyptian occupation of Syria and Mount Lebanon by Ibrahim Pasha who introduced new educational system rules that favored Western-style education! The Egyptian occupation lasted for less than a decade, but it irrevocably changed things in a way that helped the missionaries in their Cultural assault on the Muslim population of the Ottoman State.

The Cultural Invasion Backed by the American Navy

Most Americans sided with the Greek Revolt due to their religious convictions that the Greeks were nothing less than later-day Crusaders and that the war was one between Christendom and Islam. Support groups sprang up in major cities and universities. The Greeks received covert assistance from Europe, but when the Ottomans and the Egyptian forces regrouped to crush the revolt, a combined Western power naval force from Britain, France and Russia, intervened overtly and sank most of the Ottoman Egyptian flotilla on October 20 1827 in the Bay of Navarino, tilting the balance towards the Greeks. Not only did ordinary Americans cheer the European aggression at Navarino, Secretary of State John Quincy Adams considered the Greek revolt as part of an eternal struggle between Christendom and Muslims whose religion is "fanatic and fraudulent" which embraces a "doctrine of violence and lust". Bernard Lewis echoed these perceptions to his neoconservative clients of the Bush administration almost literally.

The success of the Greek revolt and Greece's secession from the Ottoman Empire signaled and hastened the process of disintegration of the Ottoman Empire and caused wars among the European powers. The Russians conquered huge parts of Bulgaria and a year later France landed 24000 troops and occupied Algeria. The Americans negotiated with a weakened Sultan the Treaty of Navigation and Commerce on May 7, 1830 in which the U.S.A.

secured extraterritorial rights – capitulations in the Ottoman Empire. Thus, the missionaries and American merchants enjoyed American protection even within the territories of the Ottoman Empire. David Porter became the first American charge d'affaires in Istanbul and then also the first ambassador. The treaty was negotiated by the commander of the U.S. Navy Mediterranean squadron. By 1830 the American Mediterranean naval force equaled and to some even surpassed the British navy.

By 1827 the missionaries' success was very modest. Though they succeeded in establishing schools in Syria, their effort to produce converts was unsuccessful. After the Ottoman defeat at Navarino, the American Board for Foreign Missions was emboldened and now it wanted to try again to establish a mission station in Jerusalem after the failure of Parsons and Fisk. They chose 30 year old Josiah Brewer to spearhead the mission and his mandate as spelled by the Board was to establish a "permanent station in the Holy Land and initiating the ingathering of the Jews". Brewer landed in Palestine just after the naval battle of Navarino in 1827. Palestinian Muslims at the time thought of themselves as devoted Ottoman subjects. They suspected all Westerners whom they called 'Franks' as enemies of the Muslim State especially after Navarino. He was evicted from one Palestinian Village after another until he gave up and and went back to Boston.

To appease the West so it would bless his occupation, Ibrahim Pasha abolished the Ottoman rules that prevented the foreigners from staying in Jerusalem and granted the non Muslims unprecedented privileges. Taking advantage of this, the American Board authorized a new Palestine mission to be led by William and Eliza Thomson. They arrived in Palestine in 1834 when a violent revolt encompassed Jerusalem and most of Palestine. The Muslim Palestinians resented, and violently rejected Ibrahim Pasha's new laws. Thomson had to flee from Jerusalem leaving his nine month pregnant wife behind. Ibrahim Pasha used all kinds of arms against the revolt including cannons. Thomson could only return to Jerusalem following a column of Ibrahim Pasha's reinforcement to find Jerusalem in ruins resulting from the harsh use of force to subdue the revolt, and his wife died shortly afterwards. Two missionaries replaced Eliza after her death but still they had no success. The American Board was finally compelled to admit, by the end of 1834 that 'not a single soul' had been 'converted to God' .The Board gave up and decided to abandon further missions to Palestine. One of the missionaries thought that Palestine was not the blessed country but 'a land of devils!' With Ibrahim Pasha cancelling the Ottoman laws that forbade foreigners from residing in Jerusalem, the tide was reversed. When Edward Robinson arrived to Jerusalem in 1838 with Eli Smith, they were greeted by eight missionaries and their wives, quite a change from only few years back! Robinson was a professor of Scripture and he was a pioneer in archeological work, by which he started to identify contemporary Palestinian sites and cities with old Hebrew sites and names mentioned in the Old Testament. He gave them their Hebrew names. The influx of Americans now became so great that Washington appointed consular agents to seven Palestinian cities. Biblical archeology was invented by Robinson and it was elevated in the West to a science.

Things did not go well for the Missionaries in Beirut also. Following the Egyptian invasion of Beirut by Ibrahim Pasha, fighting erupted between pro – Ibrahim Pasha Maronites and the Druze. The Maronites again pressed their demand to expel the missionaries and expressed their opposition to Protestantism, missionaries and their schools. With such conditions, the missionaries felt isolated and in physical danger and decided that their entire community should leave Beirut, but apparently not for long.

A New Start

The year 1840 may be considered as a landmark when Britain decided to drive Ibrahim Pasha from Syria, Palestine included. They saw in Mohammad Ali a threat to their designs in the area as he was aspiring to create an Arabic speaking Muslim Empire. He became a military and economic force beyond the limits accepted by the European powers. Also, an Arab Muslim Empire might threaten the integrity of the Ottoman Empire that they wanted to preserve until the day balance of power allowed Britain to grab the territories it desired for itself in the area. The British, with some help from the Sultan's Ottoman troops, drove Ibrahim Pasha from Syria and stability was restored. The Ottomans who regained sovereignty again over Syria, including

Palestine, maintained the equal rights for non-Muslims, allowed foreigners to reside in Jerusalem and recognized Protestantism as another religion (millet). Now the missionaries had their day. The Missionaries, who deserted Beirut, came back and they re-established their schools. Eli Smith began an Arabic translation of the Bible. He brought a printing press and he started producing about 50000 volumes per year.

Emboldened, the missionaries after their return continued to call Islam fraudulent as well as describing all forms of Eastern Christianity as decadent and outmoded .The local churchmen, especially the Maronites, were unhappy with the return of the missionaries and their new found boldness. The Maronites Patriarch petitioned the Sultan in 1841 to banish the evangelicals from the empire, and to issue them an expulsion order. The Sultan turned to the American ambassador for his comments. The ambassador asked the missionaries not to provoke the Maronites or Muslims otherwise they were doing so "at their own risk". The American Board for Foreign Missions was infuriated and intervened in Washington. The Secretary of State Webster reversed Porter's decision and instructed him to "omit no occasion … to extend all proper succor" to the missionaries. The American missionaries challenge to Ambassador Porter was the beginning of a lasting alliance between Church leaders and decision makers in the U.S.A. This was mostly due to America's embrace of expansionism that was marketed as Manifest destiny in the U.S.A and now in the Middle East. Politicians used God for ungodly purposes, especially in the decade of the 1840s.

The U.S. ruling and money classes decided to invade the rest of North America beyond the 26 states that existed by then. Their Manifest Destiny ideology laid claim to a God- given right to conquer the rest of their Promised Land, which was America. As such they invaded the territories to the South and West until they expanded from coast to coast. This ideology gave America a self-given divine right to disseminate both its secular and religious principles all over the world. Missionary Eli Smith said that the U.S. was a powerful nation and it was time for the Muslims to feel this. The missionaries now started not only to call on Washington for diplomatic help, they even started calling on the U.S. Mediterranean warships to protect them or show force when they felt it was needed. The USS Independence toured Egyptian and Syrian ports and it was ordered to,

"Inquire into the safety and prosperity of the Missions ... and to extend to them such assistance as they may require"[1]

Also in 1840, Cyrus Hamlin landed in Istanbul. He obtained permission to open a school at Bebek near Istanbul. The Armenian patriarch had protested when some Armenian children attended the school. Instead, the missionaries influence increased as they established for Sultan Abdul Majid, a school for the Ottoman military cadets, modeled after similar American schools.

1   Power, Faith and Fantasy, Michael B. Oren, W.W. Norton & Co., New York, 2007, Pg. 131

Joseph Smith, the founder of the Mormon religion dispatched Orson Hyde as his personal envoy to Jerusalem in 1841. There he prayed for God to *"restore the kingdom unto Israel-raise up Jerusalem as its capital, and continue his people (as) a distinct nation and government."*

The restorationalist ideas promoted by the early immigrants and colonial Americans became part of the American mainstream ideology after independence. It was strongly embraced by Methodists, Congregationalists and Presbyterians. A restorationalist professor of Hebrew at New York University, George Bush, the forebear of two later American presidents carrying his name, wrote a biography of Prophet Mohammad, in which he called him a false prophet. He wrote in 1844 a book titled *The Valley of Vision; the Dry Bones of Israel Revived*. In this book, George Bush called for the creation of a Jewish state in Palestine. Such a state, George Bush said, would provide a link between humanity and God.

It was another British restorationalist of those days, Lord Shaftesbury, who coined "a land without people for a people without a land", much earlier before the Zionist movement borrowed this slogan to market its ideology.

Warder Cresson, a restorationalist, was 46 when he met Secretary of State John C. Calhoun requesting to be appointed as American consul to Jerusalem. Calhoun approved Cresson's request. As he left the United States on June 22 1844, he wrote that he left his wife, children and farm because "the light...of

God's precious promise, in reference to the return of the Jews was so great…that I could no longer remain at home." [1]

As soon as Cresson arrived in Jerusalem he extended American protection to cover the city's Jews. He was openly pressing for a Jewish state in Palestine in a way that alarmed the State Department and caused his dismissal as consul. He remained in Palestine for some more years. The way the State Department described Cresson as someone who lost half his mind while the other half was erratic, may be applied to many fanatics that flooded the Holy Land after Ibrahim Pasha's permissive laws. Harriet Livermore was one of those. The daughter of a New Hampshire congressman, she established her own sect of Baptism and left for the Middle East. She met a Lady Hester, another 'weak mind'. They both decided to combine forces but finally disagreed on which one of them was elected to hold the hands of Jesus as he re-entered Jerusalem!

The first effort for Jewish colonization of Palestine took place in 1851 when Clorina Minor an Episcopalian and wife of a wealthy businessman sailed to the Holy Land to introduce the Jews to the 'set time' to favor Zion. Soon after she arrived in Jaffa, she met a British Jew, John Meshollam. Both decided to encourage the Jews and introduce them to 'the active labors of love'. They received financial backing from the Anglo-Jewish financier Baron Moses Montefiore and some American donors, and they bought a piece of land in the village of Artas, near Bethlehem and established an

---

1   Power, Faith and Fantasy, Michael B. Oren, W.W. Norton & Co., New York, 2007, Pg. 143

Agricultural School for Jews. After two years of failing to find Jews interested in agriculture, the project was abandoned, but Minor did not give up. She moved to a new orange groves farm near Jaffa, again paid for by Montefiore and she called it Mount Hope. Again the project failed and Minor died in 1855. The project was taken over by Warder Cresson who was still residing in Palestine. Cresson abandoned Christianity and became a Jew. He gave himself a Hebrew name, Michael Boaz Israel. With his farming and colonizing project failing, he left Palestine and returned to his family in the United States. Next to Mount Hope, another American named Dickson founded another colony for the Jews which was called the American Agricultural Mission. Palestinians living nearby this project exhibited their hostility so Dickson sought help from the U.S. Navy squadron in the Mediterranean. The Navy responded positively and they supplied Dickson with arms. Thus, the first American arms supply to a Jewish colonial project was recorded.

While Americans in those days were exercising their Manifest Destiny which they tailored to sanction their genocide against native Americans and to wage expansive and aggressive wars on others, and while one sixth of the American population were slaves with no human rights and were treated as animals in their plantations, Americans still braved to talk about liberty and freedom and saving souls, forgetting their famous saying that charity starts at home! Such duplicity and hypocrisy became an inseparable characteristic of Americans, and they 'never leave home without it.' Those visitors came from different professions and backgrounds, and just as the missionaries they aspired for a Middle East without Muslims or at least without Islam, which they almost unanimously called a false religion. Sara Haight called for an international "political crusade", may be not much unlike George W. Bush's crusade a century and a half later, to humble Islam and to dismantle the Ottoman Empire. Naval Chaplin Walter Colton concluded "Islamism", he said in 1838," was the grave of inspired truth and liberty." He added, "The scepter and the crescent alter and throne, will sink together." James Cooley thought that, "Muslims must adopt a more enlightened and consistent faith" so that they may join the "civilized nations". An artist, William H. Bartlett wrote after his visit to Cairo in 1849:

> "Egypt fallen and decrepit, bowed under oppression and a false religion with America, daily raising in power, a land of light, freedom, enterprise and Christianity".

But the missionaries learned the hard way that it was not possible to convert Muslims to Christianity. Their efforts in thirty years did not produce but a shady three converts from Islam! The next best thing they decided was to change the Muslim values and Americanize them, so they can remain Muslims only in name. After all, the missionaries considered Eastern Christians as Christians in name as well. This required missionaries to embark on a new grassroots cultural invasion starting from kindergarten to university to change these values. Maybe in a generation or two they will see the results. They did!

So the Middle East in general witnessed a cultural invasion by the missionaries not only from America, but from Britain, France, Russia and Prussia. The Americans though were second to none in human and financial resources.

The New Target: Secularism through Nationalism

The missionaries knew Arab history very well. They learned that Arabs, even before the Christian era penetrated Syria and Iraq and formed dynasties in these territories. They formed the Arab kingdoms of Palmyra and Hira in the third century A.D. The cultural impact of the Arabs before Islam was minimal, as the old civilizations remained unchanged: Greco-Armenian in Syria, Sassanian in Iraq, and Greco-Coptic in Egypt.

As Muslims, the Arabs now empowered by the impetus of Islam and the power of their faith spread in every direction. Within a hundred years from the death of Prophet Muhammad, they reached the borders of China on the east, and northward they advanced into Anatolia near Constantinople. Eastward they occupied all North Africa, crossed the Gibraltar into Spain and crossed the Pyrenees into France and reached not far from Paris. But unlike the Arabs before Islam, the old civilizations gave way to the new Muslim Arab civilization, and Arabic language became the language of countries between Persia and Morocco which became known as the Arab World. The Muslim world was made of the Arab world as well as the Muslim countries which did not embrace Arabic as its mother tongue. As Muslim Arabs moved into countries, two processes interacted and worked simultaneously: the Islamization process and the Arabization process. The Islamization process dominated, and the Arabization process worked at varying degrees in different territories. One of these places that Arabization did not penetrate strongly enough was with the Ottoman Turks, who adopted Islam and kept Arabic as a language of Koran and religious teaching and not the language of the state.

The missionaries came to the Middle East with two objectives: the first was to convert Muslims primarily and the 'corrupted' Eastern Christians, as they were called by the missionaries, as well. The second objective was to dismantle the Core Muslim state of the times, the Ottoman Empire. They wanted to see a secular Middle East abandoning the bond of Islam in public life and governance which is what makes Islam unique. The conversion of Muslims proved an impossible task. Author Henry Field thought that "Christian Missions make no more impression on Islam than the winds of the desert upon the cliffs of Mount Sinai". Statistics proved Fields to be correct. In forty years of hard work that on occasion proved fatal, an average of less than one convert per year was recorded, costing a prohibitive $ 16000 per convert. If they could not convert Muslims, then they would settle for diverting Muslims from practicing their Islam in life as expressed in Islamic doctrines within an Islamic state. The word "secularism" became the catch word, and the separation of Islam from the matters of state became the main objective.

Briefly, the missionaries wanted to separate the Arabization process from the Islamization process as the route to destroy the Muslim Caliphate as embodied in the Ottoman Muslim state. The vehicle to achieve this objective was the creation of an Arab national movement. This meant the destruction of the Ottoman Caliphate State that, even imperfectly, represented the temporal and spiritual Islamic bond. That mission was achieved when the Young Turks destroyed the Ottoman Muslim Caliphate, and secularism became indeed the catch word in every constitution of the newly created Arab states and mini-states that were created by the West after the defeat of the Ottoman Caliphate. The glue that kept the Arabs together was Islam, and disconnecting the bond between Arabization and Islamization would destroy the cohesive bond between the fractions of the territories of the Arab world. Today's status quo is a living proof.

Through their schools, they promoted Western secular ideology. They used nationalism as the vehicle to get them to their objectives and their instruments were their schools and colleges. The one institution that stood head and shoulder above the rest was the American Protestant College, renamed later as the American University of Beirut. About the same time, a similar institution was founded in Anatolia by Cyrus Hamlin who established the Roberts College.

Missionary Daniel Bliss arrived in Beirut in 1855 at the age of 37. He originally was to establish a mission in Mount Lebanon, but had to the abandon it in 1860 due to the fighting between the Maronites and Druze. Back in Beirut, and after consulting with the local missionary elders, on the first day of 1862, he requested permission from the American Board to open a college to instill the spirit of nationalism in the missionaries school studies. Arabic should be the language of instruction and the college was named the American Protestant College. Bliss advised the American Board that since the missionaries were not able to import their religion to the area, they should settle by accepting to instill American secularism and values instead. Secularism through nationalism will awaken the sleeping racial or even the tribal issues amongst the various ethnic groups of the Ottoman Empire, resulting in the realization of the second goal of the missionaries, dismantling the core Muslim state, the Ottoman Empire. The American Protestant College, which later on in 1920 changed its name to be the American University of Beirut, became truly the cradle of Arab Nationalism and most of the leadership of Arab Nationalist movements were graduates of that university in both the 19th and 20th centuries. Satisfied with the achievements of the American Protestant College, the evangelists established in 1919 the American University of Cairo to follow the footsteps of the older university and spread its mission. Even though in a span of 10 years between 1885 and 1895 the budget for missionary institutions increased seven times with over 400 schools and enrollments of over 20 000 students, and with missionary presses rolling out some four million text books, the progress of nationalism, however, was very slow throughout the 19th century. Oren wrote:

"Arab Muslims, however, having long rejected the missionaries religious teachings, felt little affection for secular Western ideas. They already possessed a nation- the Islamic nation (Ummah), as embodied by the Ottoman State." Oren added: "Rather than secede from the empire, they preferred to attain additional rights within it and achieve unity not through an alien philosophy but by returning to native Islam." [1]

It was members of a few minority sects who accepted the nationalist idea for most of the 19th century. To Arab Muslims, the cry of Ibrahim al Yaziji , a Maronite turned Protestant, in his poem "Arise, O Arabs, and awake" went unheeded, and to them the Ottoman State , headed by a Muslim Khalifa, was the bastion of Islam. This all changed in 1908 when a Western backed Mason-Jewish led coup took hold in Istanbul. It not only promoted Western ideas but also racial discrimination against the Arabs. A reaction was a foregone conclusion. Even the Arab revolt was not motivated by nationalism. Oren wrote:

"While the British managed to spark an Arab revolt against Turkey and to rally many nationalists to its cause, the rebellion was in fact spurred less by Arabism than by the desire to revive a purified Arab Caliphate independent from the Westernized Turks.

---

1   Power, Faith and Fantasy, Michael B. Oren, W.W. Norton & Co., New York, 2007, Pg. 167 - 168

The uprisings leader Sharif Husayn…believed that the Arabs could unify only under Islam, and not beneath some racial or cultural banner." [1]

After the allied victory, the British wanted to appoint Sharif Hussein as a secular king. He insisted he wanted to be an Arab Khalipha, so he lost his territory and throne and was deposed and exiled to Cyprus.

---

1   Power, Faith and Fantasy, Michael B. Oren, W.W. Norton & Co., New York, 2007, Pg 169

"The European powers at that time believed they could change Moslem Asia in the very fundamentals of its political existence, and in their attempt to do so introduce an artificial state system into the Middle East that has made it into a region of countries that have not become nations even today. The basis of political life in the Middle East – religion – was called into question by the Russians, who proposed communism, and the British, who proposed nationalism or dynastic loyalty, in its place." [1]

"Many of the Bolshevik leaders were of Jewish origin. So was Helphand, who had brought them German money and support – and who had come from Constantinople and was an intimate of the Young Turks. The Young Turks – according to the doctrine long held by British officials – were controlled by Jewish Freemasons who had brought the Ottoman Empire into alliance with Germany. It was a long standing British belief that Jews and Germans were intimately related. It all seemed to fit." [2]

---

1   A Peace to End All Peace, David Fromkin, Henry Holt &Co, New York,1989, Pg 17

2   A Peace to End All Peace, David Fromkin, Henry Holt &Co, New York,1989, Pg 247

CHAPTER FIVE

SULTAN ABDUL HAMID II & THE FINAL DAYS

Rejuvenating the Empire through an Islamic Agenda

American exports to the Middle East in the 1880's had exceeded imports to the Middle East by fourteen times. The commercial significance of the Middle East became more important as time went by. Also, the geographic and geopolitical importance increased as American international trade and industrial power was on the rise. The United States started to assert its power militarily and economically. Using religion to advance those agendas, Joseph Strong, a Congregationalist, proclaimed that America "must take the lead in the final conflicts of Christianity for procession of the world". Preachers acting as the priests of capitalism and in order to justify the American Spanish wars advocated "enlightened imperialism" in addition to the sophistry of White man's burden and Manifest Destiny.

As the military in America is always at the service of the business, America concluded at this time that whoever controls the Middle East will control the world. So it started constructing a state of the arts 16 battleships that became known as the Great White Fleet assigned to the Mediterranean, becoming America's first global naval fighting force, much before that fighting force became known as the sixth fleet. That was America at about the time Sultan Abdul-Hamid II became the Sultan of the Ottoman Muslim State.

Abdül-Hamid II

He was the 34th sultan of the Ottoman Empire. He ruled from August 31, 1876 until he was deposed on April 27, 1909 . He succeeded to the throne after his brother Murad was deposed. Pious and humble, he rode to the Eyup Sultan Mosque to receive the sword of Osman unattended. When he took over in 1876, his treasury was empty. He had to consent to foreign control over the national debt , thus, a large portion of the empire's revenues were handed over to the Public Debt Administration for the benefit of foreign bondholders. Like Egypt, like the Ottoman Empire, and like the IMF today.

To the West, he was anti-Western, "Abdul the Damned, or the assassin" This is how a Western historian described him:

"After he lost, at the age of seven, his devoted Circassian mother, it was said of him that "he never loved anyone, least of all himself."[1]

But who was the real Abdul-Hamid?

He was a poet, a skilled carpenter who as a hobby crafted his own furniture which is nowadays displayed at the Yildiz Palace and Beylerbeyi Palace in Istanbul. He personally wrote the Turkish translations of many opera classics and composed several opera pieces himself. He hosted several famous European performers at the Opera House of Yildiz Palace. He was a good wrestler and he organized wrestling tournaments. He was well travelled as he toured most of Europe before assuming his Sultan post. And above all, he had a determination of steel, knowledge of the fundamentals of power, and was a great politician and strategist. He assessed the dangers encompassing his empire. He realized that the Powers were disintegrating his empire and detaching one territory after the other, and he realized that the forces against him and his empire were overwhelming. He determined that it was only through Islamic unity that his empire would be saved.

A few months after he became Sultan, Russia declared war on Abdul Hamid on April 24 1877. This was after Russia ensured the neutrality of the other European powers. The Treaty of San Stefano imposed harsh terms as the Ottoman Empire had to give

---

1   The Ottoman Centuries, The Rise and Fall of the Turkish Empire, Lord Kinross, Perennial, 2002, Pg 533

independence to Romania, Serbia, and Montenegro and to grant autonomy to Bulgaria. It had also to institute reforms in Bosnia and Herzegovina; and to cede the Dobruja and parts of Armenia to Russia. An enormous indemnity was also imposed, even though the Ottoman Empire was already bankrupt. This resulted in Russia having a great influence on the new independent states of Southeastern Europe.

As Russia could dominate the newly independent states, her influence in Southeastern Europe was greatly increased by the Treaty of San Stefano. The Great Powers, Britain in particular objected and the treaty was later revised at the Congress of Berlin so as to reduce the great advantages acquired by Russia. To balance the newly acquired Russian advantages, Britain dominated Cyprus and the British forces occupied Egypt and Sudan in 1882. Technically, these territories remained as Ottoman territories until 1914 when they were annexed to Britain formally. In early 1897 a Greek expedition sailed to Crete to overthrow Ottoman rule on the island. This act was followed by war, in which the Ottoman Empire defeated Greece. England, France, and Russia only few months after the Greek defeat intervened and they appointed Prince George of Greece as ruler, so Crete was also lost. Most of the North African territories were occupied by France. One so called Western reform was imposed on his predecessors after the other, including economic reforms and free trade that accelerated the bankruptcy of the state. With a bankrupt treasury and corrupt administration that was penetrated by agents of the

European powers, the situation was tempting for most people to just give up. But this was no option for Abdul Hamid.

Late 19ᵗʰ Century American Christian Zionism Agenda

The decade of the 1880s was marked by massive Jewish immigration of Eastern European Jews who immigrated to the United States, their New Promised land which they called in Yiddish [de golden medine], the land paved with gold. Very few of them however, immigrated to the old Promised Land, Palestine. Rich Americans funded the construction of new infrastructure and neighborhoods for those immigrants in Palestine. Nathan Straus the co-owner of the famous department store Macy's bought a large tract of land near Jaffa on which a city, Netanya, adopting his name was built at a later date. The bulk of American Jews were not only neutral about Zionism, they actually opposed it. In 1885 the Union of Reformed Congregations stipulated that, *"We consider ourselves no longer a nation, but a religious community."* The Jewish scholar Abram S. Isaacs reminded the Jews that Zionism is related to Christian restorationalism, which advocates the conversion of Jews to Christianity. Probably the poor attendance of American Jews to the First Zionist Congress demonstrated Jewish Americans' lack of interest in Zionism. Only four delegates came to attend the Congress in Basel, Switzerland out of about two hundred delegates. But it was the restorationalists who continued to press for the Zionist cause.

T. De. Witt Talmage was in the last quarter of the 19th century the equivalent of Billy Graham in the twentieth century. Talmage was given high profile by the media and had large audiences and followers. He was the spiritual advisor of president Grover Cleveland. His pronouncements were widely circulated in the press. Talmage visited Jerusalem in 1889 and not unlike the rest of his country men he expressed his hatred for the Ottoman Empire which he described as "that curse of nations, that old bag of centuries." He denounced Islam and described it as the antithetical to Western Civilization. He urged Americans to lead the World to wrestle Palestine from Islam so it can be made a state for the Jews.

William Eugene Blackstone, a diehard restorationalist, after his visit to Jerusalem, wrote a letter to President Benjamin Harrison and his Secretary of State on March 15, 1891. In his letter he stated that just as Europe succeeded in detaching Serbia and Bulgaria from the Ottoman Empire, the United States should do the same and help detach Palestine to give it to the Jews. Stranger than the letter was the signatories to that letter which of course included Talmage but also included 'who is who' in the world of business, finance, clergy and journalism, such as John D. Rockefeller, and J. P. Morgan. The American presidents, since 1881 started pressing Sultan Abdul Hamid to allow more Jewish immigration to Palestine. Restorationalists and Jewish American ambassadors, such as Oscar Straus, the brother of Macy's owner Nathan, and Solomon Hirsch, both Jewish, could not undermine the resolve of Abdul Hamid. He advised them that Palestine belongs to all Muslims and no Sultan can allow a change in its status or integrity.

For nearly a decade, since the outbreak of the 1881 Russian pogroms, Washington had been urging the Porte to open Palestine to Jewish immigration. The State Department instructed America's ambassador in Istanbul, Lew Wallace, to take the issue up personally with Sultan Abdul Hamid II. An avowed restorationalist, Wallace showed no hesitation in pressing for the resettlement of Jewish refugees in Palestine. His successors, Oscar Straus and Solomon Hirsch, though both anti-Zionist Jews, also pursued the matter. None of their efforts prevailed. Justifiably fearful of Zionism and any effort to disassemble their empire, the Ottomans placed increasingly draconian strictures on all Jewish immigration to Palestine hout effect. The European powers, for their part, showed no inclination to intervene on the refugees' behalf or to follow America's lead on Palestine.[1]

American diplomats denounced these measures as "inquisitorial" and "utterly repugnant to ... out Constitution", but again the massacres continued, unabated. Abram Elkus, another Jewish lawyer from New York who replaced Morgenthau as ambassador, informed the State Department that the Turks were pursuing an "unchecked policy of extermination through starvation, exhaustion, and brutality of treatment hardly surpassed even in Turkish history". In all, as many as 1.5 million Armenians

---

1   Power, Faith and Fantasy, Michael B. Oren, W.W. Norton & Company, New York, London, P 279

were killed in a genocide that the Turkish government would never acknowledge, much less regret. But Elkus also had other catastrophes to monitor, including the mounting Turkish attacks against the Greek population of Smyrna and western Anatolia and the displacement of Arabs from border lands. "Turkish authorities appear to be pursuing (a) policy of Turkifying Syria and adjacent Arabic-speaking countries", one State Department memorandum asserted, and estimated that 250.000 Arab families were slated to be removed and supplanted by Turks.[1]

...a Different Agenda for Abdul-Hamid

Abdul -Hamid was determined not to stay the course of the weak sultans that preceded him and was determined to reunify the Ottoman state under the banner of Islam, the very opposite of what the missionaries and the West were working for, for decades. A confrontation was imminent and was in the making. The missionaries thought that their secularism through the nationalism program was only the beginning for the big event, the dissolution of the Ottoman Muslim State. Henry Jessup, a veteran missionary in Beirut put it this way: *"In the war against Islam we are only yet putting on the armor and not by any means ready to wave the ensigns of victory."* By now, the missionaries were having more than 100 churches in Greater Syria and over 200 institutions and still they were not saving souls or producing converts. To their dismay,

---

1   Power, Faith and Fantasy, Michael B. Oren, W.W. Norton & Company, New York, London, P 337

the American council to the Philippines, Alexander Russel Webb converted to Islam from Presbyterianism in 1888. He returned to his home town New York where he built America's first mosque and started America's first Muslim newspaper.

What differentiated Sultan Abdul Hamid II from other 19th century sultans was his recognition that the Young Ottomans or the Young Turks were foreign supported movements based on foreign ideology. As a pious man, but also as a strategist, he believed in a native ideology of Islam on which the Ottoman Empire zenith was accomplished. As of 1517, the Ottoman Sultans were also Caliphs, so he emphasized the role of the empire as the core state of Islam and the venue of the Muslim Caliphate. He viewed the Powers assault on his empire as an assault on Islam. He curtailed the privileges of foreigners which he considered as targeting the integrity of the state, and he sent emissaries to distant places urging Islamic unity under the Caliphate. He was everything the missionaries and the West wanted him not to be, especially on the issues of Islam and Palestine. He refused an offer from Theodor Herzl to pay most of the Ottoman debt in exchange for a charter allowing the Jews to colonize Palestine. He answered Herzl:

> "To have the scalpel cut my body is less painful than to witness Palestine being detached from the Caliphate state and this is not going to happen ...let the Jews keep their millions and once the Caliphate is torn apart one day, then they can take Palestine without a price." [1]

---

1   http://en.wikipedia.org/wiki/Abdul_Hamid_II

According to research by Harvard Professor Walid Khalidi, Die Zionistische Bewegung (The Zionist Movement), Adolf Bohm, a leading authority on early Zionism, published the full text of a remarkable document from the Herzl Archives in Vienna. This was the draft of a proposed agreement (a "Charter") between the World Zionist Organization (WZO) and the Ottoman government concerning the 'privileges, rights, liabilities, and duties of the Jewish – Ottoman Land Company (JOLC) for the settlement of Palestine and Syria'. The document does not bear a date, but seems to have been drawn up sometimes between the summer of 1901 and early 1902

It is noteworthy to pay attention that the first meetings held in Paris to organize the downfall of Abdul-Hamid were in 1902.

Abdul-Hamid Reforms

Abdul Hamid was left with little choice, so he thought he could befriend the German Empire. Kaiser Wilhelm II was hosted by Abdül- Hamid in Istanbul on October 21, 1889, and nine years later, on October 5, 1898. German officers were employed to reorganize the Ottoman army and German experts were brought to reorganize the Ottoman finances. Germany extended loans to Abdul Hamid, and constructed a railroad network, including the Baghdad Railway and the Hejaz Railway.

Lord Kinross who claimed that Abdul-Hamid loved nobody, the least himself, listed in later chapters Abdul-Hamid's reforms.

He created a Ministry of Posts and Telegraph, providing courses in the schools for telegraph operators. He linked the capital with all provincial centers and parts of Empire through 20000 miles of telegraphic lines and cables covering all parts of the Empire, thus improving communications and enabling Abdul Hamid directly to control his official bureaucracy. A governor, no longer governing at his own discretion, became more accountable for his deeds.

Though cautious in dealing with the West politically Abdul Hamid drew upon the West in his pursuit of modernization in the field of technology, as well as in the judicial and educational reform to produce more competent civil servants to administer the Empire and to ensure progress and development. He improved public education to produce able public servants and an educated class of officials to replace the uneducated and the corrupt officials. To accomplish this, he reorganized the Mülkiye, the Empire's first center of higher civil education. Its enrollment increased twelve times since the days of his father. He expanded the war college, the Harbiye, as well as the naval and military engineering and medical schools for both civil and military purposes.

> "Abdul Hamid extended his education system with eighteen new higher and professional schools, covering such subjects as finance, the fine arts, civil engineering, police and customs. Finally he founded a University of Istanbul, the ultimate materialization of a project first mooted but never launched under the Tanzimat a century earlier. To provide these new colleges with students and staff, there was also

a widespread expansion of primary and secondary schools and of teachers' training colleges …..Such, thanks to the resolute industry of Abdul -Hamid, was the long delayed consummation, in effective practical terms, of the educational ideas of the Tanzimat. Here at last was the expanding nucleus of a substantial new educated class, a civil-service elite trained professionally to staff the vast bureaucracy of the Hamidian regime—and ironically enough of the anti-Hamidian regime that was to follow it."[1]

In order to limit the privileges of the foreigners' judicial privilege, he launched new laws under the Ministry of Justice so that the privileges under former Capitulations agreements may be reduced or cancelled. But these new laws were rejected by the foreign missions and they insisted on keeping their extraterritorial privileges as before. A new reading public was created through introduction and enlargement of the media of newspapers, periodicals, and books, thus increasing and widening new branches of knowledge, a new reading public could widen its horizons. All of these accomplishments were realized at a time Abdul- Hamid's treasury was empty and the Empire defaulted on its loans payments when he ascended to his post.

"In the sphere of finance the Ottoman Empire was now more than ever at the mercy of Europe. At the

---

1   The Ottoman Centuries, The Rise and Fall of the Turkish Empire, Lord Kinross, Perennial, 2002, Pg 536

Berlin Congress, the interested powers had for the first time confronted the problem of default on the Ottoman debt. In an official protocol they provided for the establishment in Istanbul of an international financial commission, to seek means compatible with the Porte's financial situation of satisfying the claims of bondholders. Here, following losses of Ottoman territory in Europe, was the humiliating prospect of a limitation by Europe of Ottoman sovereignty at home....In 1881 he issued the Decree of Muharrem, which, in agreement with the European bondholders, set up a Council of the Public Debt. Composed of Ottoman and foreign representatives, it was to ensure henceforward the resumption of service on the debt. The Decree was so shrewdly framed by the Sultan as to reestablish a degree of European goodwill toward Turkey, without appearing to weaken his sovereign powers....Its terms favored the Ottoman treasury in that the amount of the debt was written down by half, to just over a hundred million pounds, with a rate of interest at no more than 4 and usually as .little--as 1 percent. In return, the treasury ceded to the Council a large part of the government's annual revenues, for the payment of interest and the redemption of the bonds." [1]

---

1   The Ottoman Centuries, The Rise and Fall of the Turkish Empire, Lord Kinross, Perennial, 2002, pg. 537

Under Abdul Hamid in 1888, Turkey was first connected by rail to Western Europe, with the arrival of the first through train from Vienna to Istanbul—the forerunner of the Orient Express.

....Not bad for a Sultan who inherited a bankrupt treasury!

America in Egypt & France in North Africa!

The U.S. and the missionaries showed little interest in Egypt for most of the first half of the 19th Century. A chill in American Egyptian relations occurred when Egypt collaborated with the French and sent Egyptian troops to Mexico during the American civil war, a violation of Monroe's Doctrine.

When Khedive Ismael suspected the motives of the British and French, the traditional countries that assisted Egypt's military, he sent to the United States for military assistance in the form of military advisors in 1868. Such military experts were available in great numbers after the civil war. Many former American officers arrived to reorganize the Egyptian Army, about the time the Suez Canal was inaugurated. Ismael by then acquired over a 100 million dollars of debt, a substantial amount in those days. The Americans established the first general staff in the history of the Egyptian army, brought a press, established a library and then built an Arabic language school for officers and their families at Al Abbassiyah. By 1873, Egypt had a modern Western – style army base including a naval college, and command and control centers, a system for conveying orders, but with mounting debt lacked the economic base needed to go with it. Ismael was forced to sell

Egypt shares in the Suez Canal, and in June 1878, Europeans overseeing the Egypt economy recommended drastic cuts that included the dismissal of the remaining American advisors and the closure of the schools they built under the pretext of budget cuts.

Within three years period the European powers declared Egypt insolvent, removed Khedive Ismael and installed Khedive Tawfik. The harsh economic measures and the open and direct influence of the British in Egyptian affairs led to a rebellion led by the most senior Egyptian officer, Colonel Ahmad Orabi. By 1882 Orabi's revolt was threatening the Khedive and of course the Suez Canal. In July, the British battleships aligned off Egypt's coast. Alexandria was bombarded. Hundreds of Egyptians were killed and the Egyptian resistance was silenced. Egypt became thereafter under British occupation. Meanwhile in 1881, the French troops crossed from Algeria and they occupied Tunisia.

At the request of the State Department four U.S. gunboats joined the invading British Navy of Egypt. They were in Egypt waters at Alexandria's coast during the British attack. Since the British commander was ordered to bombard but not occupy Alexandria, it was American marines who were the first ashore in the British assault in Egypt, always claiming they went to protect civilians.

The Islamic & Arab policies were working well...but

Since there is neither priesthood nor church in Islam, the state and the 'church' in Islam are one and the same. The West assumed that the Caliphate was a replica of the papacy.

> "This view of the caliphate, partly derived from a false analogy with the papacy, was altogether erroneous since it overlooked that, in Islam, church and state were closely interwoven, and the term 'caliph' synonymous in practice with that of 'ruler'. Abdul Hamid's plan was to restore the caliphate to its proper place..." [1]

This is how historian Fromkin explained it:

> "Scholars have been kept busy ever since explaining to western students of the Middle East that the split between temporal and spiritual authority, that in medieval Europe pitted pope against emperor, did not occur in the world of Islam. Kitchener, Wingate, Clayton, and Storrs were mistaken in believing that the Caliph could be spiritual leader only. In Islam, all of life, including government and politics, falls within the governance of the Holy Law; so that in the eyes

---

1   The Arab awakening, George Antonius, Simon Publications, 2001, Pg 69

of Sunni Moslems, such as the Ottoman Sultan and the Emir of Mecca, the dominion of the Caliph as upholder of the Holy Law is pervasive. What British Cairo did not see is that the Caliph is also a prince: a governor and a leader in battle as well as a leader in prayer." [1]

In the same decade that Abdul-Hamid ascended the throne, a pan-Islamic revival movement was spreading, and one of its main advocates was Sayyed Jamaluddin al-Afghani. He was an eloquent preacher and he was preaching that Muslims should free themselves from foreign domination, and he called for their moral regeneration. He called for Muslim unity under one universally acknowledged caliph. At this time, Abdul-Hamid was laying the foundation of his new Islamic policy to rejuvenate the State. He realized that the missionaries and the powers aimed at disintegrating his State and they made no secret of their resolve to see a secular Ottoman or Turkish state, not an Ottoman Muslim state. He lived through the Powers dismembering his European and then African territories through advocacy of nationalism not only in the Christian populated territories but also in the Muslim territories. Arabism was promoted by the missionaries in their institutions and Ottomanism in Anatolia. He concluded that it was Islam that contributed to the greatness of the Ottoman Muslim state, and through Islam he can consolidate the State against the aggressive assault on his Muslim nation. He was

---

1   A Peace to End All Peace, David Fromkin, Henry Holt &Co, New York,1989, Pg 104

determined to use the instrument of the Caliphate to reassert the power and prestige of the Islamic Ummah. Already, Muslims were weary of Western and Russian imperialism, with its increasing domination of Moslem territories from North Africa to Central Asia and India. With all its problems, the Muslims looked at the Ottoman Muslim State to counter Western imperialism and revive Islam. He practiced the religious observances strictly in his palace and all non-Muslim practices such as drunkenness were strictly banned. He surrounded himself with Muslim scholars and listened to their council. He founded a college for training of Muslim missionaries and dispatched them to the most remote places. He provided generous donations to religious schools inside and outside the Ottoman State. His policy greatly influenced the non-Turkish Muslims, particularly the Arabs who identified themselves with the new policies. He spent lavishly on Arab institutions of learning, formed one battalion from Arabs as his personal bodyguards, and appointed Arabs in prominent government positions. Arabs were appointed at the palace, and some claim that Arab influence overshadowed even that of the Turkish staff. Among such Arabs was Issat Pasha al-Abed, who served 13 years until the fall of Abdul-Hamid in 1908. He was regarded as the most influential official in the Empire. He oversaw the construction of the Hejaz Railroad that started construction in the spring of 1901 and reached Madina in 1908. After Abdul Hamid was deposed, the line to Mecca was never finished, and the line was damaged by Lawrence and his bandits. After a century of meetings between Syria, Jordan and Saudi Arabia, the line was never operated.

> "In the eyes of the mass of his subjects he had reestablished a strong, traditional Islamic regime, freed from foreign interference and influence, which they could understand and respect as their own. In their Sultan-Caliph his people recognized those personal qualities of austerity, sobriety, and piety which as Moslems, inspired by a Puritanical spirit, they were proud to respect. For the rest he was loyally supported not only by his own ministers and governing establishment but by such forces outside it as the ulema. Loyal to him too was a proliferating class of 'men of religion,' at various levels, respected in the name of Islamic unity whether as descendants of the Prophet or otherwise; also the scholars and mystics of the less orthodox colleges and dervish convents, several of whose orders were especially favored throughout his dominions…. Abdul Hamid turned all eyes away from the West, as a remote and alien world. Its misguided political views and institutions and actions were sternly ignored by his censored press. His intelligentsias were indoctrinated with a belief in the superior culture of a medieval Islamic past. The young Ottomans, in relating their plans for reform and modernization to the institutions of Islam, had admitted that they were in fact derived

from the West. Abdul Hamid admitted no such thing. The Hamidian line was that Arab civilization was the source of European civilization, which took over from Islam not only its constitutional system but Arab science and technology – algebra, chemistry, and physics; such modern inventions as the compass and gunpowder; literature and the writing of history; everything indeed that was admired in the West. What then did the Moslems require from Europe had since tried to improve? A book repeating this thesis opened with the words, "The bases of contemporary civilization are nothing but the actions and traditions of Mohammed."[1]

The British Ambassador to Istanbul, wrote only one year before Abdul Hamid was deposed that Abdul Hamid's Islamic,

"Policy which induced the Sultan to pose before 300,000,000 of Mohammedans as the Caliph and spiritual leader of his religion, and in bringing home to his subjects the fervor and energy of his religious feelings by the construction of the Hejaz Railway which in the near future, will afford facilities to every Moslem to perform the pilgrimage to the holy places of Mecca and Medina…The effect has been that he has commanded, to an unprecedented degree, the

---

1   The Ottoman Centuries, The Rise and Fall of the Turkish Empire, Lord Kinross, Perennial, 2002, Pg 552

blind obedience of his subjects, and reconciled them to a despotism more absolute than has perhaps ever been known in the whole course of history."[1]

This vision was Abdul Hamid's from the earliest year of his reign. He enacted this strategy with diligence, through widening contacts with various Islamic communities within or outside his State. His Islamic policy was revealed through his appointment as Grand Vezir not of a Turk, but a Circassian, General Khair–ed-Din. The Sultan explained his reason behind this appointment as proclaimed in the firman, as his right as caliph to utilize the services of the most competent Muslims anywhere throughout Islam. He made it a point to appoint in high places Muslims from all races without giving preference to Turks. He displayed a solicitous interest in the Moslem communities in his former Christian territories and in countries farther afield. He settled to become the strong man of Asia instead of the sick man of Europe. *"But in so doing he was to antagonize Europe and the civilized world of the West more than ever before"*

On the use of nationalism by the British and religion by the French to dismantle the Ottoman Muslim State, Fromkin wrote:

> "The European powers at that time believed they could change Moslem Asia in the very fundamentals of its political existence, and in their attempt to do so

---

1   Gooch and Temperley, British Documents on the Origin of the War. Vol.V,p43.

introduce an artificial state system into the Middle East that has made it into a region of countries that have not become nations even today. The basis of political life in the Middle East – religion – was called into question by the Russians, who proposed communism, and the British, who proposed nationalism or dynastic loyalty, in its place. Khomeini's Iran in the Shi'ite world and the Moslem Brotherhood in Egypt, Syria and elsewhere in the Sunni world keeps that issue alive. The French government, which in the Middle East did allow religion to be the basis of politics – even of its own – championed one sect against the others; and that, too, is an issue kept alive, notably in the communal strife that has ravaged Lebanon in the 1970s and 1980s." [1]

Young Turks without a Turkey & a Masonic Jewish coup

The famous Sir Mark Sykes, whose name became famous later on, along with Mr. Picot, because of the well known Anglo-French secret Sykes Picot agreement that subdivided the Ottoman Arab territories into states and mini-states until this day, wrote in a book when he was a Member of Parliament asking, *"How many people realize, when they speak of Turkey and the Turks, that*

---

1   A Peace to End All Peace, David Fromkin, Henry Holt& Co, New York,1989, Pg 17

there is no such place and no such people..." True, the Ottomans came from Turkestan, Central Asia, and they were of Turkish heritage, but they abandoned it for Islam many centuries ago after they immigrated to Anatolia. But a brand name was needed for the secret movements to market their coup, always hiding their real agenda. Thus, Turkey and the Young Turks came out of the blues. Nationalism after all, was the banner on which the West and their vanguards, and missionaries, adopted to destroy the Ottoman Muslim State.

The Zionists concluded that their dream in Palestine can only be attained by a 'regime change' against Abdul Hamid. The first organized meeting to depose Abdul Hamid took place a short time after he refused Herzl's offer to trade his debt for a charter for Palestine. According to Encyclopedia Wikipedia:

> "The first congress of Ottoman Opposition was held on February 4 1902, at 8 pm, at the house of Germain Antoin Lefevre-Pontalis. He was a member of the Institute France. The opposition was performed in compliance with the France government. It was closed to public.... The Second congress of the Ottoman opposition took place in Paris, France in 1907. The goal was to unite all the parties, including the CUP, in order to bring about the revolution".

A year before the second congress Mehmed Talat established in 1906 the Ottoman Freedom Society (OFS) in Salonika, which took the lead in uniting all the other secret societies under the one umbrella of the CUP. The OFS became very active in recruiting young officers from the Third Army whose base and headquarters was in Salonika. The Encyclopedia Wikipedia adds:

"Although the European public and many scholars commonly labeled the Young Turks as constitutionalists and the Young Turks employed rhetoric promoting constitutionalism, but actually they followed the principle of developing an intellectual elite to govern the Empire, never envisioning participation of the masses in policy-making or administration."

A few months after the CUP and the opposition second congress in Paris, the CUP leadership threatened the Sultan on May 13 1908 asking that he restore the Constitution, which as events proved later they shelved and enforced dictatorship to enforced their alien ideology. The Third Army in Macedonia on June 12, 1908 began its march to the Palace .The constitution was restored on July 24, 1908.

The CUP members continued to hide their anti-Islamic agenda, but enough actions exposed them for what they were. They were severely denounced by the Ulema, who accused them of *"trying to change Islam into another form and create a new religion while calling it Islam"*. A spontaneous counter-revolution sparked against the CUP in 1909 as soldiers and young officers were joined with masses of Muslims from the Society of Mohammad. The CUP officers used cannons for hours against the poorly armed and civilian counter-revolutionaries. Even though there was no proof that Sultan Abdul Hamid had anything to do with, it was used to depose him and replace him with his brother as a figure head until the day the CUP party dissolved the Ottoman Muslim State and replaced it with a secular republic.

> "The life of the Sultan was spared. He was conveyed
> late at night to the railway station...and thence to
> Salonika, where...he was interned in the villa Allatini,
> the house of a Jew."[1]

In his book *A Peace to End All Peace* Boston University history professor David Fromkin wrote this account of the roots of the Committee of Union and Progress, CUP, whose members, along with other affiliated secret sister organizations, were known as the Young Turks. Fromkin wrote:

> "They (the CUP) were viewed with sympathy by the
> Foreign Office in London, but were disliked and
> disdained in the British embassy in Constantinople.
> The ambassador, Sir Gerard Lowther, seems
> to have fallen completely under the influence
> of Gerald FitzMaurice, his First Dragoman, or
> official interpreter and adviser on oriental affairs ...
> FitzMaurice's interpretation of the events of 1908
> was colored by the fact that they had occurred in
> Salonika, about half of whose 130.000 inhabitants

---

1   The Ottoman Centuries, The Rise and Fall of the Turkish Empire, Lord Kinross, Perennial, 2002, Pg 578

were either Jews or Dunmehs (members of a Jewish sect that had converted to Islam in the seventeenth century). Salonika was also a city in which there were Freemason lodges. Emmanuel Carasso (or Karasu), a Jewish lawyer, had founded an Italian Freemason lodge in which he apparently allowed Talaat's secret society to meet when it was in hiding from the Sultan's secret police. FitzMaurice concluded that the C.U.P. was a Latin – influenced international Jewish Freemason conspiracy; and Lowther duly reported this to the Foreign Office in London. Lowther referred to the C.U.P. as "the Jew Committee of Union and Progress .....FitzMaurice later conducted an investigation of the C.U.P., the results of which were reflected in a confidential report sent by Lowther under his own name on 29 May 1910, to the official head of the Foreign Office, Sir Charles Hardinge. In his report, Lowther pointed out that "Liberté , égalité, fraternité" (liberty, equality, fraternity), words drawn from the French Revolution, were both the slogan of the Italian Freemasons (hence Karasu's lodge) and of the Young Turkey movement. The Young Turks, he claimed, were 'imitating the French Revolution and its godless and leveling methods'.... In his detailed report of more than 5000 words, Lowther alleged that Jews had taken over a Freemason network ....and through it had taken control of the Ottoman Empire. Amongst the ringleaders of the Jewish Freemason conspiracy, according to Lowther, was the U.S. ambassador to Turkey, Oscar Straus (who was a Jew), whose brothers owned the New York department stores Macy's and Abraham & Straus."[1]

It is worth noting that the United States appointed Jews for consular and ambassadorship positions in the Ottoman State for most of the 19th century as well as the last days of the Ottoman state. Ambassadors that followed Straus in Istanbul in the 20th century were also Jewish, including Henry Morgenthau and Abram Elkus.

According to Fromkin and research based on newly released secret documents:

> "Many of the Bolshevik leaders were of Jewish origin. So was Helphand, who had brought them German money and support – and who had come from Constantinople and was an intimate of the Young Turks. The Young Turks – according to the doctrine long held by British officials – were controlled by Jewish Freemasons who had brought the Ottoman Empire into alliance with Germany. It was a long standing British belief that Jews and Germans were intimately related. It all seemed to fit." [2]

---

1   A Peace to End All Peace, David Fromkin, Henry Holt &Co, New York,1989, Pg 41 - 42

2   A Peace to End All Peace, David Fromkin, Henry Holt&Co, New York,1989 , Pg 247

This is how Lord Kinross, the Ottoman Empire historian described the roots of the CUP:

> "In Salonika the vigorous Committee of Union and Progress, enlisting covert support from organized groups of Freemasons, Jews and Donmehs (Jews turned Moslem), was more practical in its effect than the organization in Paris, with which it merged in 1907." [1]

Encyclopedia Wikipedia lists some of the leaders of the Cup as such:

Marcel Samuel Raphael Cohen (aka Tekin Alp) (1883-1961), born to a Jewish family in Salonica under Ottoman control (now Thessaloniki, Greece) was one of the founding fathers of Turkish nationalism and an ideologue of Pan-Turkism.

Mehmed Cavid Bey (1875-1926) "a shrewd Dönmeh from Thessalonica, Jewish by ancestry but Moslem by religion, with a quick financial brain, who was an expert Minister of Finance.

Talat Pasha or Talaat Pasha, His role is not clear, before the revolution. It's argued that he was the one who shaped the organization according to Bektashi sect or Masonic rules, or both.

---

1   The Ottoman Centuries, The Rise and Fall of the Turkish Empire, Lord Kinross, Perennial, 2002, Pg 573

Emmanuel Carasso Efendi, Jewish from Salonika, Grand Master of the lodge known as "Macedonia Risorta".

Mehmed Talaat, who became the Minister of the Interior and the leader of the largest faction within the governing political party, was "a figure whom British diplomats did not regard as a gentleman. They believed … that he was of gypsy origin. Talaat was the single most important figure in Turkish politics.… Little is known of his origins and background except that they were humble. He is believed to have joined a Freemason lodge, is known to have organized a secret political society, and to have been imprisoned for a time for his underground activities."[1]

Among Talaat's early recruits was a young officer, Ismail Enver, who in 1908 was requested by the Sultan to return to Istanbul. He left to the hills taking his soldiers and ammunition with him. He was joined by other CUP officers and they formed the core of the rebelling forces that marched to Istanbul to subdue and then depose Abdul-Hamid.

The C.U.P. took control of Salonika at the same time. They seized the Telegraph office so they could communicate with all the CUP cells in the empire.

The year after the CUP coup in 1908 proved to be a disaster for the Ottoman Empire, as wars were lost that resulted in further territorial losses in the Balkan. Initially, the CUP managed the Empire behind the scenes, leaving chosen old politicians to be in front. But they suddenly decided in 1913 to seize control of

---

1   A Peace to End All Peace, David Fromkin, Henry Holt&Co, New York,1989, Pg 39

the government. The same Enver of Salonika led a raid on the government. He killed the Minister of War and was promoted to a field command. On 4 January 1914, when he was 31 years old he took over the War Ministry for himself. And from there he led the Ottoman Empire into World War One and into disaster.

Djemal Pasha was appointed as the Military Governor of Istanbul. Mehmed Djavid was appointed Minister of Finance. Talaat, the principal C.U.P. leader, became Minister of the Interior and the real leader of the government.

This is how Encyclopedia Wikipedia described the regime of the Young Turks:

"The new regime worked to be included in Western culture while exerting an anti-imperialist rhetoric and convened a parliament composed not of elected politicians but of virtually selected intellectuals working on behalf of the people without cooperating in any capacity with the masses. The impact of the Young Turks on shaping the official ideology of early modern Turkey went far beyond the political changes they effected."

Young Arabs and the 'Arab Revolt'

What the British ambassador to Istanbul called 'the Jewish Masonry conspiracy' in which he claimed that the Jews controlled the Ottoman empire through a network of Masonry Lodges and secret societies, resulted in the creation of the CUP and the Young Turks but also the Young Arabs, many of its leadership members were Masons or Mason controlled. The first secret society organized in the Arab World was traced back to 1875, to five young men, all graduates of the American Protestant College, later renamed the American University of Beirut. They were all Christians.

> "Freemasonry on the European pattern had just found its way into Syria, and the promoters of the secret society were able, through one of their members, to interest the recently founded Lodge in its activities." [1]

The society, created or now aided by the Freemasons, spread from Beirut, the center of their activities into Damascus, Tripoli, and Sidon. They started to post anonymous placards in the streets advocating Arab Nationalism and anti-Ottoman slogans. It was suspected that one of the Young Turks was Governor-General of Syria and he was collaborating with the secret society. The Governor, Midhat Pasha was recalled by the Sultan and the secret society burned its records and its members dispersed. A telegram traced at the Public Record Office in London [P.O.1951/1306] sent by the Beirut Consul-General, dated June 28.1880 read as follows:

> "Revolutionary placards have appeared in Beirut, Midhat suspected as the author. Tranquility, however, prevails. Details by next post."

---

1   The Arab awakening, George Antonius, Simon Publications, 2001, Pg 79

George Antonius interviewed one of the founders of that secret society at age eighty. He was Dr. Fares Nimr Pasha who immigrated to Egypt in 1883. In Egypt he was one of the founders of al-Muqtatuf and of al-Muqattam daily newspapers both published in Cairo.

The secret society was requesting local autonomy for Syria similar to that of Lebanon. In 1865, through foreign pressure, Lebanon was granted local autonomy by what became known as the 'Règlement Organique', which granted that province an administration of its own, and practically was detached from the Ottoman Empire. But Sultan Abdul Hamid's Muslim policy disarmed the secret societies from issues to rise against the Ottoman Muslim State. He assigned Arabs to high places and he used Turkish and non-Turkish subjects equally based on qualifications, including even his Grand Vasir.

This impartial policy "was bound to achieve at least partial and temporary success, and although it did not kill the movement or arrest its subterranean growth it did reduce it to impotence."[1]

During his almost three decades of rule Sultan Abdul Hamid encountered no Arab opposition except in two instances. One at the beginning of his rule by the Beirut secret society and another at the end of his rule by a shady movement of Al Kawakibi that he advocated for the caliph to be an Arab, which was the beginning of the British agenda that became British policy to disintegrate the Ottoman Caliphate. To fuel agents of disintegration, the CUP

---

1   The Arab awakening, George Antonius, Simon Publications, 2001, Pg 91

on the other side worked for the Turkification of the Empire, giving more reason for the Arab population's discontent. At best, Al Kawakibi was a shady figure who "drew a sharp distinction between the Arab and non-Arab Moslem peoples....So that... he advocated the abolition of the sultan's title to the caliphate and the setting up of a Quraish-born Arab as caliph in Mecca."[1] Was Kawakibi a prophet forecasting the British agenda for Sharif Hussain, or was he a propagandist employed by the British to promote that agenda?

1   The Arab awakening, George Antonius, Simon Publications, 2001, Pg 98

While the British managed to spark an Arab revolt against Turkey and to rally many nationalists to its cause, the rebellion was in fact spurred less by Arabism than by the desire to revive a purified Arab caliphate independent of the Westernized Turks. The uprisings of Mecca, believed that the Arabs could unite only under Islam and not beneath some racial or cultural banner [1].

---

1   Power, Faith and Fantasy, Michael B. Oren, W.W. Norton & Company, New York, London, P 369

CHAPTER SIX

DISMEMBERING THE ARAB EAST INTO MINI STATES

Deliberate Steps by CUP to alienate Arabs

The CUP appointed Sharif Hussein as the Grand Sharif of Mecca in 1908, soon after the coup against Abdul-Hamid in that same year. While in Istanbul as a representative of Hejaz Hussain

> "Entered into cordial relations with the British
> Embassy and had encountered friendliness...And he
> had learnt that his elevation to the Grand Sharifate in
> 1908 had had England's secret backing." [1]

A combination of admiration and gratitude governed Hussain's attitude during his negotiations and relations with Britain during and after the War, until experience taught him better, but after he ended up in exile in Cyprus.

---

1   The Arab awakening, George Antonius, Simon Publications, 2001, Pg 175

It is an accepted historical fact that Sultan Abdul-Hamid disarmed the enemies of Islam of causes for Arab discontent due to his Islamic and Arab policy and the equal opportunities given to Arabs and other races. This all changed when the CUP staged their coup and assumed real power, behind closed doors initially and in the open soon afterwards. Their racial policies, specifically anti-Arab policy was meant to instigate Arabs against the Ottoman Empire. The conspirators in Europe and their lodges and secret societies in the empire worked in harmony to execute the death sentence of the Ottoman Empire. For most of the 19th century, it was the powers that held it together, and Abdul-Hamid was almost successful to create cohesion. The same forces that created the conspiracies and secret societies of the Young Turks now synchronized their forces to repeat the act in the Arab World.

Through tyrannical and racial policies of the CUP discontent in the Arab territories spread and with it, secret organizations were formed. The leadership of these organizations cannot be pronounced innocent, but the majority of members were. Even some of the leadership knew little about the ultimate intentions of the West, as the societies operated in secrecy and compartments, and as known in those societies, information was on a "need to know basis" and was given in spoonful doses.

> "The CUP was a medley of races and creeds, in which
> Turks predominated and Jews came second…"[1]

---

1   The Arab awakening, George Antonius, Simon Publications, 2001, Pg 101

Few Arabs joined, and those who did, did so as Ottoman citizens not as Arabs. The CUP claimed that their revolt on July 24, 1908 against the Sultan was to reinstate the 1776 constitution of Midhat Pasha and to give liberty to the people. The first election they held which was called by the constitution was rigged. They controlled the electoral machinery and saw to it that their nominees were elected. Even though the Arab subjects of the state outnumbered the Turks by a ratio of 3 to 2, the Chamber of Deputies, which assembled in December 1908, had 150 Turkish representatives and 50 Arabs. The appointed House of Senate which numbered 40, had 3 Arabs only. On April 16, Abdul-Hamid was deposed and the rubber stamp parliament was all eager to ratify the resolution of his deposition. All non-Turkish societies were banned. The CUP promoted Turkish nationalism, and asserted their Turanian origins and claimed that the Turkish regeneration lay towards reunion with populations of Turanian origins (not Arab Muslims of course!). They adopted a repressive centralization policy in which Arabs were least represented in the administration. It clearly appeared that they planned to antagonize the Arab masses to revolt, and those who organized the Young Turks were now ready to organize the Young Arabs.

Al Fatat & al Ahd secret societies

The first secret society was al-Qahtaniya, in reference to one of the pre-Islamic ancestors of the Arab race. It was established the same year Abdul-Hamid was deposed. Its stated objective was to promote two entities out of the Ottoman empire, one Turkish and the other Arab on Austro-Hungarian model. The society was led by Aziz Ali Al Masri, an Arab out of all people who was a CUP member himself! The membership included Arab officers of very high rank in the Turkish army, and the society operated on Masonry like style as it had passwords and signals for identification. By early 1914 Aziz al Masri turned al-Qahtaniya into an all military members secret society now renamed al Ahd.

One if the most secretive and effective societies which involved civilian membership was al-Fatat, which formed in 1911 in Paris (just as the CUP was) . It played the biggest part in the Arab movement against Turkey before and during World War One. It was similar to the 1875 Beirut secret society which folded after Abdul-Hamid Arab and Islamic policy disarmed them from connecting with the population. Only after Abdul-Hamid was deposed did such societies come to life again. The founders were seven young Arab students who were studying in Paris backed by the same forces that created and backed the CUP. Young Arabs and Young Turks had the same roots, without them necessarily being aware of it, yet one was played against the other to attain the larger goal, ,namely abandoning the Caliphate system and the disintegration of the Ottoman Empire's Muslim character. Their program was a replica of the Beirut secret society which was backed by Masonry lodges in Greater Syria. They operated on Masonry procedures:

> "Each recruit was introduced by one of the sworn
> members but was kept in ignorance of the identity

of all the other members until he had been tried and proven, when he would be invited to take the oath to serve the ends of the society, to the point of forfeiting his life, if need be, in its service."[1]

The headquarters remained in Paris till 1913 when it moved to Beirut, and it again moved to Damascus in 1914 about the time al Ahd was formed. A very small number in the leadership of the secret societies belonged to both to ensure coordination and harmony. The secrecy of the societies was guarded all the way until the end of World War One and the occupation of the Arab World by Britain and France, because then the 'mission was accomplished.

Initiation of Faisal in the Secret societies

Nasib al-Bakri, one of al Fatat leaders in Damascus arranged for his younger brother Fawzi, to serve in the bodyguard of the Grand Sharif. Nasib, a sworn member of al-Fatat, in agreement with the secret society, asked his brother to pass a secret oral message to the Grand Sharif. The Arab leaders of the national movement in Syria and Iraq favored a revolt against Turkey and they wanted to know if he would accept to lead it. They could send a delegation to Mecca or he could send a representative to Damascus. The oral message was disclosed to Fawzi after he

---

1   The Arab awakening, George Antonius, Simon Publications, 2001, Pg 112

was made a sworn member of the Fatat and he was let in to its secrets.

At this time, Ahmad Jamal Pasha was appointed as Governor and military commander in Syria. Antonius described him as "an outspoken champion of Islam" and that he "was not a representative Young Turk of the CUP stamp." He believed in Ottoman nationalism under Muslim solidarity. As he arrived, documents were seized from the French consulates in Beirut and Damascus including correspondence incriminating well-know Arab personalities in the secret societies.

> "The seized documents contained evidence of activities that seemed indistinguishable from treason: but Jamal, bent on making a good impression, merely informed the Sharif (Hussein) of the discovery, locked the papers up in a drawer and turned his attention to the task of liberating Egypt."[1]

Hussein sent his son to explore things with the secret societies, in a trip that was to continue to Istanbul. He arrived in Damascus on March 26th 1915 and stayed there for a month. He was well received by Jamal Pasha who invited him to stay at the General Headquarters, but he advised him he was committed to stay with the al-Bakri family. During his month long stay, Faisal was initiated in the secret societies. Faisal, at first expressed fear about Europe's designs, and worried that maybe the Arabs would end

---

1   The Arab awakening, George Antonius, Simon Publications, 2001, Pg 151

up exchanging one rule that they knew for another occupation that they did not know. They told him that if the European designs materialize they would side with Turkey. Then Faisal was let into the secrets of the society and was made a member. He was then introduced to the al-Ahd by a high ranking member who was in both. Faisal was initiated to al-Ahd as well. He was impressed by what he found out about the membership of high ranking officers at al-Ahd and their ability to stage a revolt at a moment's notice.

The designs of European powers on the Arab territories were an open secret. When France suspected certain activities of Britain in Syria, a French representative visited London in 1912, and was assured that Britain had no political stake in Syria. The French Premier made this assurance in a statement in the Chamber on December 21st 1912, making it official. The declaration stated that Syria was a French preserve, and requested others to regard it as such. The Sultan of Morocco, a puppet of France visited Syria in 1913 and he stated to the press that the occupation of Syria by France was "necessary, inevitable and near." M. Maurice Barres openly said the same in 1914. How then, was the al-Fatat was convinced, if at all, or how did it convince Faisal to ignore his fears and become an initiate of those shady societies?

Faisal continued his trip to Istanbul where he was warmly received. He asked for assurances for the security of his father's dynasty and was given such an assurance. He was treated as a celebrity, was given audience of the Sultan, the Grand Vizir and anyone he wished to see. They did ask him for the public support of his father for Turkey in its war. He left Istanbul and went back to Damascus where he found a plan of action drawn up by his colleagues at al-Fatat and al-Ahd waiting for him. He was to take it to his father and see if it was acceptable as basis for negotiations with Britain. This became known as the Protocol of Damascus. It stipulated that Britain must recognize the independence of Arab countries involving the Arab territories of Syria and Iraq, and the abolition of all exceptional privileges granted to foreigners under the Capitulations. In return the new Arab country must give Britain an economic preference and a defense alliance.

An oath of allegiance by the leaders of the secret societies was taken, by which they bound themselves to accept Hussein as the spokesman for the Arab race and to honor an agreement with Britain reached on the basis of the Damascus Protocol. A series of correspondence began between Hussein and the colonial British 'Arab Bureau' in Cairo, which finally ended with Britain accepting the Damascus Protocol with exception to the Syrian coast which, they claimed was bound to Britain's understandings with others. The Eastern coast of Syria constituted present Palestine, Lebanon and the Syrian Latikiya strip. The British suggested that these issues could be settled best after the dust of war settled. Always believing the honorable British and their promises, Sharif Hussein accepted to go on with the revolt on these conditions. A public declaration by Britain was requested.

> "In it, Great Britain pledged herself to make it a condition of the conclusion of peace that an Arabian Peninsula should be recognized as an independent

state exercising full sovereignty over the Holy Places of Islam: and it hinted at the readiness of the British Government to welcome the proclamation of an Arab caliphate. The declaration was published early in June."[1]

Establishing a caliphate, an Arab one, was always on the mind of Sharif Hussein, although he differed in opinion with the Young Turks who deviated from true Islam. The caliphate was a pillar of Islam which had been in place since Prophet Mohammed, and he could not see himself as the one to damage such an Islamic pillar. So that was the one thing he added to the Protocol of Damascus as he started negotiating with the British. The British wanted to remain vague on this subject.

The obligations of each side were finally defined as such: The Grand Sharif would utilize all resources in the war to defeat the Turks. His forces would be supplemented as needed by Britain financially and materially. Politically, the Sharif was committed to declare a revolt against the Turks, and declare that they were enemies of Islam, which the CUP truly was. Britain accepted two obligations, the recognition of an Arab caliphate if one were proclaimed, and to recognize Arab independence in an area that was intentionally not well defined by the British. Palestine was never mentioned as an exception though the territory now called Lebanon was. This became a thorny issue. Accordingly, the Arab Revolt was declared on June the 5th, 1916, the very same day

---

1   The Arab awakening, George Antonius, Simon Publications, 2001, Pg 160

of Kitchener's death. The flag of the Faisal forces was already designed by Mark Sykes with its black, white, green and red colors.

Jemal Pasha Tightens his Reins

Jemal Pasha started to get reports from his intelligence that there existed secret national societies, and that British and French agents were in Syria instigating a revolt. The secret societies had penetrated the army which was honeycombed with revolutionary cells, so Jemal decided to change his policy of leniency and to take strong measures. He opened his drawer where he kept the incriminating documents that were seized from the French consulate, arranged a trial and hanged 11 people including some of the al-Fatat leadership. Others were jailed, and some were exiled.

During the mandate on Syria and enthroning Faisal in Iraq, members of the secret societies continued to have prominent public roles under the British and French mandates. Amongst these were Shukri al-Quowatli who became a Syrian President, and Faris Khouri who became a Syrian Prime Minister, and Nuri al-Saed who became an Iraqi Prime Minister.

When the secret Sykes Picot Agreement was made public after the Russian October Revolution, British agents quickly acted to claim that the disclosure was a fraud, and Britain was always faithful to the Arab cause. When the Balfour Declaration was made public in January, it caused confusion and discontent in the

Arab world. Sharif Hussein, now King Hussein, asked the British for an explanation! The Arab Bureau in Cairo immediately sent Commander Hogarth to Jeddah and he was instructed to put Hussein at ease. He told him that Jewish settlement in Palestine will not infringe on the political and economic rights of the Arabs of Palestine, which was untrue, as the Balfour Declaration declared 'the protection of the civil and religious rights' of the non-Jewish inhabitants. The message was delivered verbally to King Hussein and he accepted the explanation. He asked his sons to convey this message and ease the fears of the Arabs at large. This caused Faisal to call on the Arabs of Palestine through his mouthpiece newspaper al-Qibla to afford and offer hospitality and tolerance and to welcome the Jews as brothers according to our Sacred Book and traditions.

King Hussein was a principled man even when he erred in his judgment. He believed the British and he expected them to honor their commitments. Prince Faisal was a young inexperienced man who was manipulated by the secret societies and by the British at the same time. As time went by, he was their man more so than his demanding father. Hussein wanted to declare an Arab caliphate, something the British pledged, but never wanted to honor. They were after destroying the caliphate once and for all.

Hussein, From Sharif of Mecca to Arab King to Exile

Sharif Hussein never intended to be used as a tool to destroy the Muslim Caliphate institution which existed from the days of Prophet Mohammad until Hussein's days. His non suspecting character, naïve trust in Britain and its promises, and the deliberate racist excesses of the CUP all combined in his quest to ensure the caliphate institution was not destroyed, but changed from Turkish to Arab hands. This conviction never changed and was the main reason for his deposition from his throne and him being exiled to Cyprus.

It was Clayton from the Arab Bureau in Cairo who failed to reach an understanding with Arab separatist leaders from Damascus and Baghdad because they objected to being ruled by non-Muslims. The answer, wrote Clayton and Storrs to their superiors was convincing Hussein to become an Arab caliph, and the idea was accepted by Kitchener. In January 1918 King Hussein told Major Cornwallis that he was about to declare himself a caliph.

> "By January 1918, however, the Arab Bureau, which now held Hussein in low esteem, had come around to the opposite view. Cornwallis, attempting to discourage Hussein, pointed out to him that serious problems would arise if he attempted to assume the Caliphate. On receipt of Cornwallis's news, the High Commissioner, Sir Reginald Wingate, sent

off a dispatch to the Foreign Office saying that he hoped for an opportunity of 'checking premature or ill-considered action' by Hussein. This was the same General Wingate who on 17 November 1915 had induced an Arab religious leader to tell Hussein that he was 'the right man to take over his rightful heritage and verify the hopes of his people – the Mohammedans and Arabs to recover their stolen Caliphate' and calling upon the Hashemite leader to establish 'the Hashemite Arabian Caliphate'."

Historian Fromkin added:

"Kitchener's followers found it inconvenient to remember that once they and their chief had encouraged Hussein to claim the caliphate; erasing it from their minds, they would later ignore it in their books and edit it out of official documents. In memoirs published three decades later, Sir Ronald Storrs deleted the caliphate section from Kitchener's historic cable in 1914 to Hussein. T.E. Lawrence wrote that Kitchener and his followers had believed in Arab nationalism from the beginning – when in fact they did not believe in it at all. They believed instead in the potency of the caliphate; that Hussein could capture it for them; and that in the East nationalism was nothing while religion was everything.

Indeed, in 1918 politics and the desire to rewrite history both dictated a shift in emphasis: Feisal, not Hussein, began to emerge as Cairo's preferred Arab leader, for Feisal showed a disposition, lacking in his father, to accept British counsel and guidance." [1]

According to intercepted cables of King Hussein and his correspondence, Hussein complained that "they have turned my son against me…who is a rebellious & dishonest to his father." Hussein added: "Living under the orders of a disobedient son and a traitor had burdened my shoulder with this misery."

Faisal was now taking his orders from the British, not from his father anymore. The insistence of Hussein on an Arab Caliphate and on Britain to respect its pledges eventually caused King Hussein his throne and he was exiled to Cyprus. It is doubtful that Hussein ever knew how far his sons were involved in the secret societies, or at least if he ever knew the real nature and designs of these societies and the secret forces that moved them in a direction that he opposed and which led him being exiled.

The CUP Drags the Ottoman Empire to World War One

The Young Turks, or the 'Jew' Union and Progress party as the British Ambassador to Istanbul called it, got the Ottoman Empire into World War One by design more than by accident which

---

1   A Peace to End All Peace, David Fromkin, Henry Holt&Co, New York,1989, Pg 327

would result in the final dismembering of the Islamic Ottoman State. As soon as Istanbul entered the war an orchestrated campaign was waged to accomplish what Zionists could not get from Sultan Abdul Hamid: establishing Jewish settlements in Palestine as a prelude to establishing a Jewish state.

> "What is to prevent the Jews having Palestine and restoring a real Judaea? Asked H.G. Wells, in a letter he wrote as soon as Turkey entered the war."[1]

Soon afterwards, Samuel Herbert, a Jewish cabinet minister at Asquith cabinet, sent a memorandum in January 1915 to his prime minister promoting the idea of making Palestine a British protectorate to facilitate the immigration of large number of Jews and to make Palestine a Jewish Homeland. Herbert claimed that this also served Britain's best interests. The prime minister was amused that Herbert's memorandum echoed Benjamin Disraeli's novel 'Tancred" who advocated a Jewish return to Palestine. Disraeli, who also was prime minister during the British purchase of Egypt's shares of the Suez Canal, was born to Jewish parents.

The prime minister described Herbert's memo *as* "almost like a new edition of Tancred brought up to date. I confess I am not attracted by the proposed addition to our responsibilities."[2]

When a revised version of Herbert's memo was circulated in March 1915 to the cabinet, the only cabinet member besides

---

1   A Peace to End All Peace, David Fromkin, Henry Holt&Co, New York,1989, Pg 269

2   A Peace to End All Peace, David Fromkin, Henry Holt&Co, New York,1989, Pg. 269

Herbert who supported the memo was Lloyd George. War minister Kitchener was very much opposed to it arguing that Palestine has no strategic significance to Britain.

What a Coincidence! Or Was It?

The main opponents to the Zionist project in Palestine, Prime Minister Asquith and war minister Kitchener had to go if the Zionist Palestine project was to move further. Sure enough, they were both removed. Asquith was replaced by the only supporter of Herbert's Palestine proposal, Lloyd George. A trip was arranged for Kitchener and his assistants in enemy-active seas. Though British intelligence was warned about the dangers, such warning was kept in drawers of the intelligence bureaucracy.

> "At Scapa Flow, the headquarters of the Grand Fleet off the northern tip of Scotland, Kitchener and the faithful FitzGerald boarded the armored cruiser Hampshire the afternoon of 5 June 1916, bound for the Russian port of Archangel. The departure route of the Hampshire had already been plotted, but should have been changed. Naval intelligence which earlier had broken the German radio code, intercepted a message to the German mine laying submarine U75 in late May. It indicated that the submarine was to mine the passage that the Hampshire intended to follow.

Two further intercepts confirmed the information, as did sightings of the submarine"[1]

Historian Fromkin wrote that British intelligence knowledge to the mining of Kitchener route was kept a top secret until secret documents were released in 1985, some seventy years after the event.

With Lloyd George as the new prime minister and Balfour his foreign secretary, Herbert Samuel proposal was approved and the famous Balfour declaration was issued. Herbert Samuel himself was to become the first High Commissioner of Palestine under the mandate in Palestine.

Lloyd George was a self described Zionist. He actually was representative of Theodor Herzl and the Zionist Movement. After Theodor Herzl gave up on Sultan Abdul- Hamid's permission for settlements in Palestine, he approached colonial secretary Joseph Chamberlain in 1902, the father of modern British imperialism. Herzl proposed that a Jewish political entity be established across Palestine borders either at Al Arish or Cyprus. Chamberlain ruled out Cyprus, but said he would seek the advice of those responsible for Sinai in the colonial office. They rejected the idea. So Chamberlain suggested the prospect of the Jewish homeland in Uganda which happened to be under Chamberlain's own jurisdiction. The idea was passed by Chamberlain to the prime minister who was Lord Balfour at the time. Herzl agreed to the proposal and retained the law firm "Lloyd George, Roberts &

---

1   A Peace to End All Peace, David Fromkin, Henry Holt&Co, New York,1989, Pg. 217

Co." Lloyd George personally followed the matter and drafted "A Charter for the Jewish Settlement which was submitted formally to the British Government for approval. The government responded favorably in what some called the first Balfour declaration". Herzl submitted his proposal to the World Zionist Congress. However, Herzl died in 1904 and a fragmented new Zionist leadership requested Lloyd George to again request permission for colonizing Arish. Again, the foreign office rejected the proposal. Thus, Lloyd George was a representative of the Zionist movement from as early as 1903. What better position could the Zionists enjoy than having their own representative as prime minister? If the Sultan would not give away Palestine, then Palestine must not be under the Sultan. According to historians, Wellington, Canning, Palmerstone, and Disraeli policies were based on the fact that preserving the integrity of the Ottoman Empire was of importance to Britain and to Europe, as it was considered a great buffer zone, especially in the Arab territories. Time became ripe to pull the plug especially since Abdul-Hamid's policies revived Islamic fervor and restored cohesion to the empire.

"The prospect of a British capture of the Holy Land appealed to Lloyd George as a man of religious upbringing. Within days of taking office as Prime Minister he had given new impulse to plans for an advance from Egypt .

But before the campaign Lloyd George had instructed Mark Sykes to join the expedition as chief political officer, On April 5 (1917) with Curzon, he saw Sykes on the eve of his departure and instructed him to make every effort for a British Palestine, to give no pledges to the Arabs, and to do nothing to prejudice the Zionist movement." [1]

Iraq's Occupation Was First Class War Aim

From the beginning of World War One, the British cabinet agreed to annex Mesopotamia (as Iraq was called then). Already Egypt was declared a British protectorate and it had troops stationed there. Britain also made arrangements with the Gulf sheikhdoms and the Arabian Peninsula and through financial subsidies and assigned British agents secured through local rulers the interests of Britain. Palestine was considered un-strategic by Kitchener and its future remained obscure. At the start of World War One, an inter-ministerial commission was formed to discuss the future of the Ottoman territories. Palestine, the commission found was un-strategic and it did not recommend its invasion. Kitchener, being a formidable opponent to the Zionist strategy in Palestine was also so popular even the prime minister could not overrule his judgment. Some argued that Palestine was the bridge between Arab Africa and Greater Syria, and that a hostile power in Palestine could block the road to India through Mesopotamia and also through the Suez Canal. Besides, Christian Zionists like Lloyd George and Balfour wanted it as a Jewish state and the obstacle was Kitchener.

---

1   Britain's Moment in the Middle East 1914-71, Elizabeth Monroe, The Johns Hopkins University Press, 2nd edition 1981, P 38

After the drowning of Kitchener and his assistant FitzGerald in the deep sea by enemy torpedoes, his policy which was contradictory to the policy of Jewish Zionists and their supporters drowned with him and 'a regime change' occurred in Britain. After Kitchener, Sykes and his cronies in the British circles elevated Palestine, and the Middle East, to high priority, and Sykes as well as Lloyd George justified this as the result of the enormous international Jewish influence without which they may not win the war. He claimed that he felt the very high Jewish interest in Palestine during the Sykes-Picot-Sazanov agreement, which became known as Sykes-Picot after the Russian Revolution. In early 1917, Sykes felt the importance of meeting a prominent Zionist figure for coordination, and a meeting was being arranged by others for Chaim Weizmann to meet Sykes. Sykes explained that the present thinking, according to arrangements with France to create a Jewish entity in Palestine under a British and French condominium. Weizmann objected to French participation and through the Prime Minister Lloyd George it was agreed that Palestine would only be under British rule after the war. Lloyd George told Weizmann that Palestine "was to him the one really interesting part of the war." He told Weizmann that the Palestine issue was something to be decided between Britain and the Jews only. He advanced the invasion of Palestine to the top of his war objectives contrary to Kitchener's previous directives. The Zionist machine did its homework in France, which included political structural changes and Sykes wrote Lord Balfour, the British foreign secretary in April 9 1917 that France now recognized the legitimate Zionist aspirations in Palestine. Zionism was asking for a public statement from the British cabinet recognizing those rights and the new French position enforced their cause. Now in 1917, the biggest opponent to such a proclamation and the idea of Zionism came from a Jewish cabinet member, the secretary of state for India, Edwin Montagu. Coming from a family of financiers and millionaires, just like many Jews, he felt that Judaism was a religion not a nationality, and its promotion may become an instrument of anti-Semitism. And he was not alone in thinking this way.

> "As of 1913, the last date for which there was figures, only about one percent of the world's Jews had signified their adherence to Zionism."[1]

After Kitchener...

After Kitchener's obscure and sudden death, the new War Cabinet for the Middle East was under secretaries Leo Amery and Mark Sykes. William Ormsby-Gore was the third member in that secretariat. Lieutenant-Colonel John Patterson, a student of the Bible, who commanded a Jewish battalion in the Gallipoli campaign, asked Amery to ask the War cabinet for permission to form a Jewish Legion to fight under the British when Britain invaded Palestine. The idea came from a Russian Jewish Journalist

---

1   Walter Lacqueur, A History of Zionism, New York, Holt, Rinehart & Winston, 1972 p 184

named Vladimir Jabotinsky who raised the issue initially in 1915. A high British official then said, "But nobody knows yet when we shall go to Palestine and Lord Kitchener says never."

Ormsby-Gore was sent to the Middle East to work in the Arab Bureau. Under his direct command was a Jewish spying network in Palestine headed by Aaron Aaronsohn, and the network was providing critical information about the movements of the Turkish Troops. As soon as Lloyd George became prime minister, Amery initiated action to have Palestine under the British Empire. Lloyd George, already sold out on the idea of converting Palestine to a Jewish state, immediately made plans accordingly and made this an imperial British objective. Eventually, Jabotinsky's Jewish Legion was formed and it advanced with the armies of General Allenby to Palestine.

At that time, American Jews were not enthused about Zionism. New York had only 200 members, and the biggest donation received before 1914 was 200 dollars. This changed when Louis D. Brandeis joined Zionism in 1912 and became its leader in 1914. Brandeis was a politically well connected lawyer from Boston who became the first Jew to serve at the Supreme Court, and an advisor to President Wilson. When Balfour visited the United States in 1917, he met Brandeis. The Balfour declaration assisted Brandeis to forge American Jews over a concrete project that became a war aim. While American President Wilson was hesitant at first to support the Balfour declaration, with the efforts of Brandeis along with other influential Jews, Wilson endorsed the Declaration in a holiday message on the occasion of the Jewish New Year in September 1918.

The Mesopotamian (Iraq) Campaign

Persia, later on renamed Iran, was the main source of petroleum to the British Empire by 1914. Also, the Mesopotamian provinces of Mosul, Baghdad and Basra were believed to have huge oil reserves and the British oil company operating the oils fields of Persia had concessions to drill for and produce oil. So Iraq was a main war target of the highest priority by the British government.

A month before World War One broke out, Britain mobilized a standby force to initially occupy Southern Iraq, the Shat El Arab and Basra region. One day after Britain declared war on Turkey, the Turkish fort at Fao was bombarded by British gunboats and Fao was occupied. Two weeks later several thousand British troops occupied the city of Basra. The British General in command then asked his troops to march to occupy Baghdad.

General Townshend continued marching with little resistance until he reached Ctesiphon, about 25 miles southeast of Baghdad on November 25 where he lost half his army in a fierce battle which forced him to retreat.   Townshend, who had suffered a thousand more casualties, chose to retreat and make his stand at Kut el Amara. He launched several attacks and they all failed. , The British force had to surrender after several months siege.

With a change in command and more reinforcements, Baghdad was captured by British India forces led by General Stanley Maude on March 11, 1917, after opposing a poorly equipped Turkish army.

The British Conquest of Palestine

The Mesopotamian campaign was waged through the Government of India and most of the foot soldiers and casualties were Indians. Allenby started his Palestine campaign by deploying 56 000 laborers and 35000 camels to lay the train tracks and construct water pipelines behind his troops. By the time the Palestine campaign was complete, General Allenby had deployed over 350 000 troops of whom 100 000 were Egyptians, and tens of thousands of Indians as well as thousands of Australians and New Zealanders. 160 000 horses and camels were also deployed. Faisal's forces also joined Allenby as well as Jabotinsky's Jewish Legion which actually did no fighting as it was prepared to be the nucleus of the Jewish army in Palestine.

Perhaps the most concrete expression of Wilson's approval of the Balfour Declaration came in the form of American support for the Jewish Legion. A unit of the British army, the legion was organized by the headstrong Zionist leader Vladimir Jabotinsky, and was composed of armies recruited on American soil. The Wilson administration raised no objection when Jabotinsky began to enlist American Jews. Together with Ben-Gurion and other Palestinian exiles who had found refuge in the

United States, some 1,720 American Jews – the largest national contingent in the force – volunteered. In New York, Baltimore, and Boston, the inductees sang the Zionist anthem, "Hatikvah", (the Hope), as they marched past brass bands, orating politicians, and throngs of gift – giving Hadassah women en route to the ships that bore them to boot camp in Canada. Constituted as the Thirty-ninth Battalion of the Royal Fusiliers, the unit saw action only in September 1918, fording the Jordan near Jericho under fire, a month before the armistice. Nevertheless, the mere existence of a Jewish combat force – the first in nearly two thousand years – bearing Star of David flags and insignia, provided a major fillip to the hard – pressed Yishuv and was a model for later Zionist defense organizations. The Americans, in particular, gained a reputation of fortitude and elan. "The Americans brought with them a strong, often feverish interest in Palestine and everything Palestinian", commented Jabotinsky. Among the legion's American veterans were the sculptor Jacob Epstein, the future Jerusalem Mayor Gershon Agron (Agronsky), and Nehemia Rabin, whose son, Yitzhak, would one day lead the Jewish army and state.[1]

In the battle of Jerusalem, the British deployed 26000 troops including 8000 cavalry. Of these 1667 troops and 5000 horses died. Ottoman resistance was fierce, though it was fighting against great odds, and the attacking troops suffered great causalities, and in some places such as Gaza, the whole city had to be wiped

---

1   Power, Faith and Fantasy, Michael B. Oren, W.W. Norton & Company, New York, London, P 363

out before it was captured. Allenby and most of his general staff were either avid readers of the Bible or Christian Zionists who conducted the Palestine campaign with crusaders zeal. Preachers were used to give sermons to Christian troops even while being prepared in Egypt for the campaign When Moshe Smilansky met one of Allenby troops near Jaffa, a Sid Sheerson from Australia, Smilansky noted: "He had left his herd of sheep to volunteer to the army that went to conquer Palestine. As a school boy he studied the Bible and knew that the land of the Bible had been taken from the people of the Bible".

The Great War that shoved Europe into the twentieth century changed the status of Palestine as well. For more than seven hundred years the land had been under Muslim rule. In 1917, as part of the British push into the Middle East, it passed into Christian hands; indeed, many of the conquering British soldiers compared themselves to the Crusaders. [1]

The Jewish Masonry alliance provided intelligence for Allenby. One of those intelligence networks was led by Alter Levine whose cover was being an insurance salesman. When his cover was blown and Turkish intelligence was about to arrest, he sought cover in the house of Khalil Sakakini, a Christian teacher,

> "Who had joined one of the Masonic lodges in Jerusalem, and Levine also was one of the 'brothers"[2]

---

1   One Palestine Complete, Tom Segev, Henry Holt & Company, New York 1st American Edition 2000, Pg 4

2   One Palestine Complete, Tom Segev, Henry Holt & Company, New York 1st American Edition 2000, Pg. 29

The Turkish intelligence officer Zeki Bek wrote in his memoirs that Levine was running an intelligence network throughout Greater Syria, Palestine included, through setting up a network of brothels through which he was gathering intelligence using extortion. The Turkish Governor in Jerusalem got married to a Jewish girl who "people in the streets of Jerusalem said his wife was a whore…"[1]

In order to create facts on the ground, Lloyd George instructed the British Army in Egypt to invade Palestine. Led by General-Sir Archibald Murray, the British forces marched towards Palestine but were defeated in Gaza, the main city on the coastal road to Palestine. The British army losses were twice as many as the defenders. After receiving reinforcement, Murray made a second attack on April 29, 1917 and again the attack failed. This time the British army suffered three times more casualties than the defenders. Murray pulled back to Egypt where he was eventually replaced by General Allenby. Edmund Allenby was chosen in July 1917. His Mandate from the PM was to occupy Palestine and take Jerusalem before Christmas.

Sir General Edmond Allenby, a cavalry officer, was chosen in June 1917 to lead the invasion to occupy Palestine and Jerusalem before Christmas of that year. Richard Memertzbagen was appointed as head of the Intelligence Division, assisted by Wyndham Deedes as political officer and an expert on Ottoman affairs. They were assisted by Jewish spy rings of Levine and Aaron

---

1   One Palestine Complete, Tom Segev, Henry Holt & Company, New York 1st American Edition 2000, Pg. 17

Aaronsohn. With Allenby's forces were the Jewish Legion led by Vladimir Jabotinsky and the Arab forces led by Faisal who were harassing the Turkish forces at the British forces right flank. After the occupation of Jerusalem the Jewish Legion settled in Palestine to form the nucleus of the Jewish armed forces of the future, while Faisal forces continued northward fighting the retreating Turkish forces. Jerusalem was occupied on December 11, 1917. Allenby entered Jerusalem with his officers from the Jaffa gate where he proclaimed marshal law and a military administration to govern Palestine. Vivian Gilbert, a prominent officer in the British Military Administration said: "Only two bearers of the cross had succeeded in liberating the Holy City…: the crusader Godfrey of Bouillon and Edmund Allenby." In London, the bells of the Westminster Cathedral pealed for the first time in three years.

25 year old Lowell Thomas of Ohio made a show called 'The Last Crusade' after the capture of Jerusalem. The show opened in New York in March 1919, initially at the Century Theater and then in the Madison Square Garden's huge auditorium. The show then moved to London where it was shown at London's biggest halls and was seen by more than a million people in six months.

Since the French were not as supportive to a Jewish state in Palestine as the British were generally, and Lloyd George in particular, Zionists wanted Britain to occupy and keep Palestine contrary to the original Sykes Picot agreement. Lloyd George told his ambassador to France in April 1917 that Britain intended not to abide by the Sykes Picot agreement regarding Palestine. "*We shall be there by conquest and shall remain*" [1]. France had to accept that as *fait accompli* even if that was contrary to the Anglo-French agreement.

Pressure mounted on the British cabinet to publicly support the creation of a Jewish entity in Palestine. The media chorus was played into the game. The Times, on October 26 1917 published an article stating that it was no secret that Britain was considering a statement on Palestine confirming British support for a national homeland to the Jews, and it was time for such a statement to be issued. On October 31 1917 the British cabinet met, and the cabinet authorized the foreign secretary to issue such a statement. Sykes wanted to be the first to pass the news to Weizmann who was not so pleased because the statement was not as strong as he wished. Balfour wrote to the most prominent Jew in Britain. He wrote:

Dear Lord Rothschild,

I have much pleasure in conveying to you, on behalf of His Majesty's Government, the following declaration of sympathy with Jewish Zionist aspirations which has been submitted to, and approved by, the Cabinet: "His Majesty's Government view with favour the establishment in Palestine of national home for the Jewish people, and will use their best endeavors to

---

1   A Peace to End All Peace, David Fromkin, Henry Holt&Co, New York,1989, Pg. 267

facilitate the achievement of this object, it being clearly understood that nothing shall be done which may prejudice the civil and religious rights of existing non – Jewish communities in Palestine, or the rights and political status enjoyed by Jews in any other country. I should be grateful if you would bring this declaration to the knowledge of the Zionist Federation."

Many people, not the least the Palestinians, considered this declaration as absurd. It was one British politician, promising another British global financier a country of a third party. Arthur Koestler called the declaration ' a white Negro'.

Displacing Palestinians at whatever name and by all means was always central to the Zionist project:

"Authors of the Zionist project realized from the very beginning that creating a Jewish state in Palestine meant displacement of the indigenous Palestinian Arabs and their 'transfer' from Palestine. As a Colonial Secretary in 1919, Churchill worried about 'the Jews, whom we are pledged to introduce into Palestine and who take it for granted that the local population will be cleared out to suit their convenience.' "[1]

---

1   A Peace to End All Peace, David Fromkin, Henry Holt&Co, New York,1989, Pg. 494

Allenby's army carried with it a Jewish army, led by Jabotinsky, and a Jewish shadow government called the Jewish Commission headed by Chaim Weizmann.

> "The establishment of the commission, long before the British government had decided to remain in Palestine, long before it received the League of Nations Mandate to rule the country, and despite the objections of the army men in the field , was once again a reflection of the presumed power of Zionism…in London."[1]

Weizmann asked the American Zionists to raise a million dollars for the Commission's finances. During the three and a half years after settling in Jerusalem, the Commission spent 4 million dollars. The commission moved from direct hand outs to poor Jews to job creation projects. Weizmann wanted to use the donations, especially to the ultra orthodox Jews to attract them to the Zionist project which they did not support, and to change their teaching from Yiddish to Hebrew. He wanted to create a national language without which a state cannot be created. Establishing a university in Jerusalem to revive Hebrew and Jewish nationalism was decided in the first Zionist congress of 1897. A plot of land was bought by the Jewish Commission at Mount Scopus and Weizmann set 24th of July 1918 as a date for laying cornerstones of the university in a big ceremony. Allenby

---

1   One Palestine Complete, Tom Segev, Henry Holt & Company, New York 1st American Edition 2000, Pg 65

objected at first, saying the war was not yet over and politically the time was not right. Weizmann over-ruled him by going above his head to Balfour in London. Twelve stones representing the twelve tribes of Israel were laid, and a thirteenth, representing the Zionist movement was laid by Weizmann. About six thousand guests gathered at the site. Allenby brought Weizmann with him in his Rolls-Royce. Balfour cabled his congratulations!

Chaim Weizmann as head of the Jewish Commission lodged at Allenby's camp in the city of Ramle. As he was about to start his march to Jerusalem Allenby invited Weizmann to accompany him on his journey. Weizmann told Allenby that as much as he wanted to, it may be politically not right for people to see him with Allenby as he entered Jerusalem. Weizmann's assessment was that "Allenby is with us and for us." The military regime lasted for two and half years. The Egyptian pound became the legal tender during this period. The second man in the British military Administration, Wyndam Deedes, was a devout Christian Zionist. He was interested in the second coming of the Lord and believed that the quicker he got the Jews to Palestine the better. He believed there was an unwritten alliance between Britain and World Jewry and he acted accordingly. But not all British officers felt that way. Lieutenant general Sir Walter Congreve who served in Egypt and Palestine thought that the Jews were "aggressive, contentious, and unbridled." He believed that the Balfour Declaration would be revoked. "We might as well declare that England belongs to

Italy because it was occupied by Romans."[1] Congreve felt that the Jews wanted to flood Palestine with Jews from Russia, Poland and Romania so they become a majority. "Then they will crush the Arabs, expel them from their land, and get rid of the British as well."[2]

General Congreve noted that the Jewish Commission had a parallel organizational structure to the Military Administration in Palestine and wrote: "The existence of the Zionist Commission in its present form is an insult to the British administration."[3] Actually in case of conflict, the Commission prevailed, often by going directly to London. For instance, Weizmann stated in a Commission meeting that Edmund Vivian Gabriel was an enemy of Zionism and he should not remain in Palestine. He was accused of supporting the interests of the Catholic Church and the Arabs. Sure enough, Gabriel did not return from a trip to London! Weizmann spoke to Herbert Samuel who in turn spoke to Churchill about the matter. Weizmann not only succeeded in firing those he did not like, but also succeeded in appointing those he preferred to the Military administration. The chief British administration officer, General Louis John Bols, described the Zionist Commission as an administration within an administration. When he assumed his post, he was a firm

1   One Palestine Complete, Tom Segev, Henry Holt & Company, New York 1st American Edition 2000, Pg 92

2   One Palestine Complete, Tom Segev, Henry Holt & Company, New York 1st American Edition 2000, Pg. 92

3   One Palestine Complete, Tom Segev, Henry Holt & Company, New York 1st American Edition 2000, Pg 94

supporter of the Zionists, but five months later he demanded that the Commission be dismantled. He felt undignified that the Commission was giving him orders rather than the contrary, and he was sick and tired of this.

A young man in his twenties was studying in Cairo to assume his father's position as Mufti of Jerusalem. When the war broke out, he volunteered with the Turkish army but soon got himself discharged on medical basis. This young man was Haj Amin Husseini. "Apparently he made a quick recovery, for as soon as the British reached the city he helped to enlist two thousand or more volunteers into their service."

Weizmann instructed the Zionist Commission members to evade talking about Zionism's goal of establishing an independent Jewish Palestine and went to Cairo in a public relations visit. He believed that: "The Arab is primitive and believes what he is told."[1]

Weizmann planned to meet Prince Faisal at his camp near Aqaba in June 1918. He wanted to tell Faisal that it is the Jews, and the Jews only who can help him to build a modern Arab Kingdom. Mark Sykes wanted to make sure that Faisal was well prepared for Weizmann's visit. He wrote Faisal:

> "I know that the Arabs despise, condemn, and hate the Jews...Believe me, I speak the truth when I say that this race, despised and weak, is universal, is all powerful and cannot be put down..." Sykes added

---

that Jews are found "in the councils of every state, in every bank, in every business, in every enterprise."[1]

He advised Faisal that the Jews do not intend to expel the Arabs and advised him to take them as an ally just like Lloyd George did. Though Faisal reception to Weizmann was warm, he made no promises or agreement. But Weizmann thought that things would be okay with Faisal heading the Arab National movement.

Confronting the Jewish Immigrants

Early confrontations between Zionist settlers and Arab farmers started as early as the 1880's when the Jews established agricultural settlements in newly purchased lands. The tenants were ejected from the lands violently in most cases, and deadly in some other cases. From the onset of the Jewish settlement movement the conflict was between an indigenous people, the Arabs of Palestine and a new project that wanted to create a nation from foreigners on their land.

This is how Ahad Ha'am, a Jewish writer addressed the issue in his pamphlet "Truth from Palestine", published in 1891. The Jewish settlers, he wrote, "treat the Arabs with hostility and cruelty, trespass unjustly, beat them shamelessly for no sufficient reason, and even take pride in doing so". He offered a psychological explanation for the phenomenon:

---

1   One Palestine Complete, Tom Segev, Henry Holt & Company, New York 1st American Edition 2000, Pg. 111

"The Jews were slaves in the land of their Exile, and suddenly they found themselves with unlimited freedom, wild freedom that only exists in a land like Turkey. This sudden change has produced in their hearts an inclination toward repressive tyranny, as always happens when a slave rules". Ahad Ha'am warned: "We are used to thinking of the Arabs as primitive men of the desert, as a donkey-like nation that neither sees nor understands what is going on around it. But this is a great error. The Arab, like all sons of Shem, has a sharp and crafty mind ... Should the time come when the life of our people in Palestine imposes to a smaller or greater extent on the natives, they will not easily step aside". [1]

In 1899 an Arab notable in Jerusalem expressed what people of Palestine thought of the Zionist project: "The world is big enough, there are other, uninhabited lands in which millions of poor Jews could be settled ... In the name of God, leave Palestine alone!" In 1891 Palestinian Arabs sent a petition to the authorities demanding restriction on Jewish entry to Palestine and the prohibition of selling lands to foreign Jews. To Palestinians, the issue became clear: foreigners are coming to displace them from their motherland. Probably what David Ben Gurion said at a

---

1   One Palestine Complete, Tom Segev, Henry Holt & Company, New York 1st American Edition 2000, Pg. 104. Ahad Ha'am, "Truth from Palestine", in the Complete Works of Ahad Ha'am (in Hebrew) (Tel Aviv: Dvir, 1949), P. 24

later date was the truth that everybody in Britain and the West wanted to ignore. He said:

> "Everybody sees the problem in relations between the Jews and the Arabs. But not everybody sees that there's no solution to it. There is no solution! ... The conflict between the interests of the Jews and the interests of the Arabs in Palestine cannot be resolved by sophisms. I don't know of any Arabs who would agree to Palestine being ours – even if we learn Arabic ... and I have no need to learn the Arabic language. Woe to us if we have to conduct our lives in Arabic. On the other hand, I don't see why "Mustafa" should learn Hebrew ... There's a national question here. We want the country to be ours. The Arabs want the country to be theirs".[1]

In the fall of 1918, Weizmann was again in London and he was invited by Prime Minister David Lloyd George to lunch on November 11, which happened to be the day on which an armistice was declared and World War I came to an end. Already, Weizmann was preparing and coordinating the Zionist position in the coming peace conference that convened at Versailles in January 1919. Weizmann's diplomatic achievements reached its Zenith in that conference. Not only did he succeed in ensuring,

---

1   One Palestine Complete, Tom Segev, Henry Holt & Company, New York 1st American Edition 2000, Pg 116. Pollock to his father, 21 Dec. 1919, Proni D/1581/5

but he succeeded in an international ratification of the Balfour Declaration. Due to such efforts, the League of Nations granted a mandate to the British over Palestine. In this mandate it was defined explicitly that it is Britain's responsibility to help the Jews establish a national home in the country. Thus, the Balfour Declaration which was between one British Lord to another British Lord acquired international legitimacy. What Weizmann wanted Weizmann got. And why not, especially if:

> "Prime Minister Lloyd George and Foreign Secretary Balfour continued to view Weizmann as a leader possessed of some mysterious, world encompassing power to pull the strings of history. Britain, together with the rest of Europe, had endured one of the most dramatic periods in its history. Close to a million British soldiers had been killed in the war and two million wounded; the Spanish influenza epidemic had cut a swath through Europe; millions were out of work. Britain was in a state of shell shock, forced to confront a new world, new values, and new ways of life that were causing much agony. With all this, doors stayed open to Weizmann: the prime minister and all the other officials made time to see and hear him whenever he asked for their attention."[1]

---

1   One Palestine Complete, Tom Segev, Henry Holt & Company, New York 1st American Edition 2000, Pg 116

Lloyd George and Balfour were not the only ones that thought the Jews ruled the world. American President Wilson's adviser, Colonel House, thought that if the Jews were to receive their own state, this should be in exchange for their influence to halt the Bolshevik revolution, which was threatening to spread to other countries. In his diary, Colonel House summed up a conversation with Balfour on the subject.

> "{Balfour} is inclined to believe that nearly all Bolshevism and disorder of that sort is directly traceable to Jews. I suggested putting them, or the best of them, in Palestine, and holding them responsible for the orderly behavior of Jews throughout the world. Balfour thought the plan had possibilities", House wrote. House later discussed the idea with Wilson himself. [1]

With all the historical success achieved, the Zionists were disappointed that the territorial definition of their desired state was not totally accepted. The Zionist map submitted to the conference had included southern Lebanon, the Golan Heights, and a large area east of the Jordan River. The area allocated for the Mandate, however, was half the area of the Zionist map.

In the peace conference, it was suggested that a commission be formed to consult about who the Palestinians wanted as

---

1   One Palestine Complete, Tom Segev, Henry Holt & Company, New York 1st American Edition 2000, Pg 119. Intelligence report, 1 Sept. 1919, CZA L4/764. See also: Minutes of the Zionist Commission, 20 Sept. 1919, CZA L4/297; CZA L3/9I

the Mandatory power to rule their country. A commission was formed which became known as the King Crane Commission, headed by Henry Churchill King, the president of Oberlin College in Ohio, who was a church and missionary activist and the leader of the YMCA, and Charles Crane, an industrialist and businessman from Chicago and a friend of President Wilson. The Commission concluded that the great majority of the people of Palestine wanted American rule and made the recommendation accordingly. Wilson never saw the report. He became ill and the report was filed away. People knew of it only when an American newspaper revealed the report's content as a journalistic scoop.

Faisal after World War One

Prince Faisal met Weizmann in Europe and the Zionists alleged that he signed a document accepting the creation of a Jewish majority in Palestine, provided he received a large independent Arab Kingdom. Major I.N. Camp, the deputy chief political officer to Palestine thought that the agreement was not worth the paper it was written on, because if it was made public it would become a noose around Faisal's neck. He explained that nationalists followed Faisal as long as he made no concessions to Zionism, and they considered anyone who did a traitor.

After the war, Faisal travelled to Europe to attend the peace conference. In 1919, the whole area of the Middle East was classified as Occupied Enemy Territory and it was under military rule. Faisal arrived in Marseilles on November the 26th. Two

French officers introduced themselves and advised him that the French Government welcomed him as a visitor only without any official capacity whatsoever. After making a tour, he left to London where he was given a flattering welcome. But then he was introduced to one bad news after another. The Sykes Picot was a fact and not a malicious fabrication of the Bolshevik he was now told. The French strongly objected to his representation and they do not accept him as representative of Hejaz at the Peace Conference. He was asked to endorse the Zionist project in Palestine in an Agreement between him and Chaim Weizmann. Here was a man in his mid thirties, who spoke little English or French, who had no diplomatic experience or knowledge, having the disappointment of his life, and not knowing what to do. The British were very insistent on the issue of Palestine and they wanted him to yield to their and the Zionist pressure to sign a formal Agreement. Faisal did not know what to do. The Agreement he was requested to sign was outside the agenda of his trip. It will enflame the Northern Arabs if he signed it. He could not say no to his patrons, the British, especially after he saw what the French attitude towards him was. So he sought his father's instructions. His father was very straightforward and brief. He was not authorized to accept anything short of the British pledges. Faisal was given no latitude as his father's order was very clear. The Foreign office asked Lawrence to work on Faisal, and Faisal was desperate not to alienate the British. They were his only hope, he thought. Contrary to his father's order, he consented to sign the Agreement, which the Zionists wanted in anticipation of the Peace Conference. He stipulated a statement to the Agreement that this consent was conditional to Britain living up to its pledges regarding Arab independence. In a way, that was his father's instruction, since if the British did not honor their commitments, which they did not, Faisal's qualifying statement made his signature to the agreement as null and void. But the Zionist propaganda underplayed Faisal reservation and claimed he consented to their Zionist project.

After World War One ended formally, lots of horse trading took place among the allies about the spoils of the war especially the Arab territories of the Ottoman state. Even when the war was going on, secret negotiations between Britain, France, and Russia took place, which became known as the Sykes Picot Agreement in which the three countries agreed about how to divide the Ottoman occupied territories after the war.

A New Middle East at Cairo Conference

The Cairo Conference, as the meeting became known afterwards, which included forty or fifty of the 'who is who' in British diplomacy of the Middle East convened at the Sameramis Hotel on March 12, 1921. Churchill already had an agenda and Mesopotamia now renamed Iraq was the first issue to resolve. The Palestinian question was the other issue. The conference continued until March 22nd. The Next day Churchill left by train to Jerusalem.

The question of local resistance in Mesopotamia and Palestine was largely driven by Muslim resistance to foreign non-Muslim rule. Also, the cost of combating the rebellions was draining the Empire's resources. On the subject of Mesopotamia, the conference debated and agreed on the best policy to adopt. They unanimously agreed that to cut down the work expenses, Churchill's strategy of putting down the insurgency through air power was the most cost effective provided that an Arab be their proxy in governing and subduing the local population. They all agreed that Faisal would be the right person for the job. They agreed however, that all efforts were to be taken to make it absolutely clear that the appointment of Faisal as King of Iraq was a local national choice. Faisal was called from London and advised of the decision. The British High Commissioner in Baghdad who was at the Conference left for Baghdad to make the proper arrangements. Among the arrangements was the invitation of the chief opponent of such a proposal for a tea at the Commissioner's home in Baghdad with a party of others. The Commissioner, Percy Cox, left a while before the arrival of the party. Tea was served by Lady Cox and then members in the party, per prior instructions from Cox, arrested the opponent and exiled him to Ceylon. The British-appointed Council of Ministers unanimously agreed that Faisal become a King of Iraq and the minister of interior arranged a 'plebiscite' to confirm the Council of Ministers resolution. Faisal became king and the name of Mesopotamia became Iraq.

General Allenby who became the High Commissioner for Egypt insisted that Egypt should be given a limited independence to alleviate revolution and disturbances. Although Churchill objected initially, Allenby's view was accepted. He proclaimed in 1922 independence for Egypt unilaterally because he found no Egyptian who would accept the conditions attached which included British military bases and free military movement across the country, as well as foreign policy remaining under British control.

East of the Jordan River, also called East Palestine by the Zionists, was in turmoil. The Chief of the Imperial General Staff estimated that the area would need at least two battalions to keep order, but he added "which of course we have not got". Churchill suggested that Prince Abdulla, Faisal brother be given temporary governorship over the territory for six months. Herbert Samuel strongly objected, saying that that territory was defined as Palestine in the mandate of the League of Nations. Churchill said that Palestine was not defined geographically in the Balfour Declaration and that his suggestion still respected British commitment. It seems that Samuel passed the work to Zionist circles in London since Churchill received a cable from Prime Minister Lloyd George:

> *"Cabinet... discussed your proposals for Transjordania, as to which considerable misgivings were entertained."* Churchill and those at the Cairo Conference were able to press their viewpoint. In Jerusalem Churchill met Prince Abdulla four times and reached an agreement with him. His report to cabinet afterwards that Abdulla's "attitude was moderate, friendly and statesmanlike." Regarding Arab demonstrators against Zionism Abdullah "maintained a correct attitude, reproved the demonstrators, and stated that the British were his*

> *friends and that the British Government would keep*
> *their promises to Jews and Arabs alike."* [1]

Abdulla agreed to govern for a trial period of six months assisted by a British political agent and a financial subsidy but no British troops. This was the start of the Emirate of Transjordan that became Jordan after a few decades.

One week before the U.S. invaded Iraq, on March 10, 2003, Howard Fineman wrote in Newsweek as part of a special report, "Bush and God":

"George W. Bush rises ahead of the dawn most days ... he goes off to a quiet place to read alone. His text isn't news summaries of the overnight intelligence dispatches ... It is not recreational reading ... Instead, he's told friends, it's a book of evangelical mini-sermons (*My Utmost for His Highest*). The author is Oswald Chambers, and under circumstances, the historical echoes are loud. A Scotsman and itinerant Baptist preacher, Chambers died in November 1917 as he was bringing the Gospel to Australian and New Zealand soldiers massed in Egypt (in the Army of General Allenby). By Christmas they had helped to wrest Palestine from the (Muslim) Turks. Now there is talk of a new war in the Near East, this time in a land once called Babylon ... Later that day ... Bush told religious broadcasters that ... the United States was called to bring God's gift of liberty to every human being in the world." [2]

---

1   A Peace to End All Peace, David Fromkin, Henry Holt&Co, New York,1989, Pg. 506

2   Oil Crusades, America through Arab eyes, Abdulhay Zalloum, Pluto Press, London, 2007, Pg 50-51

*"We have forgotten one small matter" wrote Yitzhak Epstein, a
Zionist educator, in 1907. "There is in our beloved land an
entire nation, which has occupied it for hundreds of years
and had never thought to leave it… We are making a great
psychological error with regard to a great assertive and jealous
people…we forget that the nation that lives in (Palestine)
today has a sensitive heart and a loving soul. The Arab, like
every man, is tied to his native land with strong bonds."*

*The Jews were embarrassed when Hans Herzl, the son of the
founder of the Zionist movement, had converted to Christianity.
Itamar Ben-Avi, the editor of Do'ar HaYom commented that
unlike the Jesus of Nazareth, Herzl's son was at least not a bastard.*

CHAPTER SEVEN

THE MANDATE: BUILDING
JEWISH STATE INSTITUTIONS

On Monday morning of March 1, 1920, Arabs gathered at the gates of a Jewish settlement in the upper Galilee called Tel Hai. They demanded to search the settlement for French soldiers that they suspected were in hiding at the settlement. The Jews, it is claimed, put up no resistance to having the settlement searched by the Arabs, but one of the settlers fired the first shot. It is alleged that it was a signal for settlers in nearby Kfar Giladi for reinforcement, which consisted of ten armed settlers led by Yusef Trumpeldor, a former officer in the Russian army who immigrated to Palestine. Once he reached Tel Hai, he opened fire. Palestinian Arabs fired back and six settlers were killed including Trumpeldor. The result was the evacuation of Tel Hai and Kfar Giladi settlements. The Zionist propaganda machine needed an incident to glorify settlements and armed struggle and it made a story out of the Tel Hai incident .

> "To symbolize the principle that no settlement should be abandoned the fact that two settlements were evacuated after the attack was generally not

mentioned. The defeat was turned into victory" wrote Israeli historian Tom Segev.[1]

The Intifada of Nebi Musa

On April 4, 1920, a Sunday, some 70 000 Arabs gathered in Jerusalem to celebrate the Nebi Musa (prophet Moses) festival which always coincides with Passover, the Greek Orthodox Easter. Since Christians from the time of the crusades gather on that day from all over the world, the tradition of Nebi Musa was to ensure that Muslims are present at the Holy City for any eventuality. On that day in 1920, speeches were made from the balcony of Jerusalem's municipality condemning Zionism and demanding independence. It is claimed that a Jew spat on an Arab flag carried by an Arab youth, and riots swept the city and the Jewish Quarter was attacked. Curfews were imposed. Several Arab rioters were jailed. The next day, tension grew stronger and the Jewish quarter in Jerusalem was stormed by rioters. Two pedestrians were stabbed to death and the old city was sealed off, and martial law was declared. Some homes were set on fire. Jabotinsky and his comrades used gunfire at the Jaffa Gate and once searched, some arms were found in his apartment. He was sentenced to 15 years, and was sent to a jail in Egypt. On his train trip, his guards moved him to a first class carriage. Only one day after arrival, and for reasons unknown, but very likely

---

1   One Palestine Complete, Tom Segev, Henry Holt & Company, New York 1st American Edition 2000, Pg 125

due to instructions from London, he was sent back to Palestine to the Acre prison. The result of the Nebi Musa violence was the death of five Jews and 216 wounded, against 4 Arabs killed and 23 wounded. 7 soldiers were wounded as they were beaten by the rioters. More than two hundred people were put on trial. Arab leaders Haj Amin Husseini and Aref al-Aref were sentenced to 10 years each for inciting the crowds and Mayor Musa Kazem al Husseini was removed from his job. Historian Joseph Klausner wrote in Ha'aretz:

> "If the Arabs imagine that they can provoke us to war and that because we are few they will easily win, they are making a huge error. Our campaign will include all 13 million Jews in all the countries of the world. And everybody knows how many people of great wisdom and great wealth and great influence we have in Europe and America.[1]"

A court of inquiry was formed to investigate the Nebi Musa violence. It was made up of two generals, a colonel, and a legal counsel. They concluded that the Balfour Declaration "is undoubtedly the starting point of the whole trouble." They believed that Chaim Weizmann had lost control to the more extremist Zionist elements, and they reached the conclusion that Zionist movement was both dictatorial and nationalist with a clear plan to expel the Arabs from Palestine. Thus, the fears of the

---

1   One Palestine Complete, Tom Segev, Henry Holt & Company, New York 1st American Edition 2000, Pg 139

Arabs are not baseless. They stated that Bolshevism was entrenched in Zionism's heart and they named Lieutenant Jabotinsky's Poaler Zion Party as a "definite Bolshevik institution."The report was never published publicly and the military administration was dismissed in July 1920.

A New British Civil Administration... Tension continues

A civil administration was created in its place as was the preference of Chaim Weizmann. Weizmann, upon returning to London, petitioned Churchill for the release of Jabotinsky from prison. It was decided that since Herbert Samuel would arrive in Palestine in few weeks as the High Commissioner of Palestine, the issue of Jabotinsky would be resolved. Surely, one of Samuel first acts as High Commissioner was letting Jabotinsky out of jail. The Arabs of Palestine became furious at the appointment of Samuel as commissioner, as he was well known as a staunch Zionist Jew who participated in all stages of developing the Balfour declaration and supporting Zionism at the Peace Conference, and the assignment of Britain as the Mandatory power over Palestine.

Tension between the Arabs and Jews continued to escalate from that date. Actually, the relationship between Arabs and Jews deteriorated earlier in 1919. When Weizmann left for Europe to prepare for the peace conference, Menachem Ussishkin was appointed as head of the Zionist Commission. A confrontation occurred between him and Jerusalem Mayor Musa Kazem al Husseini. When Husseini asked Ussishkin what the news was from the peace conference, Ussishkin, a Russian immigrant, said that though a treaty had not yet been signed, things were already settled. Palestine would remain with Britain, and Syria with the French. Husseini said the Arabs would not agree to this. Ussishkin interrupted him by saying, "Look, I said everything is settled" and told him that Faisal agreed to this. Husseini answered that Arabs in Palestine did not authorize Faisal to make concessions on their behalf. When Ussishkin reminded Musa al Kazem Husseini that the Jews wondered the desert for forty years before reaching Palestine, Musa (which means Moses in Arabic} told him it was because you did not listen to Prophet Musa that you got lost, and if you do not listen to this Musa (Husseini) you may get lost for another forty years. Ussishkin wrote a report to the Zionist Commission that Mayor Husseini was anti-Zionism. Mayor Husseini was removed and was replaced by Ragheb Al Nashashibi, who was more accommodating.

When Churchill visited Jerusalem in the spring of 1921 former Mayor Musa Al Husseini demanded that Churchill revoke the Balfour Declaration, halt Jewish immigrations and cancel the borders with Syria, things Churchill said he could not do. Before Churchill left, the Mufti of Jerusalem died and the High Commissioner appointed Haj Amin al Husseini, who was also pardoned by Samuel, as the new Mufti of Jerusalem. During Samuel's years as commissioner, the Palestinian Jews and British Zionists dominated the senior positions in the

Palestine government. Lieutenant Colonel Percy Pramley, the director of public security in Palestine complained that Samuel's administration was a "Zionist-controlled government."

The Jaffa Uprising...

After the Nebi Musa and the arrival of the High Commissioner to Palestine Samuel considered things to be so quiet that the Nebi Musa bloodshed seemed like a hundred years ago. This optimism did not last long. On May 1, 1921, the Jewish Communist Party called for a May Day parade calling on the workers to topple the British Mandate and establish instead the Soviet Union of Palestine. Police gave no permission for this parade, but permission was given to a rival Jewish labor party, Achut HaAvoda, which was the major labor party at the time. As the two parades took place, the communists and the other party clashed with fist fights and the police chased the communists back to Jaffa. Tel Aviv was at that time still part of Jaffa and acquired municipality status shortly after these May Day events. A court of inquiry later on decided that the fight between the two Jewish parties was the direct cause that ignited the Arab riots that followed. The Arabs anger was directed at an immigrant's hostel run by the Zionist Commission in which about a hundred immigrants stayed. Rioters also attacked Jewish homes and shops and any Jew that was in sight. They demanded that Jewish immigration stop. It was alleged that even Arab policemen joined the rioters. Samuel sent his most trusted senior Zionist officials to Jaffa. He called

General Allenby in Cairo asking for reinforcements. Allenby sent two destroyers to Jaffa and one to Haifa. A state of emergency was called. Samuel met Arab representatives and tried to calm them down. Among them was former Jerusalem Mayor Musa Kazem al Husseini who demanded immediate suspension to Jewish immigration. Samuel instructed the Ramle commissioner to issue a statement suspending immigration and the boats on their way to Palestine were turned back to Istanbul after Allenby refused Samuel's request to temporarily permit them access to Port Said. Nachum Sokolow asked Samuel to revoke the suspension of immigration because he was rewarding terror. Sokolow said there was no reason for worry, but Samuel said he worried that Palestine was turning out to be another Ireland. When Sokolow told Samuel it was only a small band of Arab terrorists that caused the riots Samuel answered him: "You are wrong. This is a war of the Arab Nation against the Hebrew nation."

At Sarafand camp where members of the Jewish Legion resided, several soldiers left to join the riots. The next day they went to the streets of Jaffa and they attacked Arab homes, killing whole families, men, women and children. The tension spread to nearby settlements and Samuel ordered that for the Arab rioters be bombed from the air. 47 Jews and 48 Arabs were killed and 146 Jews and 73 Arabs were wounded in these disturbances.

A Zionist High Commissioner Rethinks Balfour...

The inquiry commission appointed to investigate the riots ruled that the violence was instantaneous and the rioters were not Jew haters but Zionist opponents. Zionism, the report added scares the Arabs. The commission concluded that Arabs are more obedient but prone to violent outbursts, while the Jews are inclined to violence and are less obedient. In what became known as the King's Birthday Speech at the Government House, Samuel called the dignitaries of Palestine and stated that it is his intention to start caring about the second part of the Balfour Declaration which stated that nothing to be done to infringe on the rights of the non-Jewish communities. He stated that Jewish immigration will be limited so it does not hurt the country's economy. The Zionist Commission became furious. Weizmann denounced Samuel as a coward. The Zionist movement's extremism started to take root. Weizmann stated that his enemies at home were not the Arabs but Ben Gurion and Jabotinsky who started to outbid Weizmann. Some suggested that Samuel had second thoughts about Zionism after what he had experienced on the ground. Others believe he remained as Zionist as ever, but he saw the difficulties that accompanied the Zionist ideology especially regarding the indigenous population.

On July 22, 1921, a Tuesday, Weizmann was invited to Balfour's home to discuss the situation in Palestine. Present were the Prime Minister Lloyd George and Colonial secretary

Churchill. In the meeting Weizmann criticized Samuel's King's Birthday speech, and stated that without immigration the Jews could not form a majority. Lloyd George and Balfour stated that the Balfour Declaration had always meant the eventual creation of a Jewish State. This was actually much more than the Declaration promised, and Churchill was surprised adding that 9 out of 10 British officials in Palestine opposed the Balfour declaration, that a representative government must be created in Palestine. Weizmann objected because the Jews were a minority, and Lloyd George agreed with Weizmann. In that meeting Weizmann had permission for the Zionist commission, which changed names to the Zionist Executive, to smuggle arms to Palestine. Asked by Balfour if there was anything more they could do for him, he asked that the defense of Palestine be taken from General Congreve, whom he described as an enemy. Churchill agreed. Weizmann confidentially through his 'intelligence' connections got a memorandum from General Congreve's London Headquarters stating that as the experience in Ireland showed, the British army must side with one faction against the other, and to Weizmann, the sympathy of Congreve was with the Arabs.

In early 1923 Albert Einstein was in Jerusalem as part of a public relations campaign to promote the expansion and development of the Hebrew University. He listened to many speeches in Hebrew which he did not understand and Zionism made the most out of his trip. Most of the funding for the university came from the United States.

More Jewish Immigration... The Wailing Wall Uprising

As immigration increased substantially, the Jews became more assertive and aggressive in proclaiming their ultimate goals, and Zionism itself split into ultra-fanatic brands such as Jabotinsky's Revisionists. That fanaticism extended against the Christian faith as well. The Jews were embarrassed when Hans Herzl, the son of the founder of the Zionist movement, had converted to Christianity. Itamar Ben-Avi, the editor of Do'ar HaYom commented that unlike the Jesus of Nazareth, Herzl's son was at least not a bastard. Muslims consider the Western Wall an Islamic Waqf (Islamic Trust) property and they repeatedly refused attempts by Jews to buy it. It is also a sacred place as far as Muslims are concerned. Muslims for the past centuries did not interfere in the Jews observing worship in the place as long as the Jews do not change its status quo. When the Jews constructed a screen on the afternoon of Sunday, September 23, 1928, Muslims were alarmed. As they once explained it to the new British Governor of Jerusalem when they refused to have chairs installed at the Western/Wailing Wall area they said the Jews, under the Balfour Declaration spirit will first put out chairs, then wooden benches, then more walls and a ceiling to keep them from the sun and cold, and then Muslims will find at hand a synagogue on their property and then the Jews will claim their two sacred mosques al Aqsa and Omer Mosque as theirs. This is how the Jews were taking Palestine bit by bit, starting with small settlements, then cities and then the whole country. Arabs were surprised to find that Encyclopedia Britannica included the Zionist flag (two blue stripes on a white background with a blue star of David) as the flag of Palestine among the flags of the world! When one woman challenged the encyclopedia on such misinformation, the editor apologized and called their action "somewhat premature", the next edition was corrected. But note the editor apologized because of prematurity not because of error!

Zionist aspirations to build a Third Temple over the Al Aqsa Mosque were expressed in the international Zionist publications. Arabs showed the American council in Jerusalem a drawing that appeared in an American Zionist publication, Das Yidishe Folk in which a Domed structure was shown on the premises of al Aqsa Mosque, or as it is also called Temple Mount by the Jews. The council sent the drawing to Washington. Only few months before the new screen was installed at the Wailing Wall, in a post-Passover celebration, Menachem Ussishkin, a high ranking member in the Zionist Executive declared,

> "The Jewish people want a Jewish state without compromises and without concessions, from Dan to Be'ersheva, from the great sea to the desert, including Transjordan." He concluded: "Let us swear that the Jewish people will not rest and will not remain silent until its national home is built on our Mt. Moriah" referring to the Temple Mount." [1]

---

1   One Palestine Complete, Tom Segev, Henry Holt & Company, New York 1st American Edition 2000, Pg 304

Thus, Arab fears were indeed authentic.

The screen incident caused protests and proclamations by the Arabs who also telegrammed the League of Nations. Tension was on the rise and several violent incidents occurred. At that time a Chaim Shalom Halevi wrote:

> "(The Arabs) hate us and they are right, because we hate them too, hate them with a deadly hatred." He said that was the truth regardless of the nice language of Zionists. Realizing the Zionist dream by necessity will drive them out of the country. Nothing will be left to them."

On August 14, 1929, the day marking the destruction of the Temple, thousands of Jews congregated at the wall. The next day hundreds of young Jews demonstrated at the wall. The demonstrators made political speeches, waved the Zionist flag and sang the Hatikva in defiance to police orders and provoked the Arab population. In this atmosphere, one Jew was killed near the village of Lifta in the vicinity of Jerusalem and an Arab pedestrian was assaulted by the Jews.

On Friday August 23, 1929, thousands of Arabs started coming to Jerusalem from all over the country arming themselves with sticks and knives to counter the demonstrations of a week earlier by the Jews at the Wailing Wall. The acting High Commissioner was Harry Luke, whose father was a Hungarian-born American Jew. Luke tried to conceal his faith, a fact for which Weizmann called him a coward. Luke tried to defuse the tension the day before by calling the leaders of both communities for a discussion but no agreement was reached. At about noon 2 or 3 Arabs were massacred at the Jewish quarter of Mea Sha'arim, and according to the mufti, Arabs injured by the Jews started to arrive at the Mosque as prayers were just ending at the mosque. The Jews created the Haganah defense organization after the Jaffa riots and it appeared they mobilized for action.

News of the escalating tension reached Hebron through Hebronites returning from their Jerusalem Friday noon prayers. The news that the Jews were killing Arabs, spread quickly and in no time hundreds were streaming to the municipality bus parking lot intending to travel to Jerusalem. In Hebron there was a small Jewish community, a few dozens of which lived downtown and the rest in the outskirts. Relationship prior Zionism was cordial and tension crept into the community after the British invasion. On that Friday, five Arabs and eight Jews were killed in Jerusalem. Nine Arabs and fifteen Jews were injured. The next day, Saturday, violence continued in Hebron and 67 Jews were killed and dozens wounded. The remaining Jews were evacuated to Jerusalem. The residents of the Arab village Kolonia attacked the Jewish village of Motza. They killed and burned houses. Arabs tried to penetrate Tel Aviv. In Safad, the violence took several lives. All in all, when things calmed down, 116 Arabs and 133 Jews were killed and 339 Jews and 232 Arabs were wounded.

Shmuel Yosef Agnon concluded: "In my humble opinion we should now build a large ghetto of half a million Jews in Palestine, because if we do not we will, God forbid, be lost." Israel today lives in a larger ghetto surrounded by a Separation Wall, armed to its teeth with nuclear weapons and remains as a ghetto and insecure as ever. Few thousands of Hizbollah fighters compelled the residents of this ghetto to go underground in shelters for over a month, and all hundreds of kilometers of the Separation Wall as well as the airpower and hundreds of nuclear bombs were useless and added no security.

The Jewish Agency investigated charges against Jews "who shamelessly were beyond the limits of self-defense". The Agency investigating a claim that Jews broke into a mosque and set the Quran on fire stated: "This unfortunately is true." It was also reported that Jews lynched a passerby, killed women and children and even attacked Arabs who gave them refuge. Zionist Archives kept a list of 435 Arabs in Hebron who saved Jews which resulted in saving of two third of the Hebron Jews. A Jew testified that Arab Jewish neighbors *"were hurt defending their Jewish neighbors."* Sir Harry Charles Luke, the acting High Commissioner attributed the violence to the Balfour Declaration *"as if it were an original sin"* and concluded that the war for Palestine will continue.

High Commissioner Chancellor in a Dilemma...

Out of some 700 Arabs and 160 Jews who were put on trial, 124 Arabs and 25 Jews were accused of murder. 25 Arabs were sentenced to death, while only 2 Jews were sentenced to death and their sentence was commuted to life imprisonment. High

Commissioner Chancellor felt he was in a dilemma. Should he allow the execution of the Arabs while no Jews would be executed? He decided to execute 3 Arabs and commuted the others to life in prison. Chancellor was annoyed by the pressure the Zionist organization was exerting on his administration and thought that the Jews "are an ungrateful race", though he is of Jewish extracts himself. He was very annoyed when the American consul in Jerusalem told him that the Jews had organized an intelligence network and that all his secret communications with London reached the Zionists first! Then he decided that the present situation was unattainable. Palestine cannot belong to two nations, and he wrote London suggesting that Britain be extricated from the Balfour Declaration. He suggested giving the inhabitants of Palestine, the Arabs, self-government, while the Jews may view Palestine as a national home without a state. He recommended the restriction of land sale to the Jewish, and limiting Jewish immigration as well. A copy of the report was sent to the king. The report was well received at the Colonial Office and Chancellor's Memorandum resulted in an attempt to formulate a new British policy for Palestine.

A White Paper and a New Policy...

A White Paper defining the new policy was issued by Colonial Secretary Passfield. It stated the Balfour Declaration imposed equal and binary obligation on Britain to both Arabs and Jews and that the immigration must be at a rate not to hurt the Arab population of Palestine. The paper assumed that the Jews would remain a minority and they may enjoy autonomy but not a state. The government promised to invest seven million pounds to develop the country so a maximum of tens of thousands may be absorbed. The Zionists project is based on immigration and stopping it or minimizing it was strongly against their plans. Ben Gurion, as many others, noted the tensions in Nazi Germany and he wanted to take advantages of it. He said:

> "We want Hitler to be destroyed", Ben Gurion said, "but as long as he exists, we are interested in exploiting that for the good of Palestine".[1]

A few years earlier, Ben Gurion had made the following statement about the rescue of German Jewish children:

> "If I knew that it was possible to save all the children in Germany by transporting them to England, but only half of them by transporting them to Palestine, I would choose the second – because we face not only the reckoning of those children, but the historical reckoning of the Jewish people". [2]

The British officials in Palestine supported the White Paper. As for the Jews, they called the White Paper a British betrayal. And what the Zionists want, the Zionists get. The White Paper was

---

1   One Palestine Complete, Tom Segev, Henry Holt & Company, New York 1st American Edition 2000, Pg 393
2   One Palestine Complete, Tom Segev, Henry Holt & Company, New York 1st American Edition 2000, Pg 394

revoked. As the American council told commissioner Chancellor, Zionists knew about his communications before they reached London, but in London they also knew things going on at the highest levels of government. Not trusting a friend or foe, they employed Lord Balfour's niece, a devout Christian and a Zionist. Blanche Dugdale had an intimate friendship with Walter Elliot; who served in the government in various posts during most of the 1930s. She spoke to him at least once a day and the information received from this one source proved extremely valuable.

Ben Gurion was dispatched to London by Menachem Weizmann, who was just ousted from the leadership of the Zionist movement, to convince the British prime minister to establish parity between Arabs and Jews in Palestine so they both had equal representation regardless of the number of population of each community. If the prime minister accepted that it would be a diplomatic coup. But this is what happened as recorded by Ben Gurion himself.

Ben Gurion and a Weizmann confident Lewis Namier travelled to London. An appointment was set to meet the prime minister Mac Donald, but did not take place as Ben Gurion's plane was late. The next day the prime minister invited Ben Gurion and Namier for breakfast at his residence 2 ½ hours drive from London. Jewish millionaire Israel Sieff provided his car to Ben Gurion. Present at breakfast were the prime minister's family. Namier complained about Chancellor and the prime minister said he understood and wanted to dismiss him but Chancellor was leaving his post shortly. The prime minister worried that when Chancellor got back to London he would be involved in pro-Arab activities. Anyhow, there would soon be a more sympathetic commissioner. They all disparaged Colonial Secretary Passfield. Then Ben Gurion brought up the issue of parity. The prime minister said the Jews should get more than parity but a preference. So Ben Gurion asked for that in writing and the prime minister signed the memo. For Ben Gurion, the mission was accomplished. There was no appropriate flight to Switzerland, which was Ben Gurion next destination. After suggesting to fly Ben Gurion on a Royal Air Force plane, it was finally decided that he leave by train. To secure a French visa on Sunday, the prime minister called the French Ambassador in London and a visa was issued.

We pause here to draw attention to that power that induces a prime minister to intervene in the issuance of a visa to a foreign national, and can conclude that the force behind this power was then as it is today. The venue changed to America as the seat of imperial power and global finance moved to America! Not much difference between Lloyd George, and George Bush, as both are 'actors' enforcing the real power structure agendas.

A new Staunch Zionist for a High Commissioner

In August 1934 Ben Gurion visited Musa Alami, a Palestinian Cambridge graduate working in the Attorney general's office in Shufat, a suburb of Jerusalem where Alami lived. He had two proposals for Alami to convey to the mufti; the first was a Jewish-Arab self government based on parity, and the second was the inclusion of a Jewish state in the historical borders of Eretz Izrael in a confederation of Arab states. Thus, the Arabs of Palestine would belong to an Arab majority in the confederate state. Ben Gurion also stated that Zionism is developing Palestine to the benefit of Arabs and Jews. Alami suggested an autonomous state around the Tel Aviv area as a canton in the Arab Palestine state, which is the national homeland the Zionists aspired for. He added that Palestinian Arabs would be happy to wait a hundred more years and develop their lands by themselves.

Arthur Wauchope, the new High Commissioner and a Zionist, who was briefed about that meeting, concluded that the differences between Zionism and Palestinian national aspirations were unbridgeable. This is a fact that remains until this day and will remain forever until Palestine sovereignty belongs to one party or the other!

Al Qassam and the 1936 Palestinian Revolt

Mohammed Iz-al-Din al-Qassam was born in Jablah near Latakiah in Syria. He volunteered with the Turkish army in World War One. He was a graduate of Al-Azhar University in Cairo. After the war, he organized a defense force in his hometown area to fight the French. He finally left for Haifa, Palestine and was appointed Imam at the Istiqlal mosque. He organized a local resistance and youth movement. His followers learned how to get arms and started their attacks on Jewish settlements. They first killed three members of the Kibbutz Yagur. Two more we killed at Nahalal. They attacked railroad and vandalized trees planted by the Jews. Spontaneous outbursts of violence increased reflecting the increased frustration of the Palestinian Arabs with the Jewish immigration and British policy. He suggested to the mufti a joint call for jihad and a mass rebellion. The mufti did not agree. He finally went to the mountains in November 1935 with some of his supporters, some of whom clashed with British police. After sometime, al-Qassam was killed in battle. But after his death, the resistance continued through several small groups that acted separately without a central command. Regions coordinated together but had no common headquarters. They started to ambush the British but also some face to face battles occurred. Observers noted that many of the resistance fighters were in their teens, most of them matured during the British occupation. Things escalated. A Palestine administration official wrote: *"The Palestine situation is worse today than ever,"* The roads became passable only by convoys. A British army convoy was attacked in the road between Haifa and Safad and an explosion that left a big hole in the road destroyed one of the ten trucks killing the driver, sending the truck and driver into the valley. After unloading its supplies, the same convey met a road block of stones. The convoy personnel jumped out of their vehicles, and sustained fire was aimed at them for one hour and continued until reinforcements came to save the convoy. This was how bad things became. Resistance extended to the cities. On Saturday, the night of May 16,1936, three Jews were killed in Jerusalem. The assassin fled. A few weeks later, a young Arab fired at the car of a police officer who was known for harassing Arabs and wounded him. The boy who fired at the policeman, Samia Ansari, was 19 years old and an English teacher. He was shot by a standing policeman. Before he died he called his brother and told him: "*Don't be sorry. I have done my duty.*" The next day people of Jerusalem went to congratulate his family for having produced such a hero.

The Arab Rebellion of 1936 may be considered to have started on April 19, 1936. The Zionists were always careful not to call such acts of resistance as a rebellion. They called them the 'events', just as they did not call the Stone Revolution in the 1980s a rebellion, but they devised the word Intifada, a word they introduced even to the English vocabulary. On that day nine Jews were killed and four wounded. From 1929 till the start of WWII, more than 2000 people were killed, at least half were Arabs plus about 150 Britons. More than 10000 incidents were reported in that period. In 1936 the mufti created the Arab Higher Committee which acted as a government of Palestine. It responded to a call by the Istiqlal party of Nablus and a general strike was proclaimed that began in April 1936 and lasted for 6 months. The strike came to an end when several Arab kings intervened. The Arabs now wanted independence and wanted Britain to leave since it identified itself with the Zionist project. The Palestinian Arabs, Ben Gurion noted emerged from the strike as "*an organized and disciplined community, demonstrating its national will with political maturity and a capacity for self-*

evaluation."While the Palestinian movement may have still been primitive compared to Zionism, Ben Gurion said that he learned from the days of al Qassam that it did not lack devotion, idealism and self-respect. [1]

Jewish and British state Terrorism

One may say that the worst terror act was state terrorism. In the summer of 1936 the British forces destroyed eight hundred Arab houses in the Old City of Jaffa. The Times said the number of houses destroyed were three hundred. The thousands of Arab residents were given twenty – four hours notice and ordered to evacuate their homes; and the evacuation orders were dropped from an airplane. The authorities did not provide the residents with alternate housing so the residents had to move to schools or even to the beach. The authorities claimed the demolition was part of an urban renewal project. The truth was it was motivated by security reasons as the neighborhood was used by stone throwers and snipers of the Arab resistance. Chief Justice Sir Michael McDonnell directed an embarrassing criticism at the government for deliberately lying and then evading responsibility. High Commissioner Wauchope was furious about McDonnell's behavior as the incident damaged the government's standing, Wauchope said. The judge was soon removed from

1   One Palestine Complete, Tom Segev, Henry Holt & Company, New York 1st American Edition 2000, Pg 370-371

Palestine. The Jaffa incident had inflamed the rebellion of the Arab community.

Wauchope's Zionism was described as deep as Balfour's. Ben Gurion wrote that the Jews in Palestine never felt as secure as in the days of Wauchope's administration. He authorized the Zionist Executive to form an army, the Haganah "in total secrecy, in the manner of conversation between friends." The Haganah started to guard settlements and it received its arms from the authorities at a time when an Arab would have received a death sentence if arms were found on him or on his premises. Ben Gurion and his staff met frequently with the High Commissioner and everything was coordinated between them, including plans for the suppression of the Arab uprising. Meanwhile, the revisionists founded their own force which they called The National Military Organization or Etzel. It was also call Argun by the British. The Etzel members started to perform terrorist acts, throwing bombs at market places or Arab coffee shops, killing Arabs by the tens. The Haganah was disciplined following the orders of Ben Gurion while Etzel was an extremist organization following the orders of Jabotinsky. Violent incidents occurred between the two organizations and their leaders failed to resolve the differences.

In 1939, as chairman of the Jewish Agency, Ben Gurion created the Special Operations Units under his command. The mission of these units was to avenge Arab killings of Jews, and to avenge Jewish traitors and British personnel involved in killing Jews. This is how Nachum Shadmi, a unit commander described one of his operations on the village of Lubia in the Upper Galilee:

> "The unit men sneaked to the village at night silently, in tennis shoes, pouring gasoline behind them to keep dogs from tracking them. Once in the village, they chose a house with its lights on. They peered in and saw three men and two women seated around a dead body laid out on the floor. The unit's men fired their weapons into the room through the window. One member of the unit, Yigal Allon, would go on to become a famous Israeli soldier and politician. There had been also children in the house, it turned out. Three people were killed; two men and a woman, and three were wounded including a two- year old boy and a ten -year old girl."[1]

A Commission was formed which was headed by Lord Peel, and thus became known as the Peel Commission. It concluded: "The social, moral and political gaps between the Arab and Jewish communities are already unbridgeable", the commission wrote to the colonial secretary. The report advised the Jews and the Arabs that half a loaf is better than none and recommended the Partition of Palestine into an Arab and a Jewish state. It suggested that Jerusalem remain under the British. What Ben Gurion liked most about the Commission's report was the fact

---

1   One Palestine Complete, Tom Segev, Henry Holt & Company, New York 1st American Edition 2000, pg 386-387

it recommended the transfer of Arabs from the part of Palestine allocated to the Jews.

The Peel commission recommended partition with the Jews getting 20 % of Palestine (the Galilee and much of the coastal Plain), the Arabs would get about 70% (Judea, Samaria and the Negev), which should eventually unite with Transjordan to enlarge Emir Abdulla's state. About 10% was to remain under British control including the cities of Jerusalem and Bethlehem and a corridor connecting them to the sea near Jaffa. In the Jewish state some 350000 Arabs inhabited and even in the Jewish state Arabs constituted a majority, so the Commission recommended a population transfer, which the commission called exchange as they also proposed the transfer of 1500 Jews that lived in the Arab state as well.

> "Once the peel Commission had given the idea [of transfer] its imprimatur, the floodgates were opened. Ben Gurion, Weizmann, Shertok, and others-a virtual consensus- went on record in support of transfer at meetings of the JAE the Twentieth Zionist Congress in August 1937, in Zurich and in other forums."[1]

The Arab rebellion threatened the Zionist project and it continued to escalate, so the British took drastic actions. They sent Sir Charles Tegart, one of their great experts on counterterrorism to Palestine to coordinate the various security services. Also, they

---

1   1948, The First Arab-Israeli War, Benny Morris, Yale University Press, New Haven, London,2008, Pg 18

sent some 25.000 soldiers and policemen to Palestine, the biggest force since World War One to leave Britain. Also, from the autumn of 1937, the British started to operate military courts to suppress the Arab Revolt. Arthur Wauchope was replaced by Harold Mac Michael who came from the Sudan.

Charles Tegart took several measures to combat the rebellion. To stop Mujahidin coming from Syria he built a security fence, like those built now by Israel. He created roadblocks throughout the country and built several police buildings around the country as well as a training center in Jerusalem to train interrogators on torture. He imported Doberman dogs from South Africa to complete his torture tools.

> "Suspects underwent brutal questioning, involving humiliation, beating, and severe physical mistreatment, including the Turkish practice of hitting prisoners on the soles of their feet and on the genitals. Jerusalem police chief Douglas Duff described the interrogation methods in his memoir. Beatings often left marks, Duff wrote; the "water can" method, however, left no traces. The police would lay the suspect down on his back, clamping his head between two cushions, and trickle water into his nostrils from a coffeepot. .... Some subjects were forced to stand under icy showers for extended periods."[1]

---

1   One Palestine Complete, Tom Segev, Henry Holt & Company, New York 1st American Edition 2000, pg 416-417

The swift justice of the Military law increased the number of Arab detainees in 1939 to over nine thousand, ten times the figure two years previously. Most of the detainees were held in administrative detention, without trial. The detention camps lacked adequate sanitation and were extremely overcrowded. Arabs were sentenced to death at a rate of one a week, and over one hundred were sentenced to death between 1938 to the end of 1939. Thirty were executed. Northern District Commissioner Kirkbride described a day in which three hangings took place at Acre prison.

"The prison warden began reading the sentence out loud, but the prisoner cut him short. "Get it over with, for God's sake", he shouted. His hands were handcuffed behind his back. The jailers tied his elbows together as well as covered his head with a black sack. At least he would not have to see the man's face, Kirkbride thought. The man was placed on the trapdoor; Kirkbride noticed that the precise spot was marked in chalk. The jailers tied his ankles and took a few steps back. The warden slammed a lever, the trapdoor dropped, and the young man fell forward and down through the opening, rebounding when the rope reached full extension. The entire platform trembled from the force of his fall. The young man lost consciousness but did not die immediately. His body continued to jerk for several long minutes, and his feet spread despite their having been tied. Blood dripped from beneath the black hood ... The medical officer tore open the man's shirt and listened to his heart, which was still beating at a good rate. He waited a little longer and then pronounced the man dead. ... Until the next hanging, at nine, the district commissioner sat in the warden's office, where he ate breakfast." [1]

Collective Punishment

Whole villages, neighborhoods or cities were accounted responsible for any rebel activities according to the enforced British laws and regulations, which also presumed everybody was guilty until proven otherwise. Judge Gad Frumkin claimed the 'honor' of initiating this 'justice' system of collective punishment practice after the Nebi Musa and Jaffa riots. Israel practices this system till this day. Here are two witnesses to such collective punishment:

> "Hilda Wilson, the teacher in Bir Zeit, described several searches in the village where she lived. First a plane would appear in the sky and someone would throw down a curfew order. Then the soldiers would come, sometimes in the hundreds, with dozens of vehicles. Once, Wilson counted two hundred men.

---

1   One Palestine Complete, Tom Segev, Henry Holt & Company, New York 1st American Edition 2000, pg 419

She never knew whether they had really come to conduct a search or whether the operation was aimed just at punishing, intimidating, and humiliating the villagers. Wilson loved the people of Bir Zeit, and when the army entered the village to conduct searches or mete out punishment she felt ashamed and tried to restrain the soldiers. On occasion the British closed the village off and then she walked to Jerusalem in a roundabout way, through the mountains". [1]

"In his diary, truck driver Alex Morrison described an operation in Tulkarem, a small village, 'a picture out of the Bible', he wrote. Morrison assumed that the army had entered the village to capture a wanted terrorist. But upon arriving, the soldiers found that all the men had departed, leaving only women and children and a few old men, one of them the mukhtar. The commander demanded, through an interpreter, to know where all the men were, but the mukhtar refused to say. That was typical of Arabs, Morrison commented, adding, 'I always admired them for their courage, for I have seen them die before they would betray anyone'. In this case the man was not required to die, but all the women were forced to stand in a line and bare their breasts to the solders to ensure that

---

1   One Palestine Complete, Tom Segev, Henry Holt & Company, New York 1st American Edition 2000, pg 420

240   *Abdulhay Y. Zalloum*

none of them were men dressed as women, Morrison explained. They were indeed all women. Afterward, the solders searched the houses and found nothing."[1]

Tom Segev added:

"Such operations were routine; almost every village might be searched at any time. In such situations, the men were gathered in an improvised enclosure or "cage", as the British called it. While the men were detained, the soldiers went from house to house, searching for weapons. They would break down doors, smash furniture, and ransack pantries, ripping open sacks of rice, flour, and sugar and strewing the contents all over the floor. They would also empty cans of oil. ... But the soldiers also acted maliciously; "They deliberately mixed the flour and oil and poured it all over the beds". [2]

On some occasions, the army would evacuate a village and would stay there for several months. Houses were routinely destroyed. The commissioner of Samaria received a letter of thanks for destroying 53 houses in the village of Baka al Gharbieh. More than 2000 houses were destroyed between 1936 and 1940. It is interesting again that the same policy is still adopted by Israel

---

1   One Palestine Complete, Tom Segev, Henry Holt & Company, New York 1st American Edition 2000, pg 420-421

2   One Palestine Complete, Tom Segev, Henry Holt & Company, New York 1st American Edition 2000, pg 421

with the same 'public relations denials'. The British denied that they violated civil rights, and called any news that reached the western press as 'isolated' instances, claiming that abuse is not in keeping with the character of his majesty's soldiers. The British used to burn the dead bodies of Arab rebels claiming that such acts were to prevent riots during funerals.

> "As efforts to suppress the terror intensified, relations between the Jewish Agency and the authorities tightened. During this period the Jewish Agency almost seemed like a security branch of the administration, serving as it did, as informer, subcontractor, and client. At several points the British army might almost have been acting under orders from the Jewish Agency, something like a mercenary force or security service. The agency even helped fund some of the security cost."[1]

The Origins of the Israeli Army Combat Doctrine

Orde Charles Wingate, an intelligence officer, the son of a family of colonial officers was a radical believer in Zionism to the point of addiction. When he arrived in Palestine he knew

---

1   One Palestine Complete, Tom Segev, Henry Holt & Company, New York 1st American Edition 2000, pg 426

242 Abdulhay Y. Zalloum

the country from his familiarity with the Bible. Ben Gurion and others referred to him as 'the friend.'

A lexicon issued by the Israeli Ministry of Defense many years after his death states,

> "The teaching of Orde Charles Wingate, his character and leadership were cornerstone for many of the Haganah's commanders, and his influence can be seen in the Israel Defense Force's combat doctrine". Tom Segev added that "The men who served under him portrayed him with a mixture of admiration and disgust; behind his back they said he was mad."[1]

This disgusting mad man, as stated above, became the role model of the Israeli army! The character of the Israeli army is indeed a replica of Wingate. Wingate created a special army, the Special Night Squads which made the Galilee its operating area. The Squads were made of 200 troops of whom 150 were Jews. They guarded IPC pipeline that carried oil firm Iraq to Haifa, as well as Tigart's fence. But also they committed acts of terror. One of Wingate's men, Tzion Cohen, a Jew wrote,

> "We would get close to a village where the oil pipeline had been sabotaged. We'd wait there until dawn and then enter the village, rounding up all the men and forcing them to stand with their faces to the wall and their hands behind their backs. Wingate and his

---

1   One Palestine Complete, Tom Segev, Henry Holt & Company, New York 1st American Edition 2000, pg 430

Englishmen would inflict the punishment because he did not want to fan the Arabs' hatred for us'. Cohen was referring to whip lashings on the villagers' bare backs, 'a horrifying sight' according to one member of the company. First, Wingate would stand on a rock and give the villagers a scolding in broken Arabic. As time went on, Tzion Cohen wrote, the punishments became more severe. Sometimes Wingate would make the villagers smear mud and oil on their faces. On occasion he would shoot and kill them. 'Wingate taught us to be good soldiers with values', Cohen noted.[1]

Cohen described the retaliation against the massacre of fifteen Jews in Tiberias. The action took place in a village called Hitin. Wingate and his troops rounded up all the village's men, chose ten, and ordered them to step forward. Cohen served as his interpreter. You killed women and children and old people in their sleep, Cohen said in Wingate's name. You had no mercy. You are cowards. I sentence you to death so that you may atone for your transgressions. Then the soldiers shot the ten men. One participant in the operation was Yigal Allon.[2]

1   One Palestine Complete, Tom Segev, Henry Holt & Company, New York 1st American Edition 2000, pg 430
2   One Palestine Complete, Tom Segev, Henry Holt & Company, New York 1st American Edition 2000, pg 430-431

The Jewish Agency funded the Special Nights Squads with money for salaries, training, vehicles, horses, provisions, barracks, and stables.

Montgomery Commanding the Anti-Palestinian Revolt

Regardless of these harsh executions and terror as well as the 25000 British soldiers imported to crush the Arab Revolt, the revolt continued. The British army had to bring in a new ruthless commander, Major General Bernard Montgomery, who made a long list of disagreements between the military and government officials. The new commander wanted to step up police actions and impose even harsher measures to crush the revolt. He was the same Montgomery who later led the British forces at al Alamein in North Africa. He refused to accept the administration's view that the revolt was an expression of an indigenous national movement, but instead declared it was a war and he must mercilessly treat it as such. The way to handle the revolt was to kill its revolutionaries, he instructed his soldiers. Jailed rebels should not be freed for political motives, he ordered, as in Ireland that policy failed. Now the rebels had to face a regular big army as well as the Jewish Haganah in full cooperation with the Jewish Agency.

The 1939 White Paper...

As a world war became very likely, British politicians started to worry about the backfiring of their Palestine and Arab policies. After consultations and studies, in May 1939, a White Paper was issued in which Britain announced that in ten years an independent bi-national state would be established in Palestine, and limitation was imposed on Jewish immigration suggesting a limit of 75000 immigrants in the next 5 years to allow the Jews to constitute a third of the population. Any increase was conditional to Arab consent. Restrictions were imposed on transfer of Arab properties to Jewish hands. The new White Paper promised Palestine's inhabitants statehood and independence within ten years severely curtailing Jewish immigration and placing restrictions on land sale. It was rejected by the Jewish community and Churchill denounced it as a cowardly act of "surrender to Arab violence."

The reason why the White Paper was issued just before the war was expressed by colonial secretary MacDonald:

> "If there was trouble in Palestine...there would be repercussions in Transjordan, Iraq, Saudi Arabia, and Egypt and even echoes of the trouble in India."[1]

Ben Gurion was furious. He wrote: "A more evil, foolish, and shortsighted policy could not be imagined". In his view, the

---

1   1948, The First Arab-Israeli War, Benny Morris, Yale University Press, New Haven, London,2008, Pg 22

government had essentially revoked the Balfour Declaration. He wrote in his diary: "Satan himself could not have created a more distressing and horrible nightmare". Jews everywhere were violently against the new policy. Moshe Shertok wrote that a Jewish girl from Poland who was studying at Oxford, suggested to going to the British Parliament to murder the prime minster and then commit suicide. Shortly afterwards, Ben Gurion calmed down as he was told by prime minister Neville Chamberlain explicitly that the White Paper would last at most for the duration of the war. So he wrote in his diary that the White paper *"is not the last word."* When Churchill became prime minister, he opposed the White Paper in a way that frustrated the High Commissioner who could not understand how to manage between official policy and Churchill's views. Though Churchill did not revoke the White Paper, he made so many exceptions to that it became irrelevant.

A month after the White Paper and Montgomery's harsh measures subdued the rebellion, Montgomery concluded that he had ended the rebellion but, "the Jew murders the Arab and the Arabs murder the Jew. This is what is going on in Palestine now. And it will go on for the next 50 years in all probability".

Though the rebellion was controlled nobody was optimistic about the future.

"The Arabs are treacherous and untrustworthy, the Jews greedy and, when free from persecution, aggressive ... I am convinced that the Arabs cannot be trusted to govern the Jews any more than the Jews can be trusted to govern the Arabs", wrote Colonial Secretary Ormsby – Gore. High Commissioner MacMichael thought that even a million soldiers could not prevent terrorism in Palestine." [1]

The Jewish Agency decided to join forces with the British in the Second World War against Germany. Cooperation between the British army and the Jewish forces in Palestine became official. The Jewish Agency wanted to take advantage of the war to beef up its own 'army' quantitatively and qualitatively. Four months after the war started the Jewish Agency gave the British authorities the names of 123 000 Jews who were willing to serve in the British army. Ze'ev Jabotinsky announced from New York, where he was then living, that his Revisionist Zionist movement would support Britain in the war. The Jews were used for intelligence and sabotage work in Syria and Iraq. That's where Moshe Dayan lost one eye.

As the Germans were advancing towards Egypt, the possibility of them reaching Palestine became very probable. This caused great panic for the Jews of Palestine. The Jewish Agency leaders considered going into exile. Some Jews equipped themselves with cyanide. *"One ultra-Orthodox spokesman even prepared an emotional plea to the Arabs to have mercy on those Jews who had not supported Zionism."* It was the same Montgomery that saved the Jews from the rebellion of Palestine who saved them from the Germans at al Al Alamain.

---

1   One Palestine Complete, Tom Segev, Henry Holt & Company, New York 1st American Edition 2000, pg 442

Terrorism by two future Israeli Prime Ministers

A close associate of Jabotinsky in Poland, Menachem Begin arrived in Palestine at the age of 29. He believed in Jabotinsky's brand of Zionism and wanted a Jewish state from the 'Nile to the Euphrates' and he believed that this could only be accomplished by force. His terrorist gang Etzel proclaimed its intention to build the Third Temple. Etzel's symbol was a rifle within a map of Palestine that extends to the Iraq border. Etzel's funds came in part from donations from America, but mostly from extortion of local business people and by robbing banks. Another terrorist group, Lechi that was headed by Isthak Shamir, attempted to assassinate the High Commissioner twice, and murdered Lord Moynes, Britain's senior representative in Egypt. Both Lechi and Etzel declared war on the British. The underground radio of these terrorist organizations labeled the Jewish leadership as cowards and traitors as well. Both organizations challenged the Labor movement and from here comes the roots of the Likud party after the establishment of Israel.

The rivalry between the Jewish terrorist organizations and the Jewish Agency and the labor movement escalated. The Jewish Agency asked the High Commissioner to create an anti-Jewish terrorism department. Yet, it was unwilling to throw its weight against these organizations before the British administration gave concessions on immigration, claiming that was needed to present to the Jewish community as an achievement. The High

Commissioner in a conversation with Ben Gurion told him that the Jewish race is strange because they do not appreciate that the British were the only nation that was doing everything for them, and the Jews were slandering and humiliating that nation without a word of thanks! Rather than take a stand against the Lechi and Etzel, the Haganah which was under the Jewish Agency leadership joined forces with Etzel and Lecci organizations and formed The Hebrew Resistance Movement. They continued together until after the King David was blown up, killing more than 90 people.

British experts: Time to leave Palestine...

Montgomery, in his new capacity as the Imperial General Staff, visited Palestine to assess the situation. He found that 100000 British soldiers were tied up in Palestine and were not actively crushing Jewish violence. He recommended to Prime Minister Attlee that, *"If we are not prepared to maintain law and order in Palestine, then it would be better to get out."* When General Parker used force after the King David attack, he was transferred from Palestine on the account that he gave orders for the troops to stay away from Jewish establishment, adding that this was the best way to strike at their pockets which the Jewish race dislikes. While in London he received a letter bomb which he discovered. Two Etzel men, one of them was Ezer Weizman, the nephew of Chaim Weizmann, who also became a president of Israel, went to London to check the possibility of killing the former Haifa police Chief Raymond Cafferata, who was accused of being anti-Zionist.

The Chancellor of the exchequer, Hugh Dalton also advised Attlee that the situation in Palestine was economically very costly, joining Montgomery in the recommendation to get out of Palestine.

The End of British Mandate, UN Partition Resolution

After the WWII, Jewish terrorism against the British was resumed, more violently this time. Before the war, it was Etzel and Lechi that conducted most of the terrorist acts, and they were sometimes condemned by the Jewish Agency. But after the war, the official military organization of the Jewish Agency, the Haganah joined the underground Etzel and Lechi, and once requested by the British to control Jewish terrorism, they requested the British to allow 100 000 Jewish immigrants in as their price for cooperation. The Haganah and Palmach joined Etzel and Lecci big time. They blew up on the night of 17 June, 1946 eleven bridges that connect Palestine with Transjordan, Syria, Lebanon and Egypt. Palmach squads raided the Atlit prison and freed the Jewish prisoners. A few days later, they destroyed one patrol boat and two British coast guard stations. The King David hotel which housed the British administration and military headquarters was blown up killing 91.

Here is an interesting paradox. The British paid treasure and blood to assist Zionism establish an economic, social, medical and military infrastructure that were ready to transform into Jewish state institutions, yet they were finally treated as occupiers. It is universally agreed that the Jewish agency functioned as a cabinet with all governmental institutions created ready for a declaration of a Jewish state! A National Health Care system was established. A Hebrew University and Education Department was created. An army, the Haganah was created in 1920. The Jewish intelligence network that assisted Allenby's army was reorganized and became the Haganah Intelligence Service HIS which provided intelligence to the Mandate authorities and kept an eye on Mandate personnel as well. While the Arabs were still suffering from their losses of the Revolt of 1936, the Jews of Palestine wasted no time during the war in preparation for their state. More than 26000 of its men and women had joined the British army and acquired good military training. The Haganah either stole or illegally bought arms. The Palmach was formed in 1941 with official British collaboration.

In the United States, Zionist power was becoming a force to be reckoned with. They launched an effective propaganda campaign equating those opposing the Zionist project as anti-Semitic at a time Americans were sympathetic to the Jewish plight in Europe during the war. For the 1930's and the early years of the 1940's, Roosevelt expressed no forthright commitment to a Jewish statehood in Palestine, irrespective of the Jewish clout in the United States. In 1943, Roosevelt assured King Abdul Aziz

Al Saud that the Arabs and the Jews will be consulted before the powers decided the fate of Palestine. Even when Congress was about to issue a joint resolution in March 1944, calling on Britain to rescind the White Paper and support a Jewish state, the White House intervened based on recommendations from several administration departments and persuaded congress to withdraw the resolution. During the second half of 1944 both American parties included pro-Zionist provisions and the Republican candidate Governor Dewey even stated that he supported the establishment of a Jewish commonwealth in Palestine. Even Roosevelt was pro-Zionist though he refrained from publicly advertising his Zionism.

> "Yet, At Yalta, in February 1945, Roosevelt, in conversation with Joseph Stalin, described himself as a 'Zionist' to which the Soviet dictator rejoined 'me too.' But then added that Jews were 'middlemen, profiteers, and parasites'."[1]

Britain wanted to leave the Palestine Burden

Churchill was swept away from office and a new labor government came in headed by Clement Attlee as prime minister and Ernest Bevin as foreign secretary.

---

1   1948, The First Arab-Israeli War, Benny Morris, Yale University Press, New Haven, London,2008, Pg 24

"I do not think we should take the responsibility upon ourselves of managing this very difficult place while the Americans sit back and criticize," wrote Winston Churchill on July 6 1945. "I am not aware of the lightest advantage which has ever accrued to Great Britain from this painful and thankless task. Some one else should have their turn now."[1]

After Roosevelt's sudden death Harry Truman came to the White House. "Truman had pointedly declined to support his party's pro-Zionist platform. And he reportedly told his cabinet in July 1944 that he had 'no use for them (the Jews and didn't care what happened to them' " But in August 1945, in Potsdam, he supported the resettling of the displaced Jews in Palestine.

On November 13, 1945 an Anglo-American Committee AAC was appointed. The British requested the demand for resettling 100000 Jewish displaced persons to be omitted from the committee's terms of reference, but the Americans refused. Bevin publically stated that he hoped the committee would propose to relieve Britain of the Mandate and place it with international trusteeship, after which an independent Arab-Majority state would be established. The AAC recommended that 100 000 Jewish immigrants be allowed into Palestine. As a result, U.S. Information Center in Beirut was stormed and set on fire. In Baghdad, the press called for a Jihad to save the Holy Land. The

---

1   1948, The First Arab-Israeli War, Benny Morris, Yale University Press, New Haven, London,2008, Pg 30

Jewish Agency did not accept the AAC's plan except for the part allowing Jewish immigration.

In a last effort attempt to find a compromise, and after discussing the AAC's commission report with the Americans, Britain came up with a Provisional Authority plan or as was also called the Morrison-Grady Plan. The plan left defense, foreign affairs and economics with Britain, Jews and Arabs were offered local autonomy. The plan approved the immediate transfer of 100 000 immigrants to Palestine, and promised the eventual independence of Palestine. Truman formally rejected the plan after it was rejected by the Zionists.

On 27 January, 1947, Britain called for a conference in London. The Arab representative arrived, the Zionist did not. The United States followed suit and refused to send a representative. Britain's politics reached a dead end and the British cabinet decided on February 14, 1947 to send the whole problem to the United Nations.

For this reason, the British government decided in February 1947 to hand the Mandate to the United Nations which formed a commission to study the issue. The commission decided to recommend to the General Assembly the partition of Palestine.

> "This decision prompted a worldwide campaign involving pressure, threats, promises, and bribes. The Jewish Agency budgeted a million dollars for its own campaign of bribery in official parlance the money was allocated to 'irregular political activity'."[1]

---

1   One Palestine Complete, Tom Segev, Henry Holt & Company, New York 1st American Edition 2000, pg 496

The resolution was passed 33 against 13 with ten abstentions including Britain. Even though the Jewish state area was twice as big as what the British suggested before World War Two, the number of Arab inhabitants in the Jewish state exceeded half a million which was larger than the Jewish population! The Jews had their army built and trained and the Palestinians were ill-equipped and ill-trained as more than six thousand Palestinian rebels and political activists were killed during their revolt. The leadership was fractured and organizationally dismantled, many were in jail or exiled and the Palestinian community had meager financial resources and limited military training and ammunition.

David Ben Gurion said: "Everybody sees the problem in relations between the Jews and the Arabs. But not everybody sees that there's no solution to it. There is no solution! ... ... There's a national question here. We want the country to be ours. The Arabs want the country to be theirs". [1]

*****

"--- The only way to make sense of Israel's senseless war in Gaza is through understanding the historical context. Establishing the state of Israel in May 1948 involved a monumental injustice to the Palestinians. British officials bitterly resented American partisanship on behalf of the infant state. On 2 June 1948, Sir John Troutbeck wrote to the foreign secretary, Ernest Bevin, that the Americans were responsible for the creation of a gangster state headed by 'an utterly unscrupulous set of leaders' [2]

---

1   One Palestine Complete, Tom Segev, Henry Holt & Company, New York 1st American Edition 2000, Pg 116

2   Avi Shlaim an Israeli who served in the IDF, is a professor of international relations at the University of Oxford. January 08, 2009 - The Guardian.

CHAPTER EIGHT

A JEWISH STATE IN PALESTINE (1948-1967)

The Haganah Intelligence Service assessment of the military balance on the eve of the United Nations Partition Resolution was that if the Arabs opted for war, the Arab States were disunited and the Arabs of Palestine were unprepared. Palestine Arabs were lacking the financial resources and the leadership and organizational capabilities against unlimited financial resources available to the Zionists of Palestine.

> "Palestine Arabs were generally poor...Izzat Tannous's crash effort, starting in June 1947, to assemble funds, through taxation...and voluntary contributions from the more prosperous was a dismal failure....By 1 November it has managed to raise only twenty five thousand Palestine pounds."[1]

By contrast, the Zionist community in Palestine had access to the deep pockets of the Jews around the world, foremost among them, the Jews of the United States. When Ben Gurion sent

---

1   1948, The First Arab-Israeli War, Benny Morris, Yale University Press, New Haven, London,2008, Pg 81

Golda Meyerson for fund raising for the Haganah, his target was 20 million dollars. From January to March 1948, she raised fifty million dollars. In a second tour in May and June another fifty million dollars was raised, which paid for the Czech arms deal that played a vital role in tipping the war in favor of the Haganah in the 1948 war. The North African volunteers coming to join the Palestinian resistance were turned back from Egypt. The Arab states were just emerging from British and French Mandates. They were weak and disorganized. The Jewish community had a government within the government of Palestine that had defense, treasury, education, health and infrastructure "ministries" as well as a first class intelligence service. *Its* leadership was committed, united, qualified and organized.

Unbalanced Political, Financial and Military Power

In anticipation of war the Jewish Agency created a 'secret' clandestine arms industry hidden in various settlements. Whereas an Arab who possessed even a pistol was handed a death sentence by the British authorities, the arms industry of the Jewish Agency under the Haganah command produced between October 1, 1947 and May 31, 1948 a total of 15,468 Sten guns, more than 200 000 grenades, 125 three inch mortars, with more than 130 000 rounds, and about 40 million 9 mm Sten gun bullets. The Haganah had a General Staff of an army with specialized branches such as intelligence, manpower, logistics, medical corps, even air force that was initially called air service. The Palestinian Arabs lacked leadership and resources, and the same can be said about all of the newly created Arab armies. The Haganah reorganized from a militia- like force to a regular army and by May 1948, it deployed 12 brigades, three of them Palmach and two armored. The picture on the Arab side was pitiful.

General Ismail Safwat, head of the Arab League Military Committee, wrote in November 1947:

> "Victory over the Jews – who are well trained and well equipped – by gangs and irregular forces alone is not feasible. So regular forces must be thrown into the battle, trained and equipped with the best weaponry ... As the Arab states do not have sufficient means for a protracted war, everything must be done so that the war in Palestine will be terminated in the shortest possible time".[1]

That was mission impossible. But worse yet, Safwat not only did not plan for any role for the Palestinian Arab militia, he denied its leader Abdulqader al Husseini a re-supply of arms after they were out of ammunition. Husseini returned to Jerusalem desperate even though he registered several victories in the Jerusalem area.

The most feared and disciplined armed force was the Arab Legion of Jordan, but it was led and financed by the British.

---

1   1948, The First Arab-Israeli War, Benny Morris, Yale University Press, New Haven, London,2008. Pg 180

Though some claimed that there was a general outline of a plan, General John Bagot Blubb, known as Glubb pasha later recalled: "The Arab statesmen did not intend war … But in the end they entered {Palestine} and ordered their commanders to advance as a result of pressure of public opinion and a desire to appease the 'street'".

Alan Cunningham did not think that Arab armies' invasion to Palestine was improbable because, "these armies have neither the training, equipment nor reserves of ammunition … to maintain an army in the field far from their bases for any length of time, if at all".[1]

The British and French who created the Arab armies during the Mandate years knew very well that these armies were not intended nor structured to fight external wars, but to maintain internal security and to prop up unpopular regimes installed by the Mandatory authorities before they left. To this day, that remains the basic functions of Arab states armies.

> "Only in 1945 – 1946, against the backdrop of the emergent Cold War, did the British begin to prepare or help in the conversion of the Egyptian, Iraqi, and Jordanian armies into modern fighting forces, capable of serving as auxiliaries in a fight with the Soviet Union. But lack of funds, incompetence, poverty, and suspicion of Britain's intentions frustrated the conversion in Egypt and Iraq. Similar problems

---

1   Alan Cunningham to secretary of state, 28 December 1947, Pro Fo 371 – 61583

discouraged the development, under French tutelage, of the newborn Syrian and Lebanese armies. Only the Jordanian army, and this very late in the day, began a real upgrade as May 1948 approached."[1]

Gamal 'Abdel Nasser, who fought in Palestine, later summarized the Egyptian preparations and intentions:

"There was no concentration of forces, no accumulation of ammunition and equipment. There was no reconnaissance, no intelligence, no plans ... (It was to be a 'political war'). There was to be advance without victory and retreat without defeat"[2].

The Comparative Strength of the Arab and Jewish Armies

Few days before the final withdrawal of British troops from Palestine, this was the status of the Arab armies:

- Only two days before the planned invasion of Palestine, the commander of the regular and irregular combined Arab forces was removed. What a time to change command. In his stead General Nur al Din Mahmud was appointed, and King Abdalla was the nominal Supreme Commander.

---

1   1948, The First Arab-Israeli War, Benny Morris, Yale University Press, New Haven, London,2008. Pg 183

2   Nasser, "Memories", 10

- At the last moment on May 14, 1948, Lebanese president Bishara Khoury and army chief Fuad Chehab opted to stay out of the war. Lebanon, only independent in 1946, had an army of 3500 troops in four infantry battalions.

- Glubb Pasha claimed that there was no Arab joint plan: "there had been no joint planning of any kind. The Israelis subsequently claimed knowledge of an Arab master plan, combining the strategy of all the Arab armies. No such plan existed, nor had any attempt been made to prepare one"[1].

- Syria was declared independent only in 1946. On paper the army was 10 000 strong. "In reality, owing to a lack of weapons, ammunition, and trained manpower, only one brigade, the First, commanded by Colonel Abdul Wahab Hakim was more or less ready; Hakim, indeed, apparently argued that it was not. The brigade had about two thousand troops and consisted of two infantry battalions, an armored battalion with a company of light Renault 35 and Renault 39 tanks..." [2]

- The Arab Legion – the Arab world's best army, due to many considerations changed its war objective which became to capture/save the Arab portion of Palestine assigned to the Arabs of Palestine. King Abdalla was aware of the Jewish strength in Palestine and internationally.

---

1   Glubb, Soldier, 93,

2   1948, The First Arab-Israeli War, Benny Morris, Yale University Press, New Haven, London, 2008. Pg 251

He knew the limitations of his small but efficient army in availability of ammunition which was supplied by the British. The Army commander, Glubb Pasha and most of the first line officers were also British. He also knew the limitations of the Arab armies regardless of rhetoric and he limited his objective to saving the portion of Palestine that was assigned to the Palestinian Arabs in the UN partition plan. Abdalla's father Hussain was promised to be crowned the King of the Arab World from which Greater Syria was a part. Greater Syria included present day Syria, Palestine, Transjordan and Lebanon. Also, Palestine and Transjordan had been one and the same for most of the recorded history, and the Sykes Picot borders were neither holy nor acknowledged by the Arabs, Palestinians included. Even in 1937, the Peel Commission's partition recommendations posited a union, under 'Abdullah of Transjordan and the bulk of Palestine that was assigned to the Arabs. In secret negotiations between Abdalla and Golda Meyerson on November 17, 1947, an understanding was reached that for Abdalla's acceptance of partition, the Jewish state would not object to Abdalla's takeover of the Arab portion of Palestine that was specified in the UN resolution.

On the contrary, this is how the Zionists represented by the Jewish Agency prepared for the anticipated war:

- Since 1945 Ben Gurion secretly recruited eighteen Jewish millionaires, to help provide the Haganah's needs in money and equipment. But as the Jewish Agency became certain that a partition was on the way, serious steps were taken to achieve restructuring and reorganization of the armed Jewish groups at the end of 1947. Then, the Haganah had some thirty – five thousand trained members. They were scattered in settlements. Only the Palmah, numbering 2000 were full time soldiers.

- On 7 November 1947, Ya'akov Dori, the chief of general staff, and his political superior, Yisrael Galili, head of the Haganah National staff, issued the Order of a National Structure. It stated: "The danger of an attack on the country by the armies of the neighboring Arab countries ... necessitates a different structure and deployment. Opposite regular armies it is imperative to prepare in a military (as distinct from militia) force – trained, armed, and structured along military lines".[1]

- By end of 1947, mobilization of the other members for full – time service as well as recruitment and training for more troops took full throttle in late 1947. A mobilization committee was created, and recruitment offices were set up in all towns.

- "By the end of December, some seventy – five hundred men were under arms (twenty – five hundred of them

---

1   1948, The First Arab-Israeli War, Benny Morris, Yale University Press, New Haven, London,2008. Pg 200

Palmahniks); by April, twenty – four thousand; by mid – May, about thirty thousand, about half of them veteran Haganah members; by early July (by then the Haganah had become the Israel Defense Forces), about sixty – four thousand."[1]

- At the same time the Haganah scoured the globe for arms. Its agents succeeded in circumventing the British blockade before May 15, and after May 29 in defying the UN embargo. Haganah agents collaborated with networks of Zionist officials and sympathizers, using money power coupled with all other undercover tricks including dummy companies and counterfeit letters of authorization and accreditation. They succeeded in securing arms from states as well as arms dealers.

- The Haganah for their own reasons exaggerated the Arab armies strength at 165 000! Ben Gurion claimed that the Arab Legion was made of 15-18000 troops with 400 tanks, whereas the Legion had no tanks and only 7-8000 troops. At best, the invading Arab forces added up to about 20 000 on May 15, 1948. They included 5500 Egyptians, 4500-6500 Arab Legionnaires', 2750 Syrians, and 2700 Iraqis. There were about 1000 Moslem Brotherhood volunteers and up to 3000 Arab Liberation Army irregulars. They did not have a unified command,

---

1   1948, The First Arab-Israeli War, Benny Morris, Yale University Press, New Haven, London,2008. Pg 199. Gelber, Emergence of Jewish Army, 146, 153, 159

lacked ammunition and were under-equipped and much of that equipment was unserviceable.

- 22% of the Jewish population were between the ages of 20-44. In a much accelerated way the new state was able to mobilize under uniform 13% of the whole population. Two months after May 15, the Jewish army accounted for 65000, in October, the number went up to 88 000, reaching 108 000 by January 1948. Shortly afterwards, the Israeli Defense forces, the new name for the Haganah, reached 120 000, fully armed and fully trained. The Arab forces increased slightly by small contingents from Yemen, Saudi Arabia and Morocco. They lacked co-ordination, modern arms, training and a plan!

The international arms embargo that was imposed on the warring parties crippled the Arab armies which totally depended on their armament from Britain and France, who both fully implemented the embargo. The Arabs, with insufficient stockpiles of ammunition were out of practically all types of shells, bullets, spares etc., while the Jewish army had an indigenous arms industry, and was able to keep the inflow of arms to its huge army from both East and West, and private as well as state organizations. The newly independent Arab states lacked the funds and the procurement apparatus to deal with the unexpected embargo.

The Arab Legion was the most feared in the Jewish quarters, and they judged it as both efficient and professional. The Legion enjoyed high morals, and the troops were greeted by their population enthusiastically as they were on their way to Palestine

Ma'an Abu Nowar, a young officer then, recalled the "emotions ran high ... I remember my father and mother among the crowd ... in Amman. As I was passing by in my GMC light armoured car, my mother shouted: 'God be with you, my son. Don't come back. Martyrdom my son'" The legion was led by some 50 to 70 officers most of whom at the upper echelons were British. It was highly mechanized and had effective service units. The Legion commander was Glubb Pasha, his deputy was Norman Lash. But some Jordanian officers were also deployed, and many of them, including Habis al Majali and Abdulla al Tal performed courageously and professionally. The artillery was highly professional and effective. Against very great odds, the legion performed very well and actually most, if not all the initial defeats suffered by the Jewish army were inflicted by the Arab Legion, in Jerusalem, Latrun, Bab el Wad and Kfar Etzion. However,

"The Legion was short of ammunition, especially for its artillery and mortars, and suffered severely from the British arms embargo." [1] On 30 May, the Fourth Battalion, fighting in Latrun, ran out of artillery shells. [2]

> "During the following months, especially in the
> fighting in mid – July, Glubb pleaded with Whitehall
> for resupply, only to be rebuffed with the argument

---

1   Morris, Road to Jerusalem, 172, 181
2   Ilan, Origin of Arab – Israeli Arms Race, 48-49

that if Britain violated the embargo, the Americans
would do likewise and supply arms and ammunition
to Israel in even more significant quantities "[1]

Between 1948 -1967: The Zionist Project Reached a Dead End

The Jewish community was able to emerge as an independent Jewish state on Palestinian lands that they called the State of Israel. For obvious reasons we stated earlier, it was a foregone conclusion for the Arab regimes to lose that war. Thirty years of state-building under the British Mandate on one hand and repression and dismantling of Arab organization and resistance on the other hand could not produce different results.

The new state was confronted with social, political/doctrinal, geographical, demographical and economical challenges that threatened the state in its initial days, which continued to prove aggravating until it reached alarming levels by 1966 and early 1967. Immigration was the main reason for the growth of the Jewish community in Palestine. It was not a natural growth and thus brought with it lots of problems socially, demographically and economically that almost led to the collapse of the Zionist project had it not been for the 1967 war. Three problems overshadowed all the others:

---

1   1948, The First Arab-Israeli War, Benny Morris, Yale University Press, New Haven, London,2008. Pg 208 - 209

- The western culture of the predominant Ashkenazi in the earlier days of the state was threatened.
- The Palestinian Arabs living in Israel and the new threat of Palestinian refugees' first generation of Children.
- Severe economic conditions that caused despair and reverse immigration.

Jewish Demographic Revolution: More Mizrahi than Ashkenazi Jews

As early as 1950 the Ashkenazi establishment started to express unease over what they called the destruction of the Israeli culture by the mass of immigrants from Arab countries, mostly Iraq and North Africa. A prominent establishment member, Yosef Weitz wrote, *"Indeed there is a cause for anxiety."* More and more Ashkenazi expressed concern and distaste at the Mirzrahi culture that started to make inroads in the Israeli culture. :

> "'We cannot turn into a Mizrahi people', said the author Haim Haza; what he meant was we must not become such a people. "I have a great objection", he explained. We have traveled for two thousand years to become a Jewish European cultural entity. We cannot now turn back the wheel and accept the culture of Yemen, Morocco, and Iraq". Hazaz further

cautioned, 'We are nearing the precipice with regards to Levantinism'".[1]

Considering the higher fertility of Mizrahi Jews "Shabtai Teveth feared a generation in which three out of four Israelis would lack any affinity with Western culture. Such a generation might be closer to 'the culture of our surroundings'". [2]

Even Prime Minister Eshkol felt that Oriental Jews were a burden and he urged an increase of Western immigrants. Eshkol, though a pragmatist who accepted partition, wanted Israel to be as large as possible. "The eastern bank of the Jordan has been the constant dream of every young man and woman in Eretz Ysrael since time immemorial", he wrote in 1927. [3]

In the mid 1960s, a demographic revolution occurred. For the first time since the state was established in 1948, western Jews, the Ashkenazi became less than the Oriental Jews, the Mizrahi. In 1980, 80 % of the population was Ashkenazi. Soon thereafter, the Mizrahi would become a majority. In 1967, 60 % of the children in first grade were born to Mizrahi mothers. In 1968, only 30% of the children born were of Ashkenazi parents.

1   Tom Segev, Elvis in Jerusalem (new York: Metropolitan, 2002) P. 62; Segev, 1949, P 170: Maariv, 14 Sept. 1966, P. 16

2   1967 Tom Segev, Henry Holt & Co, New York, First U.S. Edition 2007. Pg 61

3   1967 Tom Segev, Henry Holt & Co, New York, First U.S. Edition 2007, Pg 87

Discrimination against Oriental Jews and Resident Palestinians!

Walworth Barbour, the U.S. ambassador reported to Washington of a profound disparity between Ashkenazi and Mizrahi Jews or "Occidentals and Orientals" as he called them, in education, housing, and employment. In addition, he said, there was deliberate discrimination against the Orientals. There was practical segregation in housing as the Mizrahi lived in isolated ghettos. He concluded that ethnic origin determines one's future in Israel, and stated that this issue constitutes the greatest danger to the future of the State of Israel. In all professions Ashkenazi earned more at every level of employment. An average Ashkenazi family earned about 55% more than a Mizrahi family. Although in general the Ashkenazi were more qualified, and there were many reasons for this disparity, discrimination was certainly one of those reasons. By 1967 not a single general in the Army was of Oriental origins, or a chief justice. Only 25 of the Knesset's 120 members were Mizrahim and only two government ministers.

If the Jews of Arab countries were discriminated against, it should go without saying that the Arabs of Palestine who remained after Israel was established were discriminated against more strictly and inhumanly.

"These Arabs should not be living here, just as American Jews should not be living in America", said David Ben Gurion in

1950.[1] Through terror and meticulous planning of the Jewish Transfer Committee almost 80% of the Arabs of Palestine became refugees outside the borders of the Jewish state. Those remaining became citizens to a state whose culture, language and religion were foreign to them. They became about 12% of the population by 1967 or about 312 000 people. In the Galilee they were the majority. By 1967, 60% of the Arab population was born after the establishment of Israel.[2]

> "As Israeli citizens, they were entitled to vote and run for the Knesset, but they were not Israelis with equal rights, or equal duties. Very few served in the IDF. The state viewed them as a security risk, and since Israel's establishment they had been subject to martial law."[3]

The martial law that was imposed on the Palestine Arabs was the same laws that the Jewish lawyers who tried to fight them during the Mandate had imposed and they compared them to Nazi policy. These laws manifested in a restriction on mobility. When they had to leave their residences they had to obtain a permit from the military governor stating their destination, when

1   Zeev Sternhell, Nation Building or Society mending (in Hebrew) (Tel Aviv; Am Oved, 1986); Eyal Kafkafi, Lavon: Anti-Messiah (in Hebrew) (Tel Aviv: Am Oved, 1998), P. 102.

2   Establishment's Attitude Toward Arabs in Israel: Policy, Principles and Actions: The Second Decade, 1958 – 1968" (in Hebrew) (diss., Haifa University, 2002), p. 15ff

3   1967 Tom Segev, Henry Holt & Co, New York, First U.S. Edition 2007, Pg 67

they would be leaving and returning. This procedure applied for any movement whether medical, relative visits, work or even funerals.

"Obtaining permits meant standing in lines. There were different types of permits, issued on forms that periodically changed. Permits often entailed extensive interrogation and petitions. Granting and withholding permits were done at the discretion of the governor, and often depended on his mood or other arbitrary factors. Not all of the governor's representatives were immune to accepting favors of various kinds. Naturally, the travel permits served as a means of oppression and control: people were asked to spy on their neighbors, to denounce them, all in order to obtain travel permits. Thousands of people were punished by means of orders forbidding them from leaving their places of residence, or even by deportation orders that forced them to live away from their homes... Martial law was imposed not only because of security considerations but also to facilitate the state's confiscation of land from Arabs and to control their political activities. Over the years, the state confiscated roughly half of all Arab owned land and transferred it to the Jewish National Fund's authority. As a director of the JNF, Yosef Weitz had significant influence over the allocation of appropriated lands to Jewish communities. The JNF was also involved in a national campaign to destroy the remnants of Arab villages that had been emptied of their inhabitants during the War of independence."[1]

The Palestine Arabs who lost their lands had to work for Jewish employers. They were discriminated against in every aspect of life.

> "Seventy four percent of Arab villages were not hooked up to the electricity grid, 75 percent were not connected to the national water system, and 20 percent had no access roads. Not a single Arab village had paved streets, nor had sewage infrastructure been laid. Public housing was seldom built for Arabs. Only three out of ten Arabs were insured by the national health fund, whereas eight of every ten Jews were. In six out of ten Arab villages there was no clinic operated by the health fund. Fifteen percent of students in elementary schools were Arab, but the state allocated only 3 percent of its education budget to Arab education. An Arab farmer made between 30 and 50 percent less than a Jewish farmer. A Jewish construction worker made up to twice as much as an Arab. In the spring of 1966, during the economic recession, the unemployment rate among Arabs

---

1   1967 Tom Segev, Henry Holt & Co, New York, First U.S. Edition 2007, Pg 68

was twice as high as among Jews. Until then most
Israelis had tended to ignore the Arabs' plight, but it
too became unavoidable, reinforcing the sudden and
painful recognition that the Israeli success story was,
to a great extent only a myth."[1]

Economic Woes

Economists believe that the Israeli economy went into
recession in 1965 mostly due to a slowdown in population
growth from 4% in 1964 to zero in 1966, resulting mostly from
a decrease in immigration. Letters coming from Israelis to their
relatives outside were not encouraging. Low population growth
caused low construction which was a prime sector that affects all
sectors of the economy. Many businesses went bankrupt. There
was also a drop of investment of 20% in industry and 30% in
construction. Foreign investment went down by 40% in 1964
and another 15% in 1966. Prices increased by 8% in 1966. In
1964 there was a 17% decline in repatriation by Germany to
the Nazi victims. Several projects were completed such as the
National Water Carrier, the Ashdod port, and the Dead Sea
industries. New projects were not initiated. Many people were
out of jobs.

In February 1966 Eshkol, Israel's prime minister said that
Israelis were living beyond their means, and that growth was not

---

1   1967 Tom Segev, Henry Holt & Co, New York, First U.S. Edition
2007, Pg 69

fueled by Israeli labor but by the United States, Germany, Jews of the world and foreign investors. The people were living in "a fool's paradise" he said. Eshkol meant to inspire the public but instead he depressed them. Writing to his government, the U.S. ambassador quoted a report in which it was stated that the government wanted to decelerate the economy, but matters got out of control beyond what was intended. Unemployment went up to about 12% of the workforce, that's more than 100 000 people. Hardest hit were the Mizrahim.

Curiously, the government decided in November 1966 to extend the military service for men to two years and a half, keeping it at twenty months for women. This was seven months before the 1967 six day war! In February, the government offered a job to anyone who sought one, yet no plan detailing where those jobs were to be occupied.

Despair was even sensed by David Ben Gurion. He wrote in his diary there was no confidence in the future "*as if the situation is hopeless.*" A few hundred unemployed took to the streets on May Day in Ashdod and the demonstrators confronted the police. About 25 demonstrators and eight policemen were injured. An uprising seemed to take place in Ashdod that day! Elsewhere also, violent demonstrations took place.

Israel, like all capitalist states when in deep economic crisis needed a war badly. And the six day war of June 5, 1967 not only saved the Israeli economy but was a transformational event in all aspects of the Israeli life. Not by coincidence, only months before the 1967 war an Iraqi spy, a MiG jet pilot, arrived with his plane to Israel. MiGs constituted the bulk of the Egyptian, Iraqi and Syrian air forces. Having an enemy plane and assessing its capabilities and weakness few months before the war was not a coincident!

Israel needed a War, Had Plans Ready and Created Pretexts for War

Evidence is abundant that the Labor party's government territorial expansionist policy differed only in style, not in substance with the revisionists. Labor wanted to grasp more territories when an opportunity is created or presented itself. They believed in more secret planning and loss rhetoric.

In June 1963, soon after Levi Eshkol became prime minister, he discussed the possibility of expanding Israel borders with the IDF chief of staff Zvi Zur and his deputy Yitzhak Rabin. The ideal borders, the generals told Eshkol would follow the Jordan River to the East, the Litani to the north, and the Suez with Egypt. Rabin added that these borders are desirable if the opportunity arose. A few weeks later, a plan code-named Whip, to occupy the west Bank, including East Jerusalem, was presented. A plan named Bnei Or detailed how the IDF would create new borders with Syria and Egypt and how it should stay in those occupied territories until peace agreements are reached that will include changes of present borders to more secure borders. [1] Eshkol asked the army also to make a plan for the occupation of Mount Scopus and connect it to West Jerusalem, since anybody holding Mount Scopus can easily conquer and occupy the West Bank.

> "A few of the generals who believed that Israel should expand its borders discussed taking over the West Bank and even debated what to do with it once it was conquered. The options were either to annex, or to set up a Palestinian buffer state.... The discussion was always confidential and the generals' positions did not figure much in public discourse."[2]

> "Students could internalize the concept of greater Israel just by glancing at the series of blue plastic binders published by the IDF education corp. in 1959. Under the rubric 'Israel from the Dan to Eilat'. two of the booklets included the Gaza Strip and the Sinai Peninsula and three the regions of Judea and Samaria."[3]

1   Analysis of possible developments in the Jordanian situation, 9 May 1936m ISA, HZ 10/40941 Shlomo Gazit The carrot and the Stick: Israeli Governance in Judah and Samaria (in Hebrew) (Tel Aviv : Zmora – Bitan, 1985) p. 23
2   1967 Tom Segev, Henry Holt & Co, New York, First U.S. Edition 2007, Pg 176 – 177
3   1967 Tom Segev, Henry Holt & Co, New York, First U.S. Edition 2007, Pg 179

A former general felt , as many soldiers did, that Ben Gurion blocked them in the 1948 war from conquering East Jerusalem, the West Bank and Gaza at a time they could have. He said:

"I never forgave the Israeli government under Ben – Gurion for not letting us finish the job in '48-'49, both militarily and politically". Allon claimed he demanded that Ben Gurion before signing the Green Line borders with Jordan to give Israel the strategic depth up to the River Jordan . He felt that Gaza also should have been conquered and all he needed was few more days to achieve these objectives. Many of Allon's comrades shared his frustration. They resented having to live with "a fragmented, defective state that would have trouble staying alive".[1]

Begin's Herut party was committed to Ze'ev Jabotinsky's Greater Israel views since the 1920s. The party's anthem was, "Two banks have the River Jordan. One is ours, the other one too". One day after Ben Gurion declared an Independent Jewish state in 1948, Begin said,

> "'The State of Israel has been founded, but let us remember that the homeland has not yet been liberated … The soldiers of Israel will yet raise our

---

1   Allon to Ben Gurion, 24 March, 1949, BGA; Anita Shapira, Yigal Allon: The Springtime of His Universe (in Hebrew) (Tel Aviv: HaKibbutz HaMeuchad, 2004), P. 426; Allon in an interview with Reudor Manor, Institute for international Relations, Hebrew University, ISA, A-19/5001, meeting 2, P. 11. 1967 Tom Segev, Henry Holt & Co, New York, First U.S. Edition 2007, Pg 174 - 175

flag above the Tower of David; our plow will yet till the fields of the Gilead'.

Begin often demanded that territories beyond the Green Line be "liberated", and he maintained that Hebron and Bethlehem, Shechem and even Amman were all an integral part of the Jewish homeland."[1]

Twenty days before the six day war of June 5, 1967, Rabbi Zvi Yehuda Kook told students at the Mercaz Harv Yeshiva in Jerusalem how terribly he felt when the UN partition resolution was passed :

"Where is our Hebron – are we forgetting it?" he asked. "Where is our Shechem? Are we forgetting it? And where is our Jericho – are we forgetting it? And where is the eastern bank or the Jordan?". [2]

Yigal Yadin, the former chief of staff who participated in the 1948 war. Yadin , who rarely spoke to the press, three weeks before the Six Day War made an interview with the newspaper Maarev, in which he projected pain, disappointment, sorrow and regret that the Old City of Jerusalem was not conquered in 1948

1   1967 Tom Segev, Henry Holt & Co, New York, First U.S. Edition 2007, Pg 180 - 181
2   1967 Tom Segev, Henry Holt & Co, New York, First U.S. Edition 2007, Pg 181 . Ha'aretz, 25 march 1966, P. 2

Seven Months before the War

In November 1966 two working groups were formed for political and strategic review, seven months before the Six Day War! The first group examined the relationship with Jordan, the other with Egypt. Representatives from the Mossad, IDF intelligence, and Foreign Ministry participated. They completed their studies in January 1967 and they produced their documents that were approved in January by Eshkol and Rabin.

....what to do with an Occupied West Banks...before its occupation

Shlomo Gazit from army intelligence summarized the IDF position regarding the West Bank.

> "Some thought Hussein's regime was harmful to Israel because as long as he ruled, Israel could not invade the West bank, which, in the current state of unrest, constituted 'a catastrophe for Israel.'. Others believed that Hussein was 'good for Israel'. Gazit presented the compromise position. 'The IDF accepts the current situation, but would welcome an opportunity to change the status quo to create a new and more comfortable one'. Under the present conditions of hostile coexistence, he added, the Green Line represented a threat to the center of the country. But were the IDF to occupy the West bank,

> Israel would have to consider what to do with it, and more specifically whether it could annex it ' without the annexed territory becoming a cancer that would gnaw at Israel from the inside.' In any event, Israel would not be annexing empty territory. To neutralize the dangers of the West Bank, continued Gazit, Israel should found an independent Palestinian state that would be completely dependent on the IDF for defense and internal order; in addition, Israel would oversee its foreign policy. Mordehai Gazit, of the Foreign Ministry, the brother of Shlomo Gazit from military intelligence, responded unenthusiastically, that would be ' a puppet regime'" [1]

Once the nuclear age is entered, the IDF said, borders become less significant. Other members of the group objected as nuclear capability is no deterrent to acts of terrorism.

Later on, Mordehai Gazit, Shlomo's brother, and a member of the study groups mentioned in a lecture at the National Defense College that the occupation of the West Bank was a possibility. He added that **any lack of interest in the West Bank stems from the demographic problem that would result:**

---

1   1967 Tom Segev, Henry Holt & Co, New York, First U.S. Edition 2007, Pg 184

"What would we do if the population in the West Bank, our sworn enemy, did not flee across the border?".[1]

The National Defense College submitted a study on the viability and economic implication of occupying the West Bank. **The study concluded that the occupation can be economically viable, but the Jews will assume white-collar professions and the Arabs will perform manual labor.**

Further demographic studies were undertaken by the College commander, Peled. He concluded that the Arab population would most likely catch up with the Jewish population by 2035 and sooner in some areas where Arabs are concentrated. If they were not deprived of their civil rights, then the Arabs would have the second or first political party in the country and this would lead to the end of **the Jewish character of the state**

"The Arabs, Peled continued, might form opposition movements, and Israel would then have to take steps characteristic of "a Police state". If the Arabs were not enlisted in the IDF, their young people might come to constitute a hard core of national liberation fighters. The concentrated areas of Arab populations might serve as shelters for terrorist bases. It would also be necessary to provide the Arabs with

---

1   1967 Tom Segev, Henry Holt & Co, New York, First U.S. Edition 2007, Pg 184 – 185 . Gazit at the National Defense College, 13 Oct. 1966, ISA, HZ-10/4094

education. Within a short while, there would emerge an educated Arab class demanding white-collar jobs. The separation between Jews and Arabs could not be preserved for long. Arabs would begin living in the big cities along the coast, and poverty – stricken Arab suburbs would develop. This would give rise to social problems necessitating large expenditures. The Arabs would influence the culture of those Israelis with similar cultural origins, namely the Mizrahim. There would be intermarriage, Peled further cautioned."[1]

A very short time before the Six-Day War and shortly after his election as Mayor of Jerusalem, Teddy Kollek canceled a plan approved by the previous mayor to move the municipal offices from near the border. Soon he said, Jerusalem will be united and the offices will be at the center of the city! **In December 1966, he told a university student news Bat-Kol that his master plan for the city anticipates reunification of Jerusalem and plans anticipate smooth connection with the old city.**

Israeli Provocations for War

In order to provoke war, get out of the economic recession and the psychological depression which caused reverse immigration, and of course in order for the generals to conquer what they

---

1   1967 Tom Segev, Henry Holt & Co, New York, First U.S. Edition 2007, Pg 186. Peled to the Chief of Staff, 12 Dec. 1966, with the kind permission of Elad Peled

could not or were no allowed to do, Syria was to be provoked, and Nasser would be dragged to war. A demilitarized zone existed between Syria and the Jewish state. So that was a good starting point.

"Not all the incidents in the demilitarized zones were instigated by the Syrians. Moshe Dayan later claimed that 80 percent erupted as a result of Israeli attempts to farm there, and that they were unnecessary. 'It would go like this. We would send a tractor to plow the earth in some plot you couldn't do anything with, in a demilitarized zone, knowing in advance that the Syrians would start shooting. If they didn't shoot, we would tell the tractor to go farther, until finally the Syrian would lose their tempter and shoot. And then we'd fire back, and later send in the Air Force'. Dayan explained that the tension caused by Israel on the Syrian border did not reflect a strategic approach, but rather the fact that Israel did not take the cease – fire seriously. 'We thought at the time, and this went on for quite a while, that we could move the cease -fire lines by using military action that was less extreme than war. Meaning, taking over some land and holding on to it until the enemy gave up and let us keep it'. One could say this represented 'a certain naiveté on our part' Dayan conceded, but one also had to remember that the state had not existed for very long. Either way, he said, 'we thought of the cease-fire lines as a temporary arrangement'. He claimed that the Syrians did not treat the agreement seriously, either."[1]

Just as Israeli military intelligence predicted, some young Palestinians, sons of the 1948 Arab refugees of 1948 organized themselves into small commando units that crossed the borders and planted some bombs. That was the last thing Israel wanted to see or hear. But that was not unexpected. An army general, a Middle East scholar and IDF chief of intelligence in a strategic research in the 1950s noted, Israel must face the rise of a new Palestinian generation. These grew up in refugee camps and they readied themselves for a second round! Refugees generally kept the keys of their homes and they are being inherited from son to grandson. They believe that if surely Israel laid claim on their real estate after 2000 years they can wait and will ultimately prevail. The security study that was submitted to the prime minister's office concluded that terror is to be expected as long as there are refugees. Abba Eban, the Foreign Minister also concluded in a similar study that guerrilla warfare is the weapon of the weak; with small weapons not even nuclear deterrence can be effective against it.

Several steps were deliberately taken by Israel to increase tensions at the Syrian borders including fiery statements by Israeli politicians and military figures. The IDF weekly, Bamahane published an interview with Yitzhak Rabin, the chief of staff. In the interview Rabin said:

---

1   1967 Tom Segev, Henry Holt & Co, New York, First U.S. Edition 2007, Pg 193

"The response to Syrian acts, be they terrorism, water diversion, or border hostilities, should be aimed at those who carry out the attacks and at the regime that supports them … The problem with Syria, then, is essentially a clash with the regime".[1]

Israel started to fire at the Syrian farmers and shepherds at the border, so tension intensified as Syrians fired back. A Ministry of Defense book published at a later date, Rabin himself determined that if Israel had not fired on the Syrian farmers and shepherds, tension would not have escalated.

War Plans against Syria

The working committees that discussed Jordan, also discussed Syria. The IDF claimed that Fateh infiltrators are rendering Israel helpless unless a war is waged against Syria. Rabin suggested an increase of Arabic speaking spies, mining the borders heavily if the Syrians are waging a war of harassment on Israel,

"Rabin suggested inflaming the borders and 'exploiting them as an excuse to act, and described the increased number of border incidents as a gold mine".[2]

1   1967 Tom Segev, Henry Holt & Co, New York, First U.S. Edition 2007, Pg 196
2   1967 Tom Segev, Henry Holt & Co, New York, First U.S. Edition 2007, Pg 203

Already plans of attacking Syria were ready:

- ☐ Operation Ax, which involved occupying Damascus.
- ☐ Operations Tongs, an intermediate plan to occupy the Golan Heights all the way to east of Kunetra.
- ☐ Operation Concoction, a plan to take over just the Banias area. [1]

On Friday, April 7, 1967, according to plan, two Israeli tractors were sent to the no-man's land. The Syrians opened fire and Israel returned fire. The Syrians on both sides used tanks. Rabin asked Eshkol to use the air force. An air battle resulted in which two Syrian MiGs were shot down. According to an Israeli general, really the Six-Day War started that day.

> "Aharonot's military commentator, Arel Ginai, who was known for having reliable sources and who often expressed government, Mossad, and military positions, learned from Rabin and Eshkol's declarations that Israel was laying the groundwork for a large – scale operation."[2]

Israel learned that the Johnson's administration had no objection for an Israeli strike against Syria. Belligerent statements from several Israeli officials against Syria were intended to create the appropriate atmosphere for a strike against Syria. Nasser's

---

1   Matityahu Mayzel, The Battle over the Golan; June 1967 (in Hebrew) (Ma'arachot, 2001), P. 93ff.

2   1967 Tom Segev, Henry Holt & Co, New York, First U.S. Edition 2007, Pg 215

prestige would not allow him to leave Syria. So Egypt would be trapped into the war!

Israel felt that its relationship with the Johnson administration was ideal. Abba Eban who conferred with Secretary of State Dean Rusk in November 1966 reported that when the problem with Syria popped up, Rusk had nothing negative to say about Israel policy towards Syria. An Israeli beauty, Mathilde Krim, a (former) Mossad agent, and now the wife of Hollywood tycoon Arthur Krim was a regular visitor to the White House where she spent several nights on the third floor. She enjoyed intimate relationship with Johnson personally, was seen sunbathing on his boat, and spent time at Johnson's Texas ranch, sometimes with her husband and sometimes without him.

After months of studying Nasser, the National Defense College concluded that "The current regime in Egypt sees the obliteration of Israel as one of its fundamental policy objectives". [1] Yet army intelligence believed Egypt was not ready to launch an offense before 1970. When Egyptian troops marched through Cairo to Sinai so openly, Eshkol said to his cabinet that was only a show of force to deter Israel from attacking Syria. When Nasser asked a former teacher from Burma, then UN secretary General, to reassign the UN troops to Gaza, Nasser, according to Abba Eban was not asking for the UN troops' withdrawal. It was U Thant who insisted on no change or total withdrawal giving Nasser two bad extreme choices. Getting rid of the UN

---

1   1967 Tom Segev, Henry Holt & Co, New York, First U.S. Edition 2007, Pg 189

force was an unannounced Israeli objective for some time. When Dayan criticized the ongoing Israeli policy Eshkol was furious. He asked Dayan, "What are you complaining about? It was you who demanded ages ago that we do something to get rid of the UN force."

The Israel government knew well that Nasser did not want war. General Aharon Yariv, and General Dayan believed that Nasser did not intend to attack Israel, but was interested in deterring Israel from attacking Syria.

Israel created all the conditions and provocations for the Six Day War. It had the plans ready. The service in the army was again extended two months before the war, and Israel needed war economically to get out of its serious recession; socially to stop reverse immigration; and territorially to expand its border. And having a friend at the White House is always a bonus!

The War and an unimagined Easy Cheap Victory

The victory in the Six Day War was easy and complete. It could as well be named the Six Hour War, since the air forces of the Arab armies were destroyed within the first two hours. Exposed Arab armies without air cover felt helpless, and their leadership was 'shocked and awed' before this term became popular. Religious fanatics in the Zionist movement and Israel believed it was the hand of God that accomplished the victory, but researchers believed that a little help from the hands of the

CIA and the Mossad had more to do with it. Incompetent Arab leadership played a role, some of who had good intentions, but hell is full of such people. Others were pushed to war by public opinion. They neither were willing nor prepared to go to war. And yet, others wished Nasser defeat more than they wished that for the Israelis, though they gave the needed rhetoric to calm their people.

Imagine that most of the Egyptian pilots spent the night before June 5, 1967 in a party organized by the general staff of the armed forces that lasted until dawn, or that the 'secret hands' organized to have the chief of staff of the Egyptian armed forces in the air with most of his commanders when his air force was destroyed, and communications between his command and the headquarters were jammed. He found no airport to land. In less than two hours, the Egyptian air force was destroyed on the ground and the troops in the desert were left without air cover or adequate supplies! Israel's army committed a massacre, not only against the Egyptian army in battle, but even against the thirsty and hungry Egyptian prisoners.

> "But rumors of prisoner killings were circulating within days. 'We've turned the Sinai peninsula into a valley of death, into one big cemetery', wrote soldier Kobi Rabinowitz, from Kibbutz Na'an, to his girlfriend. 'Unarmed men, prisoners with their hands above their heads, cut down against orders ... I've seen too many murders to shed any tears'. Yet he was clearly

shocked, writing: 'Apparently it doesn't take years of
Nazi education to turn people into animals' [1].

Or imagine that the Jordan radar at Ajlun, which spotted the
invading Israeli planes as they took off on their first mission to
Egypt, and radioed the message to Egyptian headquarters, had the
code changed the day before and no one took notice of that. How
deep the Mossad penetrated the defense establishments in the
Arab countries could be illustrated by Ellie Cohen, an Egyptian
Jew who was sent to South America, trained as a Syrian Muslim,
and decided to return "home" to Syria. He kept going up in the
Syrian Ba'ath Party until he became a part of the inner circle. He
was about to be appointed as defense minister but was advised
by the Mossad against accepting such an appointment because
it would cause high exposure. Arabs believe that many Cohens
penetrated their leaderships. The CIA was well entrenched in
the new Pax Americana post WWII Arab World. As is known,
one cannot know where the Mossad ends and the CIA starts.
When the Old City of Jerusalem was conquered, Mathilde Krim,
a super beauty and a super spy, the wife of a Hollywood Zionist
producer, an intimate friend of President Johnson, was staying at
the third floor of the White House, lobbying Johnson for Israel.
They were in constant touch and she was coordinating with the
Israeli embassy in Washington.

It may be interesting at this point to compare the Six Day
War against three Arab armies, with the 35 Days war of a much

1   1967 Tom Segev, Henry Holt & Co, New York, First U.S. Edition
      2007, Pg 375

stronger Israel in 2006, using the world's most modern and powerful weaponry ,against Hezbollah militia of less than 5000 in Southern Lebanon, which ended in an Israeli tactical and strategic failure .

Israel's New Borders, that's the Question Now!

That Israel wanted to expand its borders and was waiting for the right time was an objective that almost all , if not all Israeli parties shared. They differed only on how much. They all desired to keep the territories they occupied, the whole West Bank of Jordan, Sinai, and the Golan. None of them worried about international pressure, UN or anything else. They figured that they had the resources and power of international Zionism to handle these "inconveniences." They worried only about the 'womb bomb', the Palestinian and Arab populations living in these territories which eventually would result in a bi-national, and not a Jewish state, thus ending the Zionist project. But an ever increasing number of fundamentalists, racists, and fanatics were on the rise and they had an answer.

> "Eshkol gathered the members of his party's political committee when they were gathered to discuss the future of the newly occupied territories, 'We've been given a good dowry ...but it comes with a bride we don't like' – the Palestinians. I have a great desire for Gaza', he added, but it was 'a rose with many thorns'-

the Palestinians. There is no choice but to give the Palestinians 'special status'...But Gaza too, in his words was ' a rose with many thorns'. A committee of experts was already looking for areas where refugees could be settled. Of the West Bank, Eshkol said that the border would be at the Jordan River, and without peace Israel would not budge. The ministers reached two decisions; : to seize all of the West Bank to the Jordan River, as Begin had demanded, and to take the demilitarized zones along the Syrian border. Eshkol said repeatedly that he also wanted the Banias. 'There was a stormy argument', wrote Herzog'". [1]

Yigal Allon had a better idea for the Golan. In a confidential memorandum to Eshkol, Allon explained that the 150 000 Druze community in south Syria be encouraged to revolt and demand independence. They needed political and military guidance and assistance and Israel should take that role. Allon suggested that Israeli Druze, especially those who served with the IDF can play an important role in this project. A Druze state will be a buffer state between Syria, Jordan and Israel and it would assist Israel to keep a permanent hold on the Golan.

Raanan Weitz, whose father headed Jewish settlement projects for so many years thought the demographic problem was very serious. Before the war, about 200 000 Arabs lived in Israel. Now more than a million do in a population of less than

---

1   1967 Tom Segev, Henry Holt & Co, New York, First U.S. Edition 2007, Pg 369

two and a half million. Due to a higher birth rate for Arabs, they would soon become a majority.

He wrote that this "problem distresses me, stifling any joy and certainly any desire to celebrate."[1]

As mentioned earlier, the IDF had plans for the occupation of the territories that were invaded in 1967. As far as December 1963, those plans assigned General Chaim Herzog as military governor of the West Bank in the event of an Israeli occupation.[2] The army already had several handbooks to be handed to future military governors, detailing fully the organizational structure of the military government and guidelines on how to handle the occupied civilian populations. So, the military government started to function even before the fighting was over!

"The governors' handbook defined their preliminary assignments, mostly related to security, the collection of weapons, the clearing of land mines, the arrest of hostile persons on the basis of lists the army had prepared, and the burial of the dead. The governor was to begin operating intelligence units that would gather information about the area, including its topography, roads and streets, squares and parks, post offices and industrial plants, schools, holy places and mosques, museums and libraries, printing houses,

1   1967 Tom Segev, Henry Holt & Co, New York, First U.S. Edition 2007, Pg 429
2   1967 Tom Segev, Henry Holt & Co, New York, First U.S. Edition 2007, Pg 458

cemeteries, and, at least according to one handbook, brothels.... The working assumption was that the IDF would remain in the territories for prolonged period... The governor must identify key figures in every area and make an effort to immediately locate potential collaborators." [1]

Chaim Herzog said he spent many years before the war trying to perfect his role as military governor of the West Bank, including reading the Jordan papers daily and keeping up to date with events.

After the occupation, Teddy Kollek, the Jewish Mayor of Jerusalem visited Rohi al Khatib, the Arab Mayor. He went out of his way to show courtesy to al Khatib only to serve him his dismissal order a few days later in a Jerusalem hotel. Since the order was in Hebrew, it was translated to al Khatib on a hotel napkin!

The argument against annexation was always motivated by the fear of the Palestinian womb bomb. Zalman Aran said categorically that Israel should not annex the West Bank, not that he did not believe in a Greater Israel, but because of demography. If annexed, it would be cause for the downfall of the State of Israel. Interior minister Shapiro said that annexation of the West Bank would result in Israel becoming a bi-national state and soon after the Jews would become a minority.

---

1   1967 Tom Segev, Henry Holt & Co, New York, First U.S. Edition 2007, Pg 459

The Ben Gurion Proposed Peace Plan

Reporters from several countries asked Ben Gurion his thoughts about what Israel should do with the occupied territories. His plan as published by a manifesto was:

- ☐ No negotiations over East Jerusalem.
- ☐ IDF will not withdraw from the Jordan River. West Bank residents would be given autonomy.
- ☐ Gas Strip would remain with Israel, its people transferred to the West Bank.
- ☐ The Jews of Hebron would be allowed to return to their homes.
- ☐ If Syria agreed for peace in direct negotiations, it would get back the Golan.
- ☐ If Egypt agreed to peace by direct negotiations, it would get back the Sinai provided free access is secured through the Straits of Aqaba and the Suez Canal.
- ☐ If Jordan made peace through direct negotiations, it would be granted access to the Mediterranean.

Moshe Dayan favored autonomy of the West bank with security and foreign issues remaining with Israel. Self-government, yes he said, independence, no.

> "If it turns out that there's no possibility of granting self – government, and I have to choose between them belonging to Jordan – with the exception of

Jerusalem – or becoming Israeli citizens, I'd prefer that they belong to Jordan" [1]

Also, a joint Israeli Jordanian rule of the West bank was discussed. In case of autonomy, Dayan had a plan where military outposts and Jewish communities were to be established at the mountaintops in the heart of densely Arab populated lands.

Menechem Begin argued against giving the West Bank again to Jordan. That was Eretz Yisrael. The most he would agree to was a peace treaty with King Hussein as the King of East Jordan. He would agree for returning Sinai to Egypt in a peace treaty. But, he said, the government had no cause to hurry and must take its time, probably for seven years. Then Palestinians can be offered Israeli citizenship or leave the country.

Dr. Israel Eldad thought that even Begin was soft. He believed in a Greater Israel from the Nile to the Euphrates and he formed his own party 'The Land of Israel Party'. In 1970, he wrote Rabbi Meir Kahane of the Jewish Defense League asking him to come to Israel so they could work to realize their dream.

An expert committee which was formed after the war, recommended in its report that:

> "The Palestinian state would be 'under IDF patronage', 'without an army but with a police force. An 'Israel military delegation' would be 'credentialed' to the government of Palestine, and the IDF would have a

---

1   1967 Tom Segev, Henry Holt & Co, New York, First U.S. Edition 2007, Pg 503 - 504

permanent presence in the Jordan Valley and would protect the state of Palestine from external threats. The border between Palestine and Israel would be 'based on' the 1947 partition borders, but Israel would annex some territories, including the Latrun corridor. To preserve Palestinian 'dignity', Israel would also 'give up' a few of its own Arab villages. The state of Palestine would have access to the sea through an Israeli port, and free passage between the West Bank and Gaza. East Jerusalem would remain in Israel, but there would be a Palestinian "sub municipality" in the Old City, and the holy sites would receive "special status". The Palestinian state would establish its capital 'at the closest possible point to Jerusalem', which would be part of 'greater Jerusalem'. Israel would undertake to solve the refugee problem by means of an international fund that would encourage the refugees to leave Gaza and the West Bank and settle in other countries. As a first step toward founding the state, Kimche and his colleagues suggested convening Palestinian public figures in a congress of sorts. The proposal was dated June 14, but even then, four days after the war, it was not the first: Dayan and Eban had started receiving proposals for a Palestinian state on June 9". [1]

---

1   1967 Tom Segev, Henry Holt & Co, New York, First U.S. Edition 2007, Pg 513 - 514

After the Six Day War, a "Special Inter-Office Committee", was set up by Prime Minister Eshkol made up of four experts, which was to operate in affiliation with the Secret Service and receive orders from the Select Committee of Heads of services. The Committee was instructed to address Palestinian leaders "politely, respectfully, but firmly and clearly", with the aim of impressing them. The committee guidelines included the prevention of contact of those Palestinian leaders and the press, and those leaders would be advised that this committee was the only channel of communication between Palestinians and Israel.

Israelis were kept uninformed about the Palestinian refugees and they were shocked after occupation to see them in refugee camps. Amos Elon wrote: "We have a moral obligation because the road to Israel's independence was paved on the backs of these people, and they paid, with their bodies, their property, and their future, for the pogroms in the Ukraine and the Nazi gas chambers" in Ha'a retz on June 18, 1967.

As time went by, this sympathy evaporated. The 'need' to believe that Zionism had caused no injustice to anybody prevailed even though it was revealed by Israeli researchers that at least half of the refugees were forced to leave, and the rest were afraid partly as a result of the massacre of Deir Yassin.

Allon suggested resettling the refugees of Gaza at al Arish in northern Sinai, which was also agreed by Begin. Dayan thought that the refugee problems were handled by UNRWA and he preferred to leave this problem alone. Minister Ze'ev Sherf, suggested starting secret negotiations with foreign governments to settle the refugees overseas. He was supported by Pinhas Sapir and Eshkol. Mexico was mentioned but also Algeria, Syria, Morocco and Iraq were mentioned.

Eshkol said: "We got population from Iraq: we got a hundred thousand Jews. They'll get a hundred thousand Arabs. It's the same language, the same standard of living, there's water and there's land".

What to do with the Gaza refugees was troubling Eshkol. He wanted to annex Gaza but he preferred Gaza without Arabs, and definitely without refugees. He called Dr. Roberto Bacci, a demographer and director of the Central Bureau of Statistics and Aryeh Dvoretsky, a Hebrew University professor on December 6 1967. Bacci was involved in a project to raise the birth rate of Jews and decrease it for the Arabs. Bacci gave Eshkol 'alarming information'. Bacci said that a survey had shown that infant mortality in the occupied territories may decrease to rival that of Israeli Arabs. He added: "this is a shocking situation". Asked by Eshkol if Westernization would result in less fertility among Arabs he said yes, but it would take 15 years to do so "unless we are able to assert more control over the Palestinian family unit". He told the prime minister that half the West Bank population was under fifteen which was another "frightening thing." Bacci listed two reasons for hope: there was reason to hope that those refugees of Gaza transferred to the West Bank may move to Jordan. Also, a third of the refugees send one of their sons abroad for work hoping they will come back, but in most cases they stay abroad. Eshkol ended the meeting by saying: "Now I am going to show you my cards. First I don't know what to do. Second, I would like to do something." One may wonder what if he did not show his cards.

Transfer in Zionism Ideology

The idea of transfer was embedded in the Zionist ideology from its inception as evidenced in Herzl's diary.

> "We shall try to spirit the penniless population (the Palestinians) across the border by procuring employment for them in the transit countries, while denying them employment in our own country".

At the beginning of the 1920s, writer Israel Zangwill argued that the Arabs should be persuaded to leave. . His argument was that the Arabs had the whole Arab world, while the Jews had only Palestine. This became an argument used by the Zionist movement again and again. The two possible alternatives available he argued were either for the Jewish minority to rule the Arabs, which is undemocratic, or for the Arabs to rule the Jews and that is unacceptable. His conclusion: the Arabs must go. Actually, transfer was practiced from the very start of the Jewish settlements in Palestine as Arab tenants were transferred from the purchased lands, mostly by force. This was acknowledged by Ben Gurion who said: "Up until now we have accomplished our settlement in Palestine by population transfer". The Zionist movement however, encouraged its members not to talk about transfer in public, or even to deny it for public relations purposes. Menachem Ussishkin, stated "I do not believe in the transfer of an individual. I believe in the transfer of entire villages". He defended the transfer morality and said: "I am prepared to stand and defend the moral aspect before God and the League of Nations."

Actually, preparations for population transfer began in the 1930s when the Zionist leaders created a special committee for the task, the Committee on Population Transfer. The sessions of the Committee on Population Transfer dealt

> "With who would be deported first, villagers or city people (preferably the farmers); the rate of the deportations (probably over a period of ten years); where the deportees would go (as far away as possible, Gaza or Baghdad); and the cost of the whole operation (close to £300 million). Ben Gurion supposed that the Zionist movement would pay for the transfer. There was also a proposal to allow only Arabs bearing special work permits, which would be issued in limited numbers, to be employed in Palestine, in the spirit of Herzl's idea. One member of the Jewish Agency suggested raising taxes, 'so that they flee the taxes'". [1]

In his diary, Ben Gurion toyed with the idea of paying Iraq £10 million sterling in exchange for absorbing 500 000 people (100 000 families). Even Chaim Weizmann explored with Harry

---

1   One Palestine Complete, Tom Segev, Henry Holt & Company, New York 1st American Edition 2000, Pg 406

St. John Philby, the possibility that Arabia's king Ibn Saud might agree to a payment of "between ten and twenty" million pounds sterling in exchange for settling all the Arabs of Palestine in his country. The idea of transfer was enforced further in World War Two since mass transfers occurred in the German occupied territories. "The world had become accustomed to the idea of mass migrations and has almost become fond of them", Ze'ev Jabotinsky wrote, adding that "Hitler – as odious as he is to us – has given this idea a good name in the world".

By the end of the war Roberto Bachi,

> "A statistician and demograher, wrote a secret report in which he sounded an alarm on the demographic danger presented by the birthrate of the Arabs in Palestine, the highest in the world. For the Jews to reach a majority of 2 of 3 percent within five years, they would need to bring in about a million immigrants, 200 000 a year. But their majority would hold for only a short time; by 2001, Bachi forecast, only 21 to 33 percent of the population would be Jewish, given the Arab birthrate. In order to achieve the Zionist objective, he proposed transferring "a large part" of the country's Arabs to Arab countries."[1]

As we will see, in the 1948 war the transfer plans were implemented which resulted in the mass transfer of hundreds

---

1   One Palestine Complete, Tom Segev, Henry Holt & Company, New York 1st American Edition 2000, Pg 407

of thousands of Palestinians that are now more than five million, many of them still holding the keys to their homes and the land titles for their farms and refusing to give up. Many claim that if the Jews claimed they waited to come back to Palestine, they are ready to wait few more decades themselves and refuse to give up their right to return.

Transfer is a Zionist policy for all Israeli Parties and for as long as there is Zionism . Ariel Sharon, Former Israeli Lukud Party Prime Minister said:

> "It is the duty of Israeli leaders to explain to public opinion, clearly and courageously, a certain number of facts that are forgotten with time. The first of these is that there is no Zionism, colonization or Jewish State without the eviction of the Arabs and the expropriation of their lands".[1]

Labor Party former Prime Minister Rabin said:

> "Israel will create in the course of the next 10 or 20 years conditions which would attract natural and voluntary migration of the refugees frm the Gaza Strip and the West Bank to Jordan."[2]

---

1   Ariel Sharon, Former Israeli Lukuk Party Prime Minister (AFP November 15 1998
2   Yitzak Rabin, former Labor Party Israeli Prime Minister.

One week before the U.S. invaded Iraq, on March 10, 2003, Howard Fineman wrote in Newsweek as part of a special report, "Bush and God":

George W. Bush rises ahead of the dawn most days ... he goes off to a quiet place to read alone. His text isn't news summaries of the overnight intelligence dispatches ... It is not recreational reading ... Instead, he's told friends, it's a book of evangelical mini-sermons (My Utmost for His Highest). The author is Oswald Chambers, and under circumstances, the historical echoes are loud. A Scotsman and itinerant Baptist preacher, Chambers died in November 1917 as he was bringing the Gospel to Australian and New Zealand soldiers massed in Egypt (in the Army of General Allenby). By Christmas they had helped to wrest Palestine from the (Muslim) Turks. Now there is talk of a new war in the Near East, this time in a land once called Babylon ... Later that day ... Bush told religious broadcasters that ... the United States was called to bring God's gift of liberty to every human being in the world.[1]

*****

As always, mighty Israel claims to be the victim of Palestinian aggression but the sheer asymmetry of power between the two sides leaves little room for doubt as to who is the real victim. This is indeed a conflict between David and Goliath but the Biblical image has been inverted - a small and defenseless Palestinian David faces a heavily armed, merciless and overbearing Israeli Goliath. [2]

---

1   Oil Crusades, America through Arab eyes, Abdulhay Zalloum, Pluto Press, London, 2007, Pg 50-51
2   Avi Shlaimm The Guardian, January 8, 2008

CHAPTER NINE

ISRAEL: THE CRUSADES REVISITED

Peace Processes without Peace

It is no secret that many Palestinians, Arabs and Muslims think of Israel as a replica of the Crusades, as much as it is no secret that many Western leaders thought of Israel's creation as such or at least they claimed it was religiously motivated. One of the very early subjects that the Hebrew University devoted special interest to was the history of the Crusades, obviously having in mind the parallels between the Western implantation by force of a foreign state amidst the Muslim World to the Crusades. At least, the crusaders had no transfer policy! As Ehud Sprinzak, a political science professor at the Hebrew University in Jerusalem wrote, Israel *"was, and still is, one of the most 'unnatural' states in history- a state of newcomers, the vast majority of whom arrived after the colonial power had clearly established itself."* It was implanted by colonial powers and Israel's survival depends on theirs.

Settlers Racism, Fascism and Terrorism Become Israel's State Policy

We noted in previous chapters that Israel provoked the 1967 war and that across the Israeli spectrum, territorial expansion was desired, the problem was the 'Arab womb bomb' of demography and how to address it. There were minimalists and maximalists. In the discussions before the war and after it, annexing 'something' was part of all plans. The problem was in defining what that something was that could be achieved with Israel becoming a bi-national state. As time went by, the maximalists had their way.

Probably the single person who most affected the post 1967 Israel policies in the occupied territories, and who led the settlement movements was Moshe Levinger of the Gush Emunim movement. Even though, it was convenient for the Israeli authorities to put the blame, at least during Labor governments, on one man, his movement and settlements were protected by the Israeli army all the way.

The Gush Emunim movement was based on the teachings of Rav Zvi Yehuda Cook, the head of the Yishiva Merkaz Harav in Jerusalem, and the son of Rav Avraham Cook, the first Ashkenazi chief rabbi of Palestine, who was the founder of modern religious Zionism. Cook contended that the occupied territories were part of the land promised to the Jews by God as recorded in the Bible. Cook declared that they must remain as part of Israel and be defended at all cost. Cook and his school became the nucleus of Gush Emunim. This movement grew slowly, and several attempts to build settlements at densely populated areas were stopped by the army. Even though the early settlements were built under Labor governments which wanted to exercise some control on the movement, the Gush members compared the Labor Government to the British Mandate.

Rabbi Moshe Levinger, "was a sickly child who suffered from crippling bouts of depression, and spent some of his youth in a Swiss sanatorium". The Israeli military governor of Hebron (1979-1981), Fredy Zack, said he knew two Levingers: the respected spiritual leader and the mad man. The Arab people of Hebron only saw the 'mad' Levinger" who can be truly called the father of the settlement movement in the occupied territories. A preview of his background may be helpful to define the character of that movement.

Robert I. Freidman described him as "an extremely odd-looking man. Tall and thin, with a skull and crossbones face…" He was described as "more stubborn than even Shamir, more passionate than Begin, more extreme than Sharon" he had done more than any to lead the settlement movement to what it is today; an illegal activity according to international law and obstacle to peace if we borrow the latest U.S. description of settlements which superseded the earlier definition of settlements as illegal!. His first act was to defy the government and establish a Jewish settlement in Hebron on Passover 1968. There were no civilian Jews living in the occupied territories until then. Now there are several hundreds of thousands of settlers made up from all walks of Israeli society. Russian immigrants flooded in during the 1990s, American immigrants and secular as well as religious Jews are flocking to these settlements due to generous government subsidies and tax breaks. To Levinger, God was the first Zionist, and it is His laws and not the government's that he obeys. He believed there was no room to compromise with the Arabs. "Even if the Arabs wanted to compromise, we couldn't," he declared.

> "If someone were to come to another person's house and want to take his house or sleep with his wife or take his children, he couldn't compromise on that! It's our country, and it's our destiny to live in our land as a 'nation of priests.' " [1]

It seems as if it matters little if The New Republic magazine called Levinger as "Israel's foremost religious fascist" since he had several hundred thousand 'fascist' followers. What matters more was an Israeli former defense and prime minister Ariel Sharon's description of Levinger and his wife as "true heroes of our generation." In a 1990 poll by the leading Israeli News Paper Hadashot, Levinger topped the list of the most influential men in the 1980s. Palestinians believe that Israel's settlement movement is commanded by 'fascists' and 'mad men' who believe their interpretation of the Bible of two thousand years gave them the right to possess their homes to which they still own the land titles and the home keys.

---

1   Zealots For Zion, Robert I. Friedman, Rutgers University Press, New Brunswick, N.J. 1992, Pg 4

Gush Emonim settlers were very aggressive against the Palestinian Arabs. They were armed to the teeth, and were protected by the army. They were backed by the leading rabbinical authorities. When thirty Yishiva students shot dead a thirteen year old Arab girl in a rampage in an Arab town, Rabbi Yitzhak Ginsberg justified the murder. He told an Israeli court that:

> "It should be recognized that Jewish blood and a goy's blood are not the same. The people of Israel must rise and declare in public that a Jew and a goy are not, God forbid, the same. Any trial that assumes that Jews and goyim are equal is a travesty of justice".[1]

Not all Israelis are Ginsbergs. Bteslem, a human rights group of Israeli doctors, lawyers, academics and even Knesset members publishes periodically reports about the excesses of occupation and torture of administrative prisoners detained without charges. They are in the minority however and are rejected by settlers and the radical right. When Shlomo Goren, a former chief rabbi was asked about one of their reports he answered: "I don't know them and I don't want to know them. They betray the people of Israel and the state of Israel; they're serving our enemies. Since they are traitors, they weren't created in the image of God."

Fanaticism is deep rooted with the radical right.

> *"There were those who felt the Jewish law – halakha –comprised racist elements, and some compared the*

---

1   The False Prophet, Rabbi Meir Kahana, Robert I. Friedman, Lawrence Hill Books, New York, Fist Edition 1990, Pg 286

rulings of the chief rabbinate to Nazi law.[1] *Dr. Israel Shahak, a chemistry professor at the Hebrew University and a Holocaust survivor, once found a visiting student from Africa unconscious on a Jerusalem Street. It was on the Sabbath and a nearby resident refused to allow Dr. Shahak to use his telephone to call an ambulance, claiming that the sanctity of the Sabbath could not be violated to save the life of a non – Jew. Shahak went to the chief rabbinate, which confirmed this interpretation of the Sabbath laws.*[2]

Settlers Lunatic Behavior and Government Collusion

The brutal behavior of settlers can best be expressed by real life stories that were taken, except when otherwise noted, from the Book *Zealots of Zion*, by Robert I. Freidmann, an investigative reporter and author. As an American Jew he investigated the settlers' movement thoroughly.

Abdul Rahman was taking a nap in his Hebron apartment when he heard screams within his apartment. He saw Levinger with three of his body guards in the middle of his living room. Levinger had his hands around the neck of Abdul Rahman's seven year old daughter and tried to kill her. She had insulted

1   Ha'aretz., 7 July 1977, p.2; 13 July 1966, p.2
2   1967 Tom Segev, Henry Holt & Co, New York, First U.S. Edition 2007, Pg 99

Levinger's daughter, his daughter complained. When her nine year old brother intervened, the rabbi punched the boy in his eye and then broke his arm. Abdul Rahman's wife snatched the little daughter and held her in her arms. The rabbi started punching the mother with his fists. Abdul Rahman said it all happened within seconds. An Israeli soldier stationed on the roof of Abdul Rahman's house in Hebron came down a ladder after he heard the commotion going on below. Levinger asked for his pistol while his young daughters were watching the episode. He smashed Abdul Rahman's television and furniture, He resisted the soldier who tried to shove him outside telling the soldier he was 'a PLO agent'. The soldier called for back up and after negotiations, Levinger agreed to leave the apartment provided they lock the Abdul Rahman family in a room so they do not see him evicted by the soldiers. Levinger's justification for the rampage was because an Arab child insulted a Jewish child. Abdul Rahman was encouraged to press charges against Levinger. He hesitated, as he did not have confidence in Israeli justice, but finally he did. The judge, Yoel Tsur acquitted Levinger on assault charges and charges of insulting an Israeli soldier. The judge rejected Abdul Rahman's family testimony because they were 'interested parties'. He dismissed the charges of insult to a soldier on duty, with the explanation that since the soldier left the roof top where he was assigned, he was no longer on duty. The prosecution was enraged probably more for the soldier than for Abdul Rahman, and an appeal of three judges reversed Tsur verdict. Shortly afterwards, three of Levinger's faithful thugs showed up at Abdul Rahman's place with clubs in hand. They beat him with their clubs until he became unconscious.

Bob Silverman, an American diplomat arrived in Hebron in his armor-plated Mercedes from his base in Jerusalem and started to take some photos for a new housing development complex. Silverman's job was tracking settlement activities. Waiving his pistol at Silverman, a settler called him "a dirty American bastard." Other settlers joined in and made a circle around him preventing him from moving or leaving. It took an Israeli army officer's intervention to save Silverman, an American Jew, from the country of 'American Bastards" who rewarded Israel with 3.5 billion dollars that year, some of which was diverted to building the housing compound the American diplomat was denied the privilege of, and the apartments owned by the same Jewish settlers who pronounced an American official as a bastard for trying to carry out his duty.

Secular settlers became a majority yet they were as hawkish as the most radical Gush Emunim members. Robert I. Freidman was taken to Ariel settlement to see for himself how settlers live and think. He was introduced to an American Jewish family that immigrated to Israel in 1969. The husband was an aeronautical engineer working at the Israel Aircraft Industries, the electronic warfare division.

"A German shepherd growled menacingly as Dina Shalit and I walked up a steep cobblestone path toward the front door of the Bernstein's sprawling home in Ariel shortly before the outbreak of the

Gulf War. Fortunately, the dog was chained to a post behind a shrub. 'It barks when it smells an Arab', said Mrs. Bernstein, a slatternly middle – aged woman who is the head nurse in an intensive-care unit in a Petah Tikva hospital. 'The dog hates Arabs. They give off a smell. It's genetic.'

'But I'm Jewish', I protested.

'Are you a leftist?' Mr. Bernstein, a tall, thin man, twittered.

'Robert sides with Peace Now', said Dina. 'But he's a serious writer, and we think it would be nice if he got to know Ariel.' 'Said Mrs. Bernstein, perturbed that I was not of her political persuasion. 'Maybe that's why the dog went crazy.'" [1]

1977 Begin's Likud Victory: A Turning point for Settlement Policy

The turning point in settlement policies and outlook to the occupied territories began in 1977 when Labor was voted out of office by the Likud and Menachem Begin became the prime minister. Begin was born in Poland in 1911 and became

[1]   Zealots For Zion, Robert I. Friedman, Rutgers University Press, New Brunswick, N.J. 1990, Pg 85

a follower of Vladimir Jabotinsky, who established Revisionist Zionism. Jabotinsky as well as Begin, believed that no concessions whatsoever should be granted regarding all the Eretz of Israel, and that Zionism must use force and move faster to achieve its objectives. He moved to Palestine only in 1942 and became the head of the terrorist organization Etzel. After his Etzel gang conducted several attacks on the Arabs of Palestine and British targets, including bombing the King David Hotel, he was listed on England's Most Wanted Terrorists List. He refused the UN partition resolution and continued to get arms even after Ben Gurion declared a Jewish state of Israel in Palestine. Ben Gurion, who labeled Jabotinsky as Hitler (while Ha'aretz called him Mussolini), decided that his successors led by Begin were not fit to join a coalition and decided to disband Begin's terrorist organization. In June 1948, Begin was inside the ship Altalena which was full of arms opposite the shores of Tel Aviv. Ben Gurion ordered the Balmach to sink the ship. While thousands of Tel Aviv residents were watching, the ship was fired upon and sank. 14 members of Begin's men were killed and sixty nine were wounded. Begin barely escaped death. The commander of Balmach who sank the ship was Itzhak Rabin. Itzhak Shamir who also headed another terrorist organization, became the Israeli prime minister after Begin. This background to the roots of the Likud and its leaders found expression in the new Likud government's planning and strategy towards the occupied territories.

After winning the 1977 election, Begin formed a right-wing coalition in which the representation of Gush Emunim was very strong. Soon after his election, Begin went to Elon Moreh, a settlement sight near Nablus on which the Gush tried to establish a settlement seven times and failed. A Torah in his hand, Begin vowed to build "many more Elon Morehs". Gush found a great supporter within the Likud, and that was Ariel Sharon. In 1977, the Likud government changed policy, and it declared that settlements would be built anywhere in the Land of Israel, and it considered the occupied territories as liberated and not occupied. Labor encircled heavily populated Arab areas with settlements, but the Likud moved settlements in their midst. Ariel Sharon as an agricultural minister in 1977, revealed a plan in that year titled 'A Vision of Israel at Century's End' calling for the settlement of 2 million Jews in the West Bank by the end of the 20th century. The new government did not lack the determination or the resources to build 'many Elon Morehs'.

Even when George Bush the first, and James Baker pressured Shamir to attend the Madrid Peace conference after the first Gulf War, and as the American administration viewed the return of the West Bank to the Arabs as best for the U.S. and Israel's future, Shamir, on the eve of the Madrid summit, told the Likud Party: "All the territories of Eretz Yisrael must be settled by Jews, more and more." Later, Shamir told Likud supporters in France: "If someone thinks that it is possible to pressure Israel (to make concessions)…the answer will be that we will always be faithful to our ideals, to Zionism, to Jerusalem, and to Eretz Yisrael." Shamir won. The president who wanted to force peace on him was denied a second term.

It is no exaggeration to say that Israel was ruled by prime ministers who were officially branded as terrorists by a world empire, and that they believed terrorism was a legitimate instrument to achieve one's objectives. Shamir told a reporter while still a prime minister, when asked how he feels about his terrorist days: "Terrorism is a way of fighting that is acceptable under certain conditions and by certain movements." To Shamir, Jewish terrorism is fine "because Jews fought for their lands, but Palestinians are not fighting for their land. The settlers, many of whom are followers of the Likud or Kach take terrorism against Palestinians for granted.

When Likud took power, only five thousand Jews lived on the West Bank. Between 1977 and 1984, successive Likud governments invested more than $1 billion in building nearly sixty new settlements, increasing the number of Jewish settlers to more than thirty-eight thousand. Also, just before the 1981 elections, the Likud expropriated more than thirty-six thousand dunams, according to a statement issued in April 1981 by the Prime Minister's Office. According to Palestinian sources, the figure was twice as much.

Settlers Terrorism after Likud Election Victory

In 1980, a plot to assassinate five Palestinian Arab mayors was executed. Two of the mayors were crippled, the other three were saved due to faulty wiring of the explosives. In April 27, 1984, a plot to blow up five Arab buses during rush hour was foiled barely in time. Within days, twenty seven members of a terrorist ring were captured and people were shocked to learn that the group had an elaborate plan to blow up the Dome of the Rock Mosque. A full attack plan was discovered that studied the structure of the Mosque and acquired the arms and explosives from a military camp at the Golan Heights. The group manufactured twenty eight precision bombs to destroy the dome with minimum damage to the surroundings. They bought special Uzi silencers to kill the guards if necessary and they secured twenty skilled reservists to participate in the operation. The group planned to carry out the attack in 1982 had it not been for a split among the group.

Harvard University conducted a simulated war game about the consequences of the operation if it were carried out, wrote Hebrew University professor Ehud Sprinzak in his book *The Ascendance of Israel's Radical Right*. The Harvard study concluded in a conservative scenario that the operation would have caused a new phase in the Middle East conflict. The resulting crisis would have been "broader, deeper, and longer lasting than anything in the past. A less conservative estimation suggested the scheme could have triggered a third world war." Settlers behaved savagely against neighboring villages, beating and shooting them many times under Israeli soldiers' watch.

Until 1977, the Settlers were mostly religious belonging to the Gush Emunim movement. After Likud took over, many white-collar non-religious Israelis moved to West Bank settlements due to the availability of larger and cheaper apartments or houses, plus additional benefits of subsidized mortgages and tax breaks introduced by the Likud. By 1990, at least 80% of the settlers were unreligious yuppies, but they were just as hawkish as the Gush Emunim settlers.

Settlements certainly had no problem to secure the cash they need from the government and from the deep pockets of American Jews. When Nachman, the Mayor of Ariel went on a month tour to the U.S., he secured $ 1.5 million for his settlement Ariel. In 1987, he set up the Ariel Development Fund and raised more than $5 million from several Jewish billionaires including Albert Reichmann, head of Olympia & York, and the convicted junk-bond swindler Michael Milken.

The victory of Begin in the 1981 election was by a bigger margin than in 1977. Six months later, Begin announced formally the annexation of the Golan Heights. Also, he appointed Menachem Milson, an Arabic Literature professor at the Hebrew University, as the head of the newly created civilian administration in the occupied territories. Milson was brought to practice what he preached in an article at Commentary in which he suggested the formation of the Villagers League to be a substitute for the PLO. The League was composed of corrupt Palestinian politicians and failed. Milson deposed elected Palestinian mayors, closed Beir Zeit University and shut down two news papers. Meanwhile, the Likud was expropriating hundreds of thousands of more Palestinian lands. When the 1967 occupation began, 0.5% of the West bank land was under Israeli control. By 1984, Israel controlled more than 40% of the land. The Likud cancelled the earlier Labor government decree forbidding Jews to buy Arab land in the West Bank. Under Milson and Sharon this was changed. There were many land fraud cases. According to the August 20 1985 issue of the New York Times, Shamir ordered police not to look deeply into West Bank land fraud cases, that *"a certain amount of sleight of hand"* was needed to secure land from Arabs. In a speech about the same time Shamir said: *"Redeeming land in the Land of Israel often necessitated crafty and tricky devices".*

Meir Kahane: From New York to the Knesset

Meir Kahane immigrated to Israel with his brand of Zionism and Mechanism. In his view, Arabs presence pollutes the very essence and spirit of Judaism, therefore they are more than just a demographic and physical threat. Their expulsion is a necessary precondition for redemption.

> "Zionism, the establishment of the State of Israel, the return of millions of Jews home, the miraculous victories of the few over the many Arabs, the liberation of Judea-Samaria, Gaza and the Golan, the return of Jewish sovereignty over the Holy City and Temple Mount are all parts of the divine pledge and its fulfillment", wrote Kahane.[1]

---

1   The False Prophet, Rabbi Meir Kahana, Robert I. Friedman, Lawrence Hill Books, New York, Fist Edition 1990, Pg 173

He argued that redemption would have already been here if the Arabs were expelled, and their Dome of the Rock Mosque destroyed.

> "Had we acted without considering the gentile reaction", Kahane wrote, "without fear of what he may say or do, the Messiah would have come right through the open door and brought us redemption". [1] He wrote in an article at the JDL publication "We are Chosen One and a Special One; selected for purity and holiness, and to rise above all others and to teach them the truth for purity and holiness that we have been taught. There is no reason or purpose to being a Jew unless there is something intrinsically different about it. No. We are not equal to the Gentiles. We are different. We are higher". Can one say this was racism at its worse? Yet, Kahane established a party, Kach, and he was elected to the Knesset! [2]

And Kahane was not alone, except he was loud. Rabbi Moshe Segal who belonged to the Irgun Terrorist gang before 1948, argued that there was nothing wrong using genocide to eradicate the "Arab Problem" in the occupied territories. He compared those Arabs to the Amalek tribe which was destroyed by the ancient Hebrews.

---

1   The False Prophet, Rabbi Meir Kahana, Robert I. Friedman, Lawrence Hill Books, New York, Fist Edition 1990, Pg 173

2   The False Prophet, Rabbi Meir Kahana, Robert I. Friedman, Lawrence Hill Books, New York, Fist Edition 1990, Pg 173

"One should have mercy on all creatures ... but the treatment of Amalek – is different. The treatment of those who would steal our land – is different". Then, quoting Numbers 33, Segal wrote: "You must drive out all the inhabitants of the land as you advance ... and settle there, for to you have I given the land to possess it .... But if you will not drive out the inhabitants of the land as you advance, any whom you let remain shall be as barbed hooks in your eyes, and as thorns in your sides. They shall continually dispute your possession of the land in which you dwell. And what I meant to do to them, I will do to you" [1]

In an interview by Robert I. Freidman in 1991, Matityahu Drobles, co-chair of the World Zionist Organization said:"Judea and Samaria (West Bank) are part of the Land of Israel. If we want to achieve Jewish sovereignty, we have to settle. Those who have the power here will prevail- and we have the strength...According to the Bible, I have the right to the East Bank of Jordan. For my generation the West Bank is enough."

Likud's vision was to create an enormous number of settlements to the extent that no Israeli future government, regardless of its orientation would dare to evacuate the settlements without provoking a civil war.

---

1   The False Prophet, Rabbi Meir Kahana, Robert I. Friedman, Lawrence Hill Books, New York, Fist Edition 1990, Pg 260

Temple Mount Zealots & Al Aqsa Mosque

To dispel any claim, the destruction of the Al Aqsa Mosque to build the third temple is only toyed with by few fanatics, but is deeply entrenched in religious Zionist ideology. This story about Israel's Army chief rabbi during the six day war is very revealing. As soon as he entered the Al Aqsa Mosque he asked Israeli troops to fly the Star of David atop the Dome of the Rock golden spire. Sensing political trouble Dayan ordered it down.

Then General Solomon Goren approached General Uzi Narkis, the commander who occupied Jerusalem "and told him, this was the moment to blow up the Dome of the Rock. 'Do this and you will go down in history, 'Goren said, and explained that such a thing could only be done under the cover of war. 'Tomorrow might be too late.'" [1]

An arson fire was set inside the mosque on August 21, 1969. An Australian torched Al Aqsa Mosque, then started photographing the blazing mosque. Police and fire fighters took their time to arrive. The damage was restored. On May 12, 1980 Rabbi Meir Kahane and Andy Green were imprisoned after conspiring to blow up the Mosque. In 1980, one Orthodox Jew from America, Alan Goodman, entered the Mosque with his M-16 rifle and shot dead one Palestinian Arab and wounded another. A few months later, four Orthodox Jewish youths armed with Uzi submachine guns and hand grenades, attempted to break into

---

1   1967 Tom Segev, Henry Holt & Co, New York, First U.S. Edition 2007, Pg 379

an underground passageway that opens onto the Temple Mount compound. Israeli police caught the youths before they could plant their explosives inside the mosques. At a later date, police rounded up more than forty people including a well know rabbi in connection with the plot to blow up the Mosque. Police found at the rabbi's apartment diagrams of the Mosque and a weapons cache. On August 9, 1990, Shimon Barda, a leader of a mystical Jewish group was arrested for conspiring to blow up the Dome of the Rock Mosque after they discovered stockpiles of weapons, including U.S. made TAW shoulder-held missiles. The gang, including its leader was committed into a mental institution. Palestinians believed Israel has not enough space in such institutions for its fanatics.

It was during the early days of Menachem Begin that solid ties were forged with the evangelicals. They were pressing Begin to rebuild the temple no less than the fundamentalist Jews. Begin worked hard to cultivate their political and economical support as they were almost eight times more numerous than the U.S. Jews. The Evangelicals or Christian Zionists became financiers for West Bank Jewish settlements and the Likud Party. Jim Falwell was a staunch supporter of Begin and his projects:

> "Falwell openly supported Likud during the 1984 Israeli elections. 'I would sincerely hope no government could be elected in Israel which could freeze the settlements and reverse the trend toward irrevocable control that will come in the West Bank

in three to five years'", Falwell told several hundred members in a political conference in 1984.[1]

The Christian Zionists interpret the Bible literally and believe the restoration of the Jews to Palestine will speed up the second coming of Christ. Then the Jews will be forced to convert. When a high ranking member of AIPAC was reminded that the Fundamentalists will seek to convert the Jews after the second coming of Christ, he said he will worry when he sees Jesus wondering over the mountains of Jerusalem, but now, he will take all the support for Israel that he can get.

Gershon Solomon's Temple Mount Faithful Movement found more support in the U.S. among Christian Zionists than in Israel. He created Jewish chapters of the Temple Mount Faithful in major American states including New York, Florida, Texas and California. When he visited the Bible Belt in 1991 the Christian Evangelical leaders urged him to build the Third Temple now. One of his main supporters is Pat Robertson whose talk show is telecast over 200 TV stations as well as in sixty foreign countries. Patterson promotes the view that Israel is God's favorite nation and the United States will be blessed by supporting it. "During Israel's 1982 invasion of Lebanon, Robertson spent several weeks explaining to millions of viewers how Jewish soldiers in Lebanon were fulfilling the apocalyptic vision of the prophet Ezekiel"

Monroe Spen, a very rich Florida stockbroker and an Orthodox Jew, a self-declared "extremely Zionistic Jew" supported Israeli

---

1   Zealots For Zion, Robert I. Friedman, Rutgers University Press, New Brunswick, N.J. 1990, Pg 143

extreme right causes and people. He supported the successful campaign of Kahane to the Knesset. And he supported the Solomon movement and took it from a poor adjunct of Tehiya extremist Party to a well funded movement. He even wrote to Teddy Kollek, the Mayor of Jerusalem asking him to use the municipality funds to build the Third Temple and demolish the Dome of the Rock Mosque.

On August 17, 1986, Spen gathered various Temple Mount groups in the Old city Jewish Quarter, hoping to unite them and develop a conduit for funding them. The group included among others, Kach party activists, including Kahane himself, Stanley Goldfoot, a wealthy South – African born Jew, and Peter Goldman, head of Americans for a Safe Israel. Kach and Goldfoot wanted a speedy confrontation with the Israeli government to allow them to pray at the Temple Mount while Solomon favored a step by step approach

> "first winning the right to pray, perhaps through the
> Israeli courts, later erecting a small synagogue on the
> grounds of the Temple Mount, and finally razing the
> mosques and building the Third Temple." [1]

A former member of the Stern terrorist gang who bragged about his involvement in the assassination of UN mediator Count Bernadotte, as well as his role in the bombing of the King David Hotel, Goldfoot forged ties with the Christian Zionists

---

1   Zealots For Zion, Robert I. Friedman, Rutgers University Press, New Brunswick, N.J. 1990, Pg 146

with whom they formed a tax-exempt organization for the Temple Mount project. Of those American activists was Terry Reisenhoover, an Oklahoma gas and oil millionaire who was jailed in 1987 for four years for selling worthless oil exploration leases in Alaska!

The profile of the supporters of the radical right is peculiarly interesting. One such backer was Bernard Bergman, one of the richest and most powerful Orthodox Jews in the world. He had close ties to Israel's National Religious Party and the settlements projects.

> "He made his fortune from a national conglomerate of Medicaid nursing homes, where infirm patients were left unattended to soak in their own urine. The New York Daily news characterized the homes as warehouses where the aged were dumped to die. No doubt Bergman learned his business ethics from his parents, who not only were bootleggers, but also were convicted in 1941 of smuggling eight kilos of heroin from France in the bindings of Hebrew prayer books. 'Bernard Bergman was into all kinds of dirty business', said Sonia. 'He kept dead bodies in freezers in his nursing home to collect their Social Security payments. Then, after he was indicted (in 1974 for fraud), he stood in front of television cameras and said, 'As God is my witness, I'm innocent'. Bergman

later pleaded guilty to fraud and bribery and spent one year in prison ..." [1]

Goldfoot came to the United States to spread 'The Jerusalem Temple Foundation' and the Temple Mount gospel and to help catalyze the movement. This is how he claimed he addressed the Christian Zionists:

"I told the Goyim in America that the Temple Mount is the highest mountain on the face of the earth because it represents the moral and spiritual Everest of mankind", recalled Goldfoot. "I was astounded by the reception. Not because it was because I was somebody from Jerusalem who had come to talk about the temple". Goldfoot larded his speeches with fire and brimstone. "I told the goyim that they have a tremendous debt to us Jews. And that I doubt that they can never repay this debt; that they persecuted us; they murdered us; they've stolen from us for centuries. They have even stolen our religion, which they distorted and called Christianity. But I told them if they make retribution sufficiently, strongly, and long enough, maybe they will be forgiven and accepted in the sight of the Lord. God does not accept you, I told them. But if you help us build the temple, you can be saved. I'm not sure God will forgive you, but you've got to try. They

---

1   The False Prophet, Rabbi Meir Kahana, Robert I. Friedman, Lawrence Hill Books, New York, Fist Edition 1990, Pg 17

loved it. They cried, 'Hallelujah! Hallelujah!' Then I told them that they have to go immediately and spread propaganda all over America in favor of Jewish sovereignty on the Temple Mount and moving the American embassy to Jerusalem – to put pressure on Congress (and) on the president himself". [1]

What was not funny was the fact that even American president Ronald Reagan had been a strong believer of the Armageddon theory since 1968 up until he was in the White House

"When, on separate occasions, Frank Carlucci and Caspar Weinberger talked to Reagan about the importance of nuclear deterrence, he gave them a lecture about Armageddon. On May 5, 1989, Reagan told Cannon [his biographer] that Israel's possession of the Temple Mount is a sign that Armageddon is near."[2]

Peace Processes without Peace

The first Gulf War exposed the weakness of the Zionist Lobby argument of the strategic importance of Israel to the United States. Arming Israel to the teeth, and spending hundreds of billions for economic and military aid and grants could not make

1   Zealots For Zion, Robert I. Friedman, Rutgers University Press, New Brunswick, N.J. 1990, Pg 148
2   Zealots For Zion, Robert I. Friedman, Rutgers University Press, New Brunswick, N.J. 1990, Pg 151

Israel useful to the United States in its plans for the invasion of Iraq on the pretext of its expulsion from Kuwait. It was proxy Arab regimes that had to be mobilized, whose land and resources utilized, that the net cost of that war was paid by U.S. proxies in the Arab and Western world. Actually, considering the currency fluctuation, especially on the yen, the United States had all the Desert Storm campaign paid for by others, with some surplus! The Bush senior administration was emboldened to request Israel to start negotiating for peace against the occupied territories.

U.S. Secretary of State James Baker made eight trips to the Middle East in eight months after the first Gulf War to convince Shamir mostly, and to negotiate an agenda for the conference. Israel, Syria, Jordan, Lebanon and the Palestinians were invited to attend what became known as the Madrid Conference to be held on October 30, 1991. The conference was jointly sponsored by the United States and the Soviet Union months before its disintegration. Shamir was buying time as the American presidential elections was months away, and that's a good time for AIPAC and Israel to show presidents who really holds the ropes of power in Washington.

The Madrid Conference

The structure of the Madrid Conference apparently was heavily influenced by Shamir demands. The terms of reference were:.

- An opening conference having no power to impose solutions. In plainer language, the balance of power greatly favored Israel and Israel must get what it wants or everybody can go home.
- Bilateral talks with the Arab states bordering Israel. That's Israel's way of playing one Arab country against the other. Also, Egypt was absented as if the Palestinian problem is none of its business.
- Talks with the Palestinians on 5-year interim self-rule, to be followed by talks on the permanent status. That was meant for Palestinians to have autonomy on part of the West Bank in a self-government that can act as a security sub-contractor to Israel. After five years who knows?
- Multilateral talks on key regional issues, like refugees. Now other nations may be involved so they can settle the Palestinian refugees and pay the bill.

Only few days after the opening of the conference George Bush the First was voted out of office, and the USSR disintegrated! Secret negotiations between an inexperienced, uncommitted and some say unauthorized Palestinian delegation and an expert team of Israelis negotiated a secret agreement in Oslo, undermining a more credible, officially appointed team headed by Dr. Haider Abdul Shafi who was totally surprised that such a secret team existed and more surprised about the terms negotiated.

As the Madrid Peace Conference was going on, and Mahmud Abbas was secretly negotiating the Oslo Agreement, Sharon was pressing his earlier plan to have two million settlers by the end of the 1990s. In 1991, Sharon greatly increased subsidies for settlers in the West Bank. Settlers buying a 71 000 dollar home in the West bank can pay only 17 000 dollars at 4.5 % interest, and the remaining amount is on an interest free mortgage. After five years, 10 000 dollars of the mortgage becomes a gift! "When you look at the mortgages, a young couple that doesn't move into the territories is an idiot", said left-wing legislator Dede Zucker. Starting from November 1990, free housing plots were given to settlers, and this program was secretly implemented until it was exposed by the Davar newspaper in July 1991.

The sitting Israeli prime minister in 1991 was Itzhak Shamir, a former acknowledged terrorist and head of the Mossad who thought that even Menachem Begin was soft in negotiating the Camp David Accord with Sadat, an accord he never accepted. He and his minister Ariel Sharon had plans to settle more than two million Jewish settlers in the West Bank, and here comes this goy, James Baker, the Secretary of state of George Bush the First, who organizes a peace conference that many hoped would result in Israel's withdrawal to its 1967 borders, which means a withdrawal from the West Bank as well. At first, Shamir objected, but he was confronted by a determined U.S. president whose popularity was at a record high after his victory in Desert Storm. His victory against a third world power whose population was only one-fifth of the USA's population, and whose GNP barely exceeded two percent of that of the USA. So Shamir accepted the invitation to Madrid vowing, as he told some confidents, to make the negotiations last forever. In the meantime, the president requested freezing settlement activities and made that a condition for an Israeli request for a 10 billion dollar loan guarantee. To Shamir and AIPAC, Bush committed an unforgivable sin by standing in the way of Israeli financial demands. The Israeli Lobby and its backers will pay a few million dollars to get politicians elected (or unelected) and these politicians will open the flood gates of American treasury to Israel by billions instead.

What a viable formula indeed to Israel, but not to the American tax payer, who is kept busy in a hand - to - mouth daily routine. Barbara Bush noted thereafter, that there is something about the media that changed afterwards. His popularity sank, as a negative orchestrated media campaign against Bush, succeeded to elevate an unknown young governor of the poorest state in the United States, Bill Clinton to the presidency of the United States. Grudgingly, Shamir went to the Madrid conference against the violent oppositions of many Likudists including Ariel Sharon and Benyamin Netanyahu. Both became Israeli prime ministers and they had to undo what little efforts were made towards peace.

The Oslo Accords

On September 13, 1993, the Oslo Accords were signed. It was officially called the "Declaration of Principles on Interim Self-Government Arrangements" also referred to as DOP. The Oslo Accords contain a set of mutually agreed-upon general principles regarding a five year interim period of Palestinian self-rule, whereby the new Palestinian authority to be created was to be a security contractor to Israel, plus municipal duties. During this period, the Israeli government retains sole responsibility for foreign affairs, defense and borders. As for the major issues, which were termed Permanent Status issues, they were to be negotiated later. Such issues included borders, Jerusalem, security issues, settlements, and refugees. The concessions given by both sides was incredibly unbalanced.

A letter on key issues of the PLO and Israel, addressed to Prime Minister Yitzhak Rabin, was signed by Yasser Arafat on September 9, 1993. The letter says specifically that:

- The PLO recognizes the right of the State of Israel to exist in peace and security.
- The PLO accepts United Nations Security Council Resolutions 242 and 338
- The PLO commits itself to the Middle East peace process... all outstanding issues :.. will be resolved through negotiations
- ... the PLO renounces the use of terrorism and other acts of violence and will assume responsibility over all PLO elements and personnel in order to assure their compliance, prevent violations and discipline violators
- ... those articles of the Palestinian Covenant which deny Israel's right to exist, and the provisions of the Covenant which are inconsistent with the commitments of this letter are now inoperative and no longer valid

- ... the PLO undertakes to submit to the Palestinian National Council for formal approval the necessary changes in regard to the Palestinian Covenant.

- Rabin gave a letter in exchange to Arafat, also dated September 9, saying:

- ... Israel has decided to recognize the PLO as the representative of the Palestinian people and commence negotiations with the PLO.

The head of the Palestinian delegation that produced this imbalanced agreement was Mahmud Abbas, but it was adopted by Yasser Arafat and his companions!

In order for this peace process to last a thousand years like Shamir wanted, one agreement after another was signed but not implemented until Sharon came to power and tore Oslo apart. Before Sharon ascended to the premiership of Israel, a team of neoconservatives, including Richard Pearle wrote a paper recommending to Netanyahu to that he dump the Oslo Accord, a plan that was enforced by Sharon starting 2001 when these same neoconservatives became the new rulers in Washington in the George W. Bush administration. It is worth noting that from 1977 when the Likud took power for the first time, Israel was ruled by hardliners except for small intervals in between. Each new Likud (or Kadima) government was more hawkish than the one before. And they all did not fail to make a pile of accords that they signed but did not fulfill, as tactical steps to buy more time, and build more settlements.

The prime minister that produced Oslo, Yitzhak Rabin was assassinated by Israeli extremists. There was nothing left to negotiate for. They participated in a peace process with lots of conferences and lots of witnesses while more land grabs were exercised and group gang terrorism was elevated to become state terrorism.

... *Oslo II*

Oslo II was an agreement signed September 24, 1995 in Taba, Egypt, and countersigned in Washington four days later. It called not for Israeli withdrawal but 'redeployment' in the west Bank. After Oslo I, Israeli army 'redeployed' from Gaza and Jericho and now such redeployment characterized the West bank territories into areas A, B, &C.

- Area A: includes all the areas from which Israeli military control has been transferred to the administration of the Palestinian Authority, including the areas of Gaza and Jericho, and the seven major Palestinian population centers in the West Bank -- Nablus, Kalkilya, Tulkarem, Ramallah, Bethlehem, Jenin and Hebron. In these areas, the Palestinian Authority now has full responsibility for internal security and public order, as well as full responsibility for civil affairs.
- Area B: includes 450 Palestinian towns and villages in the West Bank. In these areas, as in Area A, the Palestinian Authority controls all civil authority. However, it differs

from Area A in that Israel maintains overriding security authority in order to safeguard its citizens and to combat terrorism.

- Area C: comprised of the unpopulated areas of the West Bank, including areas of strategic importance to Israel and the settlements, where Israel retains full responsibility for security.

This agreement gave the security burden of the populated areas to the authority while most of the West Bank remained under Israeli military direct control.

... *The Wye River Memorandum*

A Wye River Memorandum was signed on October 23, 1998 by Netanyahu and Arafat which was brokered by Bill Clinton. A Palestinian State was supposed to come into existence by May 4, 1999 and the Memorandum was to detail the disputed points that arose as a result of Oslo II. In order to offset claims of Palestinian security violation the memorandum introduced the direct involvement of the Central Intelligence Agency as a monitor and arbiter on security issues. The CIA accordingly had some of its personnel embedded with Palestinian security. It is said that Netanyahu was pressured to sign the agreement. He told reporters that he was capable of inflaming the political scene in Washington to counter Clinton's pressure. Soon after, the National Security Agency advised Clinton that a foreign Embassy in Washington was listening to his midnight love conversations with Monica Lewinsky and suggested he take notice. The Lewinsky affair exploded. It is to be noted that the three main participants in the Lewinsky Affair, Lewinsky, Linda Tripp and Paula Jones were all Jewish.

...*Barak, Arafat and Camp David*

None of the Wye River articles were carried out by Israel. A new prime minister, Ehud Barak was elected. Since Oslo set May 4, 1999 as the final date in which final status issues should have been completed, a Sharm el-Sheikh Memorandum was signed by Barak and Arafat delaying that date to September 13, 2000 and reiterating the obligation of both parties to put the peace talks timetable back on track. Barak seemed more serious to reactivate the peace process, at his own terms obviously. The following actions took place in chronological order:

- November 14, 1999: Barak and Arafat met in Tel Aviv
- January 4, 2000: Steering committee agreed on 5% redeployment, part of the second redeployment
- January 30, 2000: Multilateral track per Madrid Conference resumed in Moscow
- March 9, 2000: Barak-Arafat Ramallah agreement on completing the second redeployment; permanent status talks to resume
- March 21, 2000: Palestinian and Israeli negotiators resumed permanent status negotiations at Bolling Air Force Base in Washington, DC

- April 11, 2000: Clinton-Barak met in Washington, DC
- May 15, 2000: Interim Agreements Steering and Monitoring Committee met in Jerusalem after new fighting
- May 22, 2000: Barak cut off talks due to violence in territories
- June 6, 2000: U.S. Secretary of State Madeleine Albright met with Barak and Arafat (separately) to push for progress toward framework agreement
- July 5, 2000: President Clinton invited Barak and Arafat to summit at Camp David

At Camp David there were two Jewish teams: one Israeli representing Israel and one American representing the United States of America. The Secretary of State Albright, Sandy Berger, the National Security Advisor, and Dennis Ross were Zionist American Jews leading the American delegation. The so called concessions much talked about said no to the return of the refugees, gave 'religious sovereignty over the Aqsa Mosque (Temple Mount), and kept the major settlements under Israeli control. But while negotiations were going on, Ariel Sharon had better ideas.

As the Wye River specified, September 2000 was the final date for concluding final status issues, and as Clinton was pushing for final settlement, Sharon chose the same month of September 2000 to visit the al Aqsa Mosque compound with a huge delegation of Likud and right wing extremists under cover of about 2000 policemen and a permit for the visit by Barak.

Jerusalem and the al Aqsa compound called Temple Mount by Israel were among the hot disputed issues at Camp David. What better provocation than a visit to Islam's third holiest place by people who time and again called for its destruction to replace it with a Third Temple?

A Sharon Plan Backed by Bush Neoconservatists

By 2001, the Palestinian Authority had a security apparatus that was cooperating fully with the Israel security apparatus which was directly monitored by the CIA. With CIA assistance, interrogation techniques, first class prisons and a police force were created. Some necessary infrastructure for the Palestinian authority was built to aid it to act as a security subcontractor as per the various memorandums and agreements. Municipalities were created, and even a Gaza airport was built to connect it with the outside world.

In 2001, the neoconservatives of America, made mostly from American Zionists supportive of the Likud extremist positions, and Ariel Sharon came to power at about the same time, just a few weeks apart. The American neoconservatives even when in transition advised Clinton and Barak that they would not be bound by any agreement the parties may reach in Camp David. They were apparently more patriotic to the Israeli cause than Israel's prime minister! When acting as advisors to Netanyahu in the late 1990's, these same neoconservatives advised Israel to tear the Oslo agreement apart. And that was exactly what Sharon was up to as he became the new Israeli prime minister. Sharon was given the green light to destroy Oslo, the infrastructure that came with it, and Arafat who was judged as uncooperative enough as a security subcontractor to Israel in the West Bank.

...a second (Aqsa) intifada & reoccupying the West Bank

The European Institute for research on Mediterranean and Euro-Arab Cooperation defined the Aqsa intifada and its causes as such: "The second Intifada, also known as the Intifada Al-Aqsa, erupted on the 28th of September 2000, as a result of the controversial visit of Arial Sharon, then leader of the opposition party Likud, to the al-Aqsa / Temple Mount complex in Jerusalem. The visit,... stirred an outburst of anger amongst Palestinians, exasperated by the stagnation of the peace process, as well as by the continuing occupation and settlement expansion... The violent repression of Palestinian demonstrations demanding the immediate ending of the occupation killed more than 200 Palestinians in one month, of which one third were under 17 years old. To respond to this brutality, the Intifada became militarized as from the beginning of November 2000. Arafat's Fateh Party was no longer in total command of the revolt. Hamas and Islamic Jihad had a lot to do with the armed struggle that began against the occupation."

Tel Aviv and Washington and the allied corporate media called the intifada violence rather than resistance to occupation. They preferred to blame Arafat for this 'violence' and claimed that Israel was acting in self defense, conveniently dropping the fact it was acting in 'occupation defense'. Corporate media completely ignored that:

- It is the Palestinians that have been under military occupation for 33 years.
- Settlement programs have continued, even though they were denounced by the UN, USA and were violating recent Oslo agreements.
- The Israelis have delayed their military withdrawals or redeployments   as required by those accords.
- Israel still occupied 60 per cent of the West Bank and 20 per cent of Gaza, while 100% should have been transferred to Palestinian control before 2000.
- Jerusalem was made off-limits to those Palestinians who do not carry Israeli residence permits in Jerusalem.
- They are adding one demand after the other contrary to previous agreements and UN resolutions.
- The number of Jewish settlers in the West Bank and Gaza has grown by more than 70 per cent since and contrary to the Oslo Accord of 1993. Settlements were expanded and new settlements were projected even when Barak was claiming he was offering a generous offer to Arafat.

Professor of International Law and Practice at Princeton University, author of Human Rights Horizons [London:

Routledge, 2000] wrote: "Though the Israeli government and the U.S. media persist in describing the second Palestinian intifada as a security crisis or a disruption to the 'peace process,' in international law, Palestinian resistance to occupation is a legally protected right. For 33 years, Israel has administered a military occupation of the West Bank, the Gaza Strip and East Jerusalem in consistent and relentless defiance of the overwhelming will of the organized international community. The international consensus has been expressed through widely supported resolutions passed by the Security Council and the General Assembly of the United Nations (hereafter UNSC and UNGA). UN Resolutions 242 and 338 affirmed the legal obligation of Israel to withdraw from Palestinian territories obtained in the 1967 Six Day War. This must be the end point of any peace process that can bring lasting peace. Until such time as Israel respects this obligation, the relevant principles of international law are contained in the Fourth Geneva Convention concerning the Protection of Civilian Persons in Time of War (August 12, 1949), in particular those provisions of the Convention that require an occupying power to protect the status quo, human rights and prospects for self-determination of the occupied people, and oblige all signatories to enforce the Convention in the face of 'grave breaches.' Since 1967 and during the current uprising, Israel has refused to accept this framework of legal obligations. Its refusal has been pronounced, blatant and undisguised. Not only has Israel failed to withdraw from the Occupied Territories, during the occupation Israel has 'created facts' -- heavily armed settlements, bypass roads and security zones in the midst of a future Palestinian state -- that seriously compromise basic Palestinian rights." He added: "The events of the Oslo "peace process" do not alter the Palestinian right of resistance to the occupation, due to the Israeli refusal to implement the underlying legal directives established by a consensus within the UN"

In the spring of 2002, and with at least tacit approval of the Bush administration Sharon launched an operation to re-occupy all the West Bank and to destroy the newly built Palestine Authority infrastructure and institutions, especially those that were built after Oslo, including Yasser Arafat's compound in Ramallah.

The title of the Los Angeles Times article written by Tracy Wilinson on April 09, 2002 titled "Arafat, Oslo Accord Are Sharon's Prime Prey" summed up Sharon motives in collusion with George W. Bush and his neoconservatists Likudists running Washington. Tracy wrote:

"The designs of Israel's vast military offensive are etched in the dust and debris of the battered landscape here. The greatest destruction, by far, has been visited on symbols of Palestinian self-rule.

The sprawling if ramshackle headquarters of Palestinian Authority President Yasser Arafat is in ruins, its walls toppled and replaced by barbed wire. The Palestinians' most important West Bank security compound, an elaborate multimillion-dollar manse, was ravaged by one of the army's most relentless aerial assaults in the current campaign. Army raids have repeatedly targeted police who, Israel has said in the past, were never involved in terrorism..."

The Israeli invasion started on March 29, 2002. Roads, electricity and water infrastructure were smashed by Israeli tanks, armored bulldozers and combat helicopters. The Education ministry, the statistics department, and local radio and television stations were destroyed. In Ramalla alone, more than 1000 Palestinians were arrested including police officers who were singled for humiliating treatment. According to Tracy Wilkinson of the Los Angeles Times, police officers "were forced to strip to their underwear and turn in their weapons. Once in detention camps, they were forced to sit with their heads in a downward position,... By hitting steadily at the police forces, Sharon is undermining the very pillars of the Palestinian Authority. Nothing more symbolizes the autonomy of the aspiring Palestinian state than its own security services. The war on the police forces culminated last week with an eight-hour bombardment of the elegant U.S.-built headquarters of the Preventive Security Service complex of Col. Jibril Rajoub, one of the most powerful Palestinians in the West Bank. Rajoub's police force is precisely the body that would have to enforce a cease-fire and crackdown on terrorists. Rajoub has long maintained close contacts with American and Israeli security officials and is seen as a protégé of the CIA. One of the few photographs on his desk before his office was destroyed was one of himself with the CIA Director George J. Tenet.... In addition, Rajoub embodied the kind of Israeli-Palestinian security cooperation enshrined in the Oslo accords. Sharon's post-Arafat vision may not have room for such cooperation, preferring to leave security exclusively in the hands of Israel. That in turn implies a long-term reoccupation of the West Bank and Gaza Strip by Israel."

Mahmud Abbas after Yasser Arafat

The West Bank and Gaza were re-occupied and Oslo became history. And shortly, Arafat who was captive in his Ramalla compound, would become history too. He died in November 2004 of a mysterious illness and many believed he was poisoned. The death toll during the intifada rose to 4,046 in May 2004, of which 3,057 were Palestinians, and 918 Israelis. The hero of Oslo, Mahmud Abbas, became the next president, but the president of what? There was no autonomy, no Oslo, and no infrastructure or institutions of governance. But did Abbas learn any lessons from the Oslo fiasco?

Sharon, and Olmert after him decided they could not afford to keep occupying Gaza, so Israel made a unilateral withdrawal because they claimed they was no Palestinian partner to negotiate with. But how about Abbas whom Bush certified as" a good man"?. Avi Shlaim explained:

> "In August 2005 a Likud government headed by Ariel
> Sharon staged a unilateral Israeli pullout from Gaza,
> withdrawing all 8,000 settlers and destroying the
> houses and farms they had left behind. Hamas, the
> Islamic resistance movement, conducted an effective

campaign to drive the Israelis out of Gaza. The withdrawal was a humiliation for the Israeli Defence Forces. To the world, Sharon presented the withdrawal from Gaza as a contribution to peace based on a two-state solution...Israel's settlers were withdrawn but Israeli soldiers continued to control all access to the Gaza Strip by land, sea and air. Gaza was converted overnight into an open-air prison. From this point on, the Israeli air force enjoyed unrestricted freedom to drop bombs, to make sonic booms by flying low and breaking the sound barrier, and to terrorize the hapless inhabitants of this prison."[1]

Judeo-Christian culture and justice was demonstrated in the Gaza settlements. The Jewish settlers numbered only 8,000 in 2005 compared with 1.4 million local residents. Yet the settlers controlled 25% of the territory, 40% of the arable land and the lion's share of the scarce water resources.

Elections were held in the West Bank and Gaza and Hamas won a majority in the Legislative Council. They formed a government after Abbas refused to participate in a national unity government. The U.S. and Israel were not happy with the election results. Their preferred democracy in heads I win, tails you lose. Tension between Mahmud Abbas Fateh and Hamas reached new highs. King Abdulla of Saudi Arabia, to the dismay of the Bush administration and Israel, succeeded to broker an

---

1   Avi Shlai, professor of international relations at the University of Oxford January 08, 2009 at The Guardian

agreement between Fateh and Hamas which resulted in a short lived national unity government. The U.S. and Israel displeasure was due to their intentions to have Hamas destroyed and not accommodated. As we recalled earlier, the United States had CIA agents officially posted within the Palestinian Authority security forces and through some of these security leaders, the CIA, in league with Israel, started to escalate friction between Fateh and Hamas. This is how Avi Shlaim described this in his January 08, 2009 Guardian article.

> "Israel likes to portray itself as an island of democracy in a sea of authoritarianism... Despite all the handicaps, the Palestinian people succeeded in building the only genuine democracy in the Arab world with the possible exception of Lebanon. In January 2006, free and fair elections for the Legislative Council of the Palestinian Authority brought to power a Hamas-led government. Israel, however, refused to recognize the democratically elected government, claiming that Hamas is purely and simply a terrorist organization... It continued to play the old game of divide and rule between rival Palestinian factions. In the late 1980s, Israel had supported the nascent Hamas in order to weaken Fatah, the secular nationalist movement led by Yasser Arafat. Now Israel began to encourage the corrupt and pliant Fatah leaders to overthrow their religious political rivals and recapture power. Aggressive American neoconservatives participated in the sinister plot to instigate a Palestinian civil war. Their meddling

was a major factor in the collapse of the national unity government and in driving Hamas to seize power in Gaza in June 2007 to pre-empt a Fatah coup."[1]

Washington Promoting a Palestinian Civil War

American investigative reporter David Rose had access to confidential documents that exposed what really happened in Gaza and resulted in Hamas' takeover of Gaza. It was published in the April 2008 issue of the American magazine 'Vanity Fair' from which we will make relevant quotations. The magazine introduced David Rose's report as such:

"After failing to anticipate Hamas's victory over Fatah in the 2006 Palestinian election, the White House cooked up yet another scandalously covert and self-defeating Middle East debacle: part Iran-contra, part Bay of Pigs. With confidential documents, corroborated by outraged former and current U.S. officials, David Rose reveals how President Bush, Condoleezza Rice, and Deputy National-Security Adviser Elliott Abrams backed an armed force under Fatah strongman Muhammad Dahlan, touching off a bloody civil war in Gaza and leaving Hamas stronger than ever." Rose explained that in the January 2006 elections Hamas won majority to the surprise of the Bush

---

1   Avi Shlai, professor of international relations at the University of Oxford January 08, 2009 at The Guardian

administration. Mohamad Dahlan was Mahmud Abbas' strong man in Gaza who led the security forces in Gaza.

The American magazine, in its April 2008 issue published what it called a 'bombshell', written by investigative reporter David Rose, that revealed how the United States was dictating to the PA president Mahmud Abbas and his staff "instructions" almost daily on how to effectively make a coup against the democratically elected government of Hamas. Condoleezza Rice told reporters: "I don't know anyone who wasn't caught off guard by Hamas's strong showing." Some points revealed in Rose's report:

- "Vanity Fair has obtained confidential documents, since corroborated by sources in the U.S. and Palestine, which lay bare a covert initiative, approved by Bush and implemented by Secretary of State Condoleezza Rice and Deputy National Security Adviser Elliott Abrams, to provoke a Palestinian civil war. The plan was for forces led by Dahlan, and armed with new weapons supplied at America's behest, to give Fatah the muscle it needed to remove the democratically elected Hamas-led government from power."

- Bush publicly praised Dahlan as "a good, solid leader" According to multiple Israeli and American sources Bush described him in private as "our guy." Rose wrote that Dahlan worked closely with the FBI and the CIA and that "he developed a warm relationship with Director of Central Intelligence George Tenet..."

- When Yasser Arafat believed in Oslo, while Hamas did not, Dahlan, as head of the paramilitary Preventive Security Service and acting on instructions from Arafat, arrested more than 2000 members of Hamas because they did not trust Israeli promises and believed in armed struggle as the way to deal with Israel. Many Hamas members were tortured in jail.

- The United States, according to Rose, spoke with one voice: "We have to squeeze these guys," Rice told Abbas. The United States expects him to dissolve the Hamas government as soon as possible and hold fresh elections.

- Abbas, one official says, agreed to take action within two weeks. It happened to be Ramadan, the month when Muslims fast during daylight hours. With dusk approaching, Abbas asked Rice to join him for *iftar*—a snack to break the fast. Afterward, according to the official, Rice underlined her position: "So we're agreed? You'll dissolve the government within two weeks?" "Maybe not two weeks. Give me a month. Let's wait until after the Eid," he said, referring to the three-day celebration that marks the end of Ramadan. ... Rice got into her armored S.U.V., where, the official claims, she told an American colleague, "That damned *iftar* has cost us another two weeks of Hamas government."

- When few weeks past and Abbas was not acting to do America's bidding, Jake Walles, the consul general in

Jerusalem, was instructed to go and see Abbas to deliver a
barely varnished ultimatum to the Palestinian president.

- There was still no sign that Abbas was ready to bring
matters to a head by dissolving the Hamas government,
wrote Rose. Against this darkening background, the U.S.
began direct security talks with Dahlan...."

- Lieutenant General Keith Dayton, who had been
appointed the U.S. security coordinator for the
Palestinians in November 2005, advised Dahlan that all
the 14 security forces must be unified under him as a
national security advisor and that the United States was
ready to supply him with training and arms. When the
aid package promised to Dahlan was rejected by Congress,
Rice secured the money from friendly Arab regimes in
the region.

- Also, in late December 2006 "four Egyptian trucks
passed through an Israeli-controlled crossing into Gaza,
where their contents were handed over to Fatah. These
included 2,000 Egyptian-made automatic rifles, 20,000
ammunition clips, and two million bullets.

- On February 1, 2007, Rose wrote Dahlan took his "very
clever warfare" to a new level when Fatah forces under his
control stormed the Islamic University of Gaza, a Hamas
stronghold, and set several buildings on fire.

- Rose added: Unwilling to preside over a Palestinian
civil war, Abbas blinked. For weeks, King Abdullah of
Saudi Arabia had been trying to persuade him to meet

with Hamas in Mecca and formally establish a national unity government. On February 6, Abbas went, taking Dahlan with him. Two days later, with Hamas no closer to recognizing Israel, a deal was struck. Under its terms, Ismail Haniyeh of Hamas would remain prime minister while allowing Fatah members to occupy several important posts.

- Once again, wrote Rose, the Bush administration had been taken by surprise. According to a State Department official, "Condi was apoplectic." A remarkable documentary record, revealed here for the first time, shows that the U.S. responded by redoubling the pressure on its Palestinian allies. The State Department quickly drew up an alternative to the new unity government. Known as "Plan B," its objective, according to a State Department memo that has been authenticated by an official who knew of it at the time, was to "enable [Abbas] and his supporters to reach a defined endgame by the end of 2007". Plan B called for Abbas to "collapse the government" if Hamas refused to alter its attitude toward Israel. From there, Abbas could call early elections or impose an emergency government.

- Security considerations were paramount, and Plan B had explicit prescriptions for dealing with them. For as long as the unity government remained in office, it was essential for Abbas to maintain "independent control of key security forces." He must "avoid Hamas integration with these services, while eliminating the Executive Force or mitigating the challenges posed by its continued existence."

- Rose wrote: The Bush administration's goals for Plan B were elaborated in a document titled "An Action Plan for the Palestinian Presidency." The "desired outcome" was to give Abbas "the capability to take the required strategic political decisions ... such as dismissing the cabinet, establishing an emergency cabinet."...

- On April 30, 2007, a portion of one early draft was leaked to a Jordanian newspaper, *Al-Majd*. The secret was out. From Hamas's perspective, the Action Plan could amount to only one thing: a blueprint for a U.S.-backed Fatah coup... On June 7, there was another damaging leak, when the Israeli newspaper *Haaretz* reported that Abbas and Dayton had asked Israel to authorize the biggest Egyptian arms shipment yet—to include dozens of armored cars, hundreds of armor-piercing rockets, thousands of hand grenades, and millions of rounds of ammunition.

- Hamas decided to act. Rose conducted interviews with Hamas' leaders: "Fawzi Barhoum, Hamas's chief spokesman, says the leak in *Al-Majd* convinced the party that 'there was a plan, approved by America, to destroy the political choice.' The arrival of the first Egyptian-trained fighters, he adds, was the 'reason for the timing.' About 250 Hamas members had been killed in the first six months of 2007, Barhoum tells me. 'Finally we decided to put an end to it. If we had let them stay loose in Gaza, there would have been more violence.'

On paper things looked favoring Fateh which had 70 000 in the 14 security agencies, half in Gaza at least, against 6000 Al Qassam militia of Hamas and newly formed 6000 Executive Force. The fighting started June 7 2007 and was over in less than five days. It began with attacks on Fatah security buildings, in and around Gaza City and in the southern town of Rafah. Fatah attempted to shell Prime Minister Haniyeh's house, but by dusk on June 13 its forces were being routed.

The siege on Gaza was tightened. Israel and Arab States willing to conclude a final settlement to the Palestine problem on American/Israeli terms found in Hamas and other resistance movements a real obstacle to "their peace" Gaza was since turned into the biggest prison in the world with 1.5 million people. Some 70 % of Gazans are unemployed. People were dying from lack of medical supplies and were undernourished as Israel prevents food supplies except in meager quantities. Insufficient fuel is allowed, even ambulances run out of gas, and power stations shut down due to lack of fuel.

Eighteen months of CIA Israeli conspiracies against Hamas after which pro Israeli CIA forces were defeated in Gaza. Another eighteen months of siege by Israel and other pro American 'moderate' Arab states did not break the will of Gaza. With Mahmoud Abbas presidency over on January 8th 2009, the Bush administration second term is over January the 20th, and Israeli election coming on February 10th the alliance of these forces went for an all out war against Gaza. Avi Shalaim explained:

> "The war unleashed by Israel on Gaza on 27 December (2008) was the culmination of a series of clashes and confrontations with the Hamas government. In a broader sense, however, it is a war between Israel and the Palestinian people, because the people had elected the party to power. The declared aim of the war is to weaken Hamas and to intensify the pressure until its leaders agree to a new ceasefire on Israel's terms. The undeclared aim is to ensure that the Palestinians in Gaza are seen by the world simply as a humanitarian problem and thus to derail their struggle for independence and statehood…The army top brass had been champing at the bit to deliver a crushing blow to Hamas in order to remove the stain left on their reputation by the failure of the war against Hezbollah in Lebanon in July 2006. Israel's cynical leaders could also count on apathy and impotence of the pro-western Arab regimes and on blind support from President Bush ..". [1]

---

1   Avi Shlai, professor of international relations at the University of Oxford January 08, 2009 at The Guardian

He added:

> "A wide gap separates the reality of Israel's actions from the rhetoric of its spokesmen. It was not Hamas but the IDF that broke the ceasefire. It did so by a raid into Gaza on 4 November that killed six Hamas men. Israel's objective is not just the defense of its population but the eventual overthrow of the Hamas government in Gaza by turning the people against their rulers. And far from taking care to spare civilians, Israel is guilty of indiscriminate bombing and of a three-year-old blockade that has brought the inhabitants of Gaza, now 1.5 million, to the brink of a humanitarian catastrophe." Any wonder why Gazans had to express their anger by firing crude homemade rockets hoping this may give them some deterrence capability?

Avi Shlai, professor of international relations at the University of Oxford January 08, 2009 at The Guardian:

> Israel exclaims what it did to Palestinians to deserve all this! This reminds us of the old tale about a Jewish mother taking leave of her son, who has been called up to serve in the Czar's army against the Turks.

"Don't exert yourself too much," she admonishes him, "Kill a Turk and rest. Kill another Turk and rest again…"

"But mother," he exclaims, "What if the Turk kills me?"

"Kill you?" she cries out, "Why? What have you done to him?"

This is not a joke (and this is not a week for jokes). It is a lesson in psychology."

In its December 27 2008 genocide against Gaza, Israel killed and wounded about 5000 Palestinians, half of whom were children and women, but Israel will never rest!

Resisting occupation, a legal right under international law was called terrorism. Yet state terrorism exercised by Israel and pre-judicial assassinations are called acts of self-defense. Why do Palestinians rebel is because after their country was occupied and a state of apartheid was imposed on them.

Ahad Ha'am, wrote in his "Truth from Palestine":

"The Jews were slaves in the land of their Exile, and suddenly they found themselves with unlimited freedom, wild … This sudden change has produced in their hearts an inclination toward repressive tyranny, as always happens when a slave rules". Ahad Ha'am warned: "We are used to thinking of the Arabs as primitive men of the desert, as a donkey-like nation that neither sees nor understands what is going on around it. But this is a great error. The Arab, like all sons of Shem, has a sharp and crafty mind ... Should the time come when the life of our people in Palestine imposes to a smaller or greater extent on the natives, they will not easily step aside".[1]

General Moshe Dayan, former Israeli Defense Minister once said: "Israel must be like a mad dog, too dangerous to bother." Israel is indeed a mad dog! But what are people supposed to do with mad dogs?

---

1   One Palestine Complete, Tom Segev, Henry Holt & Company, New YorkIst American Edition 2000, Pg 104, Ahad Ha'am, "Truth from Palestine", in the Complete Works of Ahad Ha'am (in Herbre) (Tel Aviv: Dvir, 1949), P. 24

Israeli Hebrew University professor Sprinzak wrote:

"The Jewish state that reached independence in 1948 did not emerge normally out of an indigenous anti-colonial struggle against the British in Palestine. Rather, it was, and still is, one of the most 'unnatural' states in history- a state of newcomers, the vast majority of whom arrived after the colonial power had clearly established itself." He added, *"The post-1948 Israel was not perfect democracy. It was ruled for many years by one party... The Arab minority, which could vote and elect its representatives to the Knesset, was for many years kept under strict military government ..."* [1]

An anonymous Chinese saying [2] *"We are like a big fish that has been pulled from the water and is flopping wildly to find its way back in. In such a condition the fish never asks where the next flip or flop will bring it. It senses only that its present position is intolerable and that something else must be tried".*

---

1   Ehud Sprinzak, a political science professor at the Hebrew University in Jerusalem (The ascendance of Israel's Radical Right, Oxford University Press, 1990, p 11,12

2   Quoted by Perry Link in China in Transformation – Daedal us (spring 1993) and printed before chapter one of "The Future of Capitalism".

OUR CONCLUSION: THE PARTY IS OVER

On March 18, 2008, I made a speech at Harvard's Kennedy School of Government and I will quote some relevant, but edited paragraphs due to space considerations, from that speech:

As a young student in elementary school in Jerusalem, our history teacher taught us about the Balfour Declaration, the document in which Lord Balfour, the British Secretary, wrote to another British and global financier, Lord Rothschild, promising to create a Jewish homeland in someone else's country which happened to be mine. To my young, inquisitive mind I wondered about the relationship between financiers and politicians, and how can one who does not own something give it away.

Later, I was told that Palestine was given to the Jews by God, not by Mr. Balfour, and I wondered if God was in the real estate business. If he was, that would have been the first sub-prime deal ever transacted, some 2000 years ago and look what such deals are doing now to America. Here again God was invoked to bless an imperial act. Then, I was told that the evil done to Palestinians by giving their country to another people was a result of the evil done by the Christian Europeans against European Jews, a logic I could not understand or believe. Then I learned that the prominent Zionist founding father David Ben Gurion, did not understand it either. He said, as was quoted in the Mearsheimer-Walt study on the Israeli lobby of March 2006:

> "If I were a (Palestinian) Arab leader I would never make terms with Israel. That is natural: We have taken their country....We come from Israel. But two thousand years ago, and what is that to them? There has been anti-Semitism, the Nazis, Hitler, Auschwitz, but was that their fault? They only see one thing: we have come here and stolen their country. Why should they accept that?" [1]

The majority of Arabs and Palestinians are not impressed by the sophistry justifying the occupation of their lands even if it is presented as pseudo-scholarship. They are also not impressed by the hallucinations of end - timers who are supporting the Jews of Israel today to convert them or murder them at the end of times. What they see is a nation state that was created over their dead bodies and lands; with unparalleled financial backing from the United States, approaching 160 billion of U.S. tax payers' money, and unlimited military and political cover including vetoing the World community resolutions 42 times since 1972, protecting Israel's occupation and human rights excesses.

Palestinian Arabs, who comprised 65% of Palestine Population when Israel was created in 1948, were systematically ethnically cleansed and they are in millions as refugees till this

---

1   The Israel Lobby and US Foreign Policy, March 2006 on www.lrb.co.uk

day. The Palestinian Arabs that escaped expulsion are treated as third class citizens. Between 1948 and 1963, 531 Arab villages were completely destroyed. Transfer, the Israeli word for ethnic cleansing is official policy among Israeli leadership; they only differ on the way to do it. Palestinian lands are being confiscated and new settlements are littering their occupied lands. Palestinians are dehumanized in action and in words. A state of apartheid is being created.

I claim that the practices of America and Israel defy all religions.

Criticizing Israel's occupation of Palestine territories and the idea of Israel's rule over the Palestinian, Britain's Chief Rabbi Dr. Jonathan Sacks said:

> "You cannot ignore a command that is repeated 36 times in the Mosaic books: 'You were exiled in order to know what it feels like to be an exile.' He added: 'And therefore I regard the current situation as nothing less than tragic, because it is forcing Israel into postures that are incompatible in the long run with our deepest ideals.' "[1]

Of course Britain's Chief Rabbi, Dr. Sachs is right. But I will go further. Just as I argued that the Anglo-Saxon capitalism party is over, I will argue that Zionism's party is also over. Even Ehud Olmert had to admit this fact. Again, I quote Israeli writer and peace activist Yuri Avnery's article of October 8, 2008:

---

1   Guardian, August 27, 2002

"At the end of (Olmert's) political career …he said some astounding things – not astounding in themselves, but certainly when they come from his mouth.

For those who missed it, here is what he said:

- 'We must reach an agreement with the Palestinians, the essence of which is that we shall actually withdraw from almost all the territories, if not from all the territories. We shall keep in our hands a percentage of these territories, but we shall be compelled to give the Palestinians a similar percentage, because without that there will be no peace.'

- '… Including Jerusalem. With special solutions, that I can visualize, for the Temple Mount and the historical holy places. … Anyone who wants to keep all the territory of the city will have to put 270,000 Arabs behind fences within sovereign Israel. That won't work.'

- 'I was the first who wanted to impose Israeli sovereignty on all the city. I admit … I was not ready to look into all the depths of reality.'

- 'Concerning Syria, what we need first of all is a decision. I wonder if there is one single serious person in Israel who believes it is possible to make peace with Syria without giving up the Golan Heights in the end.'

- 'The aim is to try and fix for the first time a precise border between us and the Palestinians, a border that all the world [will recognize]."

- 'Let's assume that in the next year or two a regional war will break out and we shall have a military confrontation with Syria. I have no doubt that we shall smite them hip and thigh [an allusion to Judges 15:8]. ... [But] what will happen when we win? ... Why go to war with the Syrians in order to achieve what we can get anyway without paying such a high price?'

- 'What was the greatness of Menachem Begin? [He] sent Dayan to meet with Tohami [Sadat's emissary] in Morocco, before he even met Sadat ... and Dayan told Tohami, on behalf of Begin, that we were prepared to withdraw from all of Sinai.'

- 'Arik Sharon, Bibi Netanyahu, Ehud Barak, and Rabin, his memory be blessed ... each one of them took a step that led us in the right direction, but at some point in time, at some crossroads, when a decision was needed, the decision did not come.'

- 'A few days ago I sat in a discussion with the key people in the decision-making process. At the end [I told them]: listening to you, I understand why we have not made peace with the Palestinians and the Syrians during the last 40 years.'

- 'We can perhaps take a historic step in our relations with the Palestinians, and a historic step in our relations with the Syrians. In both cases the decision we must make is the decision we have refused to face with open eyes for 40 years.'

- 'When you sit on this chair you must ask yourself: where do you direct the effort? To make peace or just to be stronger and stronger and stronger in order to win the war? ... Our power is great enough to face any danger. Now we must try and see how to use this infrastructure of power in order to make peace and not to win wars'

- 'Iran is a very great power. ... The assumption that America and Russia and China and Britain and Germany do not know how to handle the Iranians, and we Israelis know and we shall do so, is an example of the loss of all sense of proportion.'

- 'I read the statements of our ex-generals, and I say: how can it be that they have learned nothing and forgotten nothing?'

One can ask: Why do such people reach their conclusions only on finishing their term of office, when they can no longer do much about the wise things they are proposing? Why did Bill Clinton come to formulate his proposals for Israeli-Palestinian peace during his last days in office, after wasting eight years on irresponsible games in this arena? And why, for that matter, did Lyndon Johnson admit that the Vietnam War has been a terrible mistake right from the beginning only after he himself had brought about the deaths of tens of thousands of Americans and millions of Vietnamese?...

That is the importance of this interview: the speaker is a person who stood for two and a half years at the center of national and international decision-making, a person who was exposed to the pressures and the calculations, who had personal contact with the leaders of the world and of the Palestinians. ...

He has delivered a kind of state-of-the-nation report to the public, a summary of the reality of Israel after 60 years of the state and 120 years of the Zionist enterprise."

Not only Olmert and his conservative party reached the conclusion that the Zionist Greater Israel dream is over, but even the American Neocons who unleashed Israel, the 'mad dog' for eight years also concluded that the Zionist project has reached a dead end. The demographic problem of Palestinians to them, or the womb bomb as they called it also, is now pressing especially after eight years of free hand given to Israel only aggravated the problem. John Bolton, a hawk even among Neocons had this to say(The Three –State Option, By John R. Bolton wrote:, [1]

"Let's start by recognizing that trying to create a Palestinian Authority from the old PLO has failed and that any two-state solution based on the PA is stillborn. Hamas has killed the idea, and even the Holy Land is good for only one resurrection. Instead, we should look to a "three-state" approach, where Gaza is returned to Egyptian control and the West Bank in some configuration reverts to Jordanian sovereignty. Among many anomalies, today's conflict lies within the boundaries of three states nominally at peace. Having the two Arab states re-extend their prior political authority is an authentic way to extend the zone of peace and,

---

1   January 5, 2009; Page A11, The Washington Post

more important, build on governments that are providing peace and stability in their own countries. "International observers" or the like cannot come close to what is necessary; we need real states with real security forces.

This idea would be decidedly unpopular in Egypt and Jordan, which have long sought to wash their hands of the Palestinian problem. Accordingly, they should not have to reassume this responsibility alone. They should receive financial and political support from the Arab League and the West, as they both have for years from the United States. Israel should accept political and administrative roles by Jordan and Egypt, unless it intends to perform such roles itself (which it manifestly does not)."

We argued that a politician cannot reach a high ranking position in the American political system without being endorsed politically and financially by the invisible power structure of the global barons and the American permanent establishment. One can conclude that Barrack Obama was sky-rocketed politically to be elected as U.S. president only by the blessing, financing and media and 'marketing' support of the establishment, and it is to be expected from him to implement a two state or a three state ; peace plan' designed for him by the establishment based on Israeli specifications. Thus Obama, like Sharon , who was labeled by Bush as a man of peace becomes 'a man of peace'. As we explained elsewhere, presidents and their administrations come to implement the agenda of the invisible and permanent establishment, and the price for their fame and glory that they must accept all the evils of the invisible establishment agenda that was implemented under their watch and by their own names, while the invisible establishment tells the people all they have to do for things to go right to just wait for the next administration.

The Zionist enterprise, as we explained earlier, progressively moved to the extreme right, from socialism, to labor that called Jabotinsky ' Vladimir Hitler' and accused his zealots as fascists, to terrorism against the Palestinians then the British, to a state formed in 1948. It was a state without borders or a constitution. Borders were left to be expanded whenever the opportunity arose as professed by the Israeli leaders and historians. Then came the 1967 war, and the minimalists were replaced by maximalists, and expansionism that was a hidden agenda became an open secret when Jabotinsky's zealots took over the premiership of Israel in 1977. Jabotinsky believed in forceful treatment of Palestinians to create a psychological "iron wall". That worked for some time, certainly with Arab rulers who cared first and last about preserving the seat of their power, but such policy failed against people at large. Palestinian children rose up against Israeli occupation, stones being their only available weapon. When TV news around the world telecasted a 7 year old Palestinian boy jumping on an Israeli Merkava with a stone in his hand, Jabotinsky's Iron Wall was gone forever. Instead, Sharon's Separation Wall was erected. And even that will be destroyed even if Ehud Olmert's vision for a 1967 borders is implemented.

Therefore we concludethe Zionism party is over... Even highly respected Israeli academics and authors question the very basis of Zionism.

Ofri Ilani wrote in Ha'aretz as updated on March 21, 2008, under the title 'Shattering a 'national mythology''

"Of all the national heroes who have arisen from among the Jewish people over the generations, fate has not been kind to Dahia al-Kahina, a leader of the Berbers in the Aures Mountains. Although she was a proud Jewess, few Israelis have ever heard the name of this warrior-queen who, in the seventh century C.E., united a number of Berber tribes and pushed back the Muslim army that invaded North Africa. It is possible that the reason for this is that al-Kahina was the daughter of a Berber tribe that had converted to Judaism, apparently several generations before she was born, sometime around the 6th century C.E.

According to the Tel Aviv University historian, Prof. Shlomo Sand, the queen's tribe and other local tribes that converted to Judaism are the main sources from which Spanish Jewry sprang. This claim that the Jews of North Africa originated in indigenous tribes that became Jewish - and not in communities exiled from Jerusalem - is just one element of the far- reaching argument set forth in Sand's new book. He is the author of *Matai ve'ech humtza ha'am hayehudi?* ('When and How the Jewish People Were Invented?'); Resling.

In this work, the author attempts to prove that the Jews now living in Israel and other places in the world are not at all descendants of the ancient people who inhabited the Kingdom of Judea during the First and Second Temple period. Their origins, according to him, are in varied peoples that converted to Judaism during the course of history, in different corners of the Mediterranean Basin and the adjacent regions. Not only are the North African Jews for the most part descendants of pagans who converted to Judaism, but so are the Jews of Yemen (remnants of the Himyar Kingdom in the Arab Peninsula, who converted to Judaism in the fourth century) and the Ashkenazi Jews of Eastern Europe (refugees from the Kingdom of the Khazars, who converted in the eighth century).

He tries to prove that the Jewish people never existed as a "nation-race" with a common origin, but rather is a colorful mix of groups that at various stages in history adopted the Jewish religion. He argues that for a number of Zionist ideologues, the mythical perception of the Jews as an ancient people led to truly racist thinking: 'There were times when if anyone argued that the Jews belong to a people that have gentile origins, he would be classified as an anti-Semite on the spot. Today, if anyone dares to suggest that those who are considered Jews in the world ... have never constituted and still do not constitute a people or a nation - he is immediately condemned as a hater of Israel.'

According to Sand, the description of the Jews as a wandering and self-isolating nation of exiles, 'who wandered across seas and continents, reached the ends of the earth and finally, with the advent of Zionism, made a U-turn and returned en masse to their orphaned homeland,' is nothing but 'national mythology.' Like other national movements in Europe, which sought out a splendid Golden Age, through which they invented a heroic past - for example, classical Greece or the Teutonic tribes - to prove they have existed since the beginnings of history, 'so, too, the first buds of Jewish nationalism blossomed in the direction of the strong light that has its source in the mythical Kingdom of David.'"

Professor Sand believed that the Diaspora was an invention. So the professor was asked"

If the people were not exiled, are you saying that in fact the real descendants of the inhabitants of the Kingdom of Judah are the Palestinians?". He answered:

"No population remains pure over a period of thousands of years. But the chances that the Palestinians are descendants of the ancient Judaic people are much greater than the chances that you or I are its descendents."

Describing the ethics of capitalism, the backbone of America's global empire, MIT professor Lester C. Thurow wrote:

> "In the most rigorous expressions of capitalistic ethics, crime is simply another economic activity that happens to have a high price (jail) if one is caught. There is nothing that one (ought) not to do. Duties and obligations don't exist-only market transactions exist". [1]

---

1   Lester C. Thurow: The Future of Capitalism, Penguin books USA, New York 1996

Such processes of Anglo-Saxon capitalism produced and are producing wars, genocides and indeed crimes as per Professor Thurow's definition, not only in Palestine but even in America. More than 40 million Americans are classified officially as poor in the richest country on earth. It is producing a child poverty rate of 22.4 percent while in Denmark it is 5.1 percent, 4.4 percent in Belgium, 4.3 percent in England, and 2.6 percent in Sweden. One percent of Americans owns more than 80 percent of Americans. Thurow concluded:

> "Capitalism's nineteenth and twentieth century competitors – fascism, socialism and communism – and all gone. Yet even as the competition fades into history books, something also seems to be shaking the foundations of Capitalism". [1]

One of the world's leading historians, Eric Hobsbawm, was reported in the Harvard Crimson (October 20, 2005) as saying:

> "The American empire may actually cause disorder, barbarism, and chaos rather than promote peace and order"; To Hobsbawm, this empire will almost certainly fail. He added: "Will the U.S. learn the lessons of the British Empire, or will it try to maintain an eroding global position by relying on a failing political force and a military force which

---

1   Lester C. Thurow, The Future of Capitalism, Penguin Books, 1997

is insufficient for the present purposes for which the current American government claims it is designed?"

It is interesting to pay attention to Hobsbawm's use of the word 'barbarism' to describe the America's present order, which happens to be exactly what a Jeffersonian populist from Alabama described America's order in the last quarter of the 19th century. Then the populist said:

"Any nation that holds property rights above human rights is practicing barbarism."

As Mr. Hobsbawm and many others believe, we also believe that for America the party is over. We are at the age of sudden collapse whether for corporations as evidenced in the 2008 economic crash or just like we saw with the USSR.

Avi Shlaim wrote

"This brief review of Israel's record over the past four decades makes it difficult to resist the conclusion that it has become a rogue state with "an utterly unscrupulous set of leaders". A rogue state habitually violates international law, possesses weapons of mass destruction and practices terrorism - the use of violence against civilians for political purposes. Israel fulfils all of these three criteria; the cap fits and it must wear it. Israel's real aim is not peaceful coexistence with its Palestinian neighbors but military domination. It keeps compounding the mistakes of the past with new and more disastrous ones."[1]

After the supposedly 'only democracy in the Middle East' was unpleased with the truly democratic and free elections that brought Hamas to power, Israel took dozens of Hamas elected officials as hostages including members of the Legislative Council and other Hamas Ministers and kept them in jail. Ha aretz, an Israeli daily wrote"

"But this is not faulty reasoning: arresting people to use as bargaining chips is the act of a gang, not a state." .

The British Newspaper 'The Independent' published an interview with Avraham Burg on November 1, 2008 and its opening paragraph was: "Avraham Burg was a pillar of the Israeli establishment but his new book is causing a sensation. It argues that his country is an "abused child" which has become a "violent parent". He was a pillar of the Israeli establishment indeed as he "was quickly swept into mainstream public life, becoming first an adviser to the then Prime minister Shimon Peres, then a Knesset member, then Speaker of the Knesset, head of the Jewish agency and the World Zionist Organization and the almost-victorious candidate for the Labor Party leadership in 2001.... In 2003 he wrote a widely publicized and much argued-over piece in Israel's mass circulation Yedhiot Ahronot in which he said that Israel had to choose between 'racist oppression and democracy' and that 'having ceased to care about the children of the Palestinians,

1   Avi Shlaim, Professor of International Relation, Oxford University. January 08, 2009 at The Guardian

should not be surprised when they come washed in hatred and blow themselves up in the centers of Israeli escapism'....But in his book 'The Holocaust is Over: We Must Rise from its Ashes' ...Burg argues that Israel has been too long imprisoned by its obsessive and cheapening use – or abuse – of the Holocaust as 'a theological pillar of Jewish identity". He argues that the living role played by the Holocaust ... in everyday Israeli discourse, has left Israel with a persistent self-image of a 'nation of victims', in stark variance with its actual present-day power. Instead, the book argues, Israel needs finally to abandon the 'Judaism of the ghetto' for a humanistic, 'universal Judaism'."

The problem for Palestinians and Arabs is not Israel, the Small America, the 'abused child', or the rogue state, or the gangster state or the mad dog! It is mainly America the big Israel.

If one accepts Hebrew University professor Ehud Prinszak conclusion that Israel had an unnatural birth, one may also conclude that such creatures end up, sooner than later, in unnatural death.